Good Housekeeping
ALL COLOUR
FAMILY
COOK BOOK

Good Housekeeping

ALL COLOUR

FAMILY
COOK BOOK

EBURY PRESS
LONDON

First published in 1994

1 3 5 7 9 10 8 6 4 2

The Good Housekeeping Institute is the food and consumer research
centre of *Good Housekeeping* magazine.

First published in the United Kingdom in 1994 by
Ebury Press
Random House, 20 Vauxhall Bridge Road, London SW1V 2SA

Random House Australia (Pty) Limited
20 Alfred Street, Milsons Point, Sydney
New South Wales 2061, Australia

Random House New Zealand Limited
18 Poland Road, Glenfield
Auckland 10, New Zealand

Random House South Africa (Pty) Limited
PO Box 337, Bergvlei, South Africa

Random House UK Limited Reg. No. 954009

A CIP catalogue record for this book is available from the
British Library

ISBN: 0 09 178452 2

Photography by Jan Baldwin, Martin Brigdale, Laurie Evans, Melvin Grey,
John Heseltine, James Jackson, David Johnson, Paul Kemp, Peter Myers.

Illustrations by Kate Simunek, John Woodcock, Bill le Fever

Filmset by AFS Image Setters, Glasgow

Printed and bound by New Interlitho S.p.a., Milan

CONTENTS

COOKERY NOTES

Follow either metric or imperial measures for the recipes in this book as they are not inter-changeable. Sets of spoon measures are available in both metric and imperial size to give accurate measurement of small quantities. All spoon measures are level unless otherwise stated. When measuring milk we have used the exact conversion of 568 ml (1 pint).
* Size 4 eggs should be used except when otherwise stated.
† Granulated sugar is used un-less otherwise stated.
• Plain flour is used unless otherwise stated.

OVEN TEMPERATURE CHART

°C	°F	Gas mark
110	225	$\frac{1}{4}$
130	250	$\frac{1}{2}$
140	275	1
150	300	2
170	325	3
180	350	4
190	375	5
200	400	6
220	425	7
230	450	8
240	475	9

KEY TO SYMBOLS

$\boxed{1.00*}$ Indicates minimum preparation and cooking times in hours and minutes. They do not include prepared items in the list of ingredients; calcu-lated times apply only to the method. An asterisk * indicates extra time should be allowed, so check the note below symbols.

⊟ Chef's hats indicate degree of difficulty of a recipe: no hat means it is straightforward; one hat slightly more complicated; two hats indicates that it is for more advanced cooks.

✳ Indicates that a recipe will freeze. If there is no symbol, the recipe is unsuitable for freezing. An asterisk * indicates special freezer instructions so check the note immediately below the symbols.

$\boxed{309 \text{ cals}}$ Indicates calories per serving, including any sugges-tions (e.g. cream, to serve) given in the ingredients.

METRIC CONVERSION SCALE

LIQUID				SOLID		
Imperial	Exact conversion	Recommended ml		Imperial	Exact conversion	Recommended g
$\frac{1}{4}$ pint	142 ml	150 ml		1 oz	28.35 g	25 g
$\frac{1}{2}$ pint	284 ml	300 ml		2 oz	56.7 g	50 g
1 pint	568 ml	600 ml		4 oz	113.4 g	100 g
$1\frac{1}{2}$ pints	851 ml	900 ml		8 oz	226.8 g	225 g
$1\frac{3}{4}$ pints	992 ml	1 litre		12 oz	340.2 g	350 g
				14 oz	397.0 g	400 g
				16 oz (1 lb)	453.6 g	450 g

For quantities of $1\frac{3}{4}$ pints and over, litres and fractions of a litre have been used.

1 kilogram (kg) equals 2.2 lb.

INTRODUCTION

This bumper cookbook is packed with imaginative dishes that all the family will enjoy. In addition to recipes for everyday meals there are recipes for all those special family occasions. Every possible mealtime is covered—from snacks and suppers to main courses, desserts and barbecues.

Every one of the 206 recipes in the main section of the book is illustrated with a colour photograph so that you can see at a glance the finished dishes. There are also helpful step-by-step illustrations to guide you smoothly through the method, ensuring that all the recipes are simple to follow. Special symbols indicate how long each recipe takes to make, the degree of difficulty involved, whether it will freeze and the calorie count. What's more, all the recipes have been double-tested so you can be absolutely sure of achieving successful results every time.

We hope very much that you enjoy these recipes and feel sure that they will become all-time family favourites.

Soups and Starters

MINESTRONE
(MIXED VEGETABLE AND PASTA SOUP)

| 2.30* | £ | ✳ | 332 cals |

* plus overnight soaking

Serves 8

50 g (2 oz) butter

50 g (2 oz) pancetta or unsmoked streaky bacon, rinded and finely chopped

3 onions, skinned and sliced

1 garlic clove, skinned and crushed

2 carrots, peeled and diced

2 sticks celery, washed and diced

225 g (8 oz) dried haricot beans, soaked in cold water overnight, drained and rinsed

350 g (12 oz) fresh tomatoes, skinned and roughly chopped, or 226 g (8 oz) can tomatoes with their juice

2.3 litres (4 pints) beef stock (see page 350)

100 g (4 oz) shelled fresh or frozen peas

350 g (12 oz) potatoes, peeled and diced

175 g (6 oz) short cut macaroni or small pasta shapes

175 g (6 oz) French beans, topped, tailed and sliced

225 g (8 oz) cabbage, shredded

15 ml (1 tbsp) chopped fresh parsley

salt and freshly ground pepper

40 g (1½ oz) freshly grated Parmesan cheese

1 Melt the butter in a large saucepan, add the pancetta, onions and garlic and fry for 5 minutes until golden brown. Add the carrots and celery and cook for 2 minutes.

2 Stir in the haricot beans, tomatoes and stock. Bring to boil and simmer, half covered, for 1½–2 hours or until the haricot beans are tender. If using fresh peas, add these with the potatoes after the beans have been cooking for 1 hour.

3 Add the pasta, French beans, cabbage, parsley and seasoning. If using frozen peas, add them at this stage. Simmer for 15 minutes or until the pasta is just tender. Serve immediately in a warmed soup tureen, with the Parmesan cheese handed separately.

Menu Suggestion
Serve for a winter lunch or supper meal with fresh bread.

MINESTRONE

Correctly speaking, this soup should be called Minestrone alla Milanese because it is the classic soup from Milan—a thick, wintry vegetable soup with dried beans and pasta. There are numerous variations, depending on the availability of the vegetables, and sometimes rice is used instead of pasta. Minestrone alla Genovese is perhaps the most famous of these variations, with its addition of basil and garlic sauce (pesto) and Pecorino cheese at the end.

CIPOLLATA
(ONION SOUP WITH BACON, TOMATOES AND PARMESAN)

| 2.00 | 🗇 £ ✳ | 519 cals |

Serves 4

45 ml (3 tbsp) olive oil

100 g (4 oz) unsmoked streaky bacon, rinded and finely diced

800 g (1¾ lb) onions, skinned and finely sliced

1 litre (1¾ pints) chicken stock (see page 350) or two 450 ml (15 fl oz) cans chicken consommé

396 g (14 oz) can tomatoes with their juice

1 small fresh chilli, seeded and finely chopped

salt and freshly ground pepper

30 ml (2 tbsp) roughly chopped basil leaves

45 ml (3 tbsp) freshly grated Parmesan cheese

8 slices French bread, toasted

1 garlic clove, skinned and halved

1 Heat the oil in a large saucepan and fry the bacon for 2–3 minutes, but do not let it brown.

2 Add the onions, stir, then cover the pan and cook on a very low heat for about 1 hour, until the onions are almost melted. Watch the onions carefully and stir them frequently in case they catch and burn.

3 Add the chicken stock, tomatoes, chilli, salt and pepper to taste, cover and cook gently for 30 minutes.

4 Just before serving, stir in the roughly chopped basil leaves and the grated Parmesan cheese.

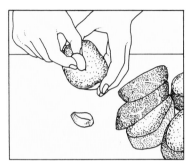

5 To serve. Rub the toasted bread with the cut sides of the garlic. Put two slices of bread per person in each of four warmed soup bowls.

6 Taste and adjust the seasoning of the soup, then pour over the bread. Serve immediately.

Menu Suggestion
Serve this meal-in-a-bowl soup for lunch or supper with a selection of Italian cheeses to follow and fresh fruit to finish.

CIPOLLATA

Soups are usually eaten with the evening meal in Italy. The main meal of the day is at lunchtime, so in the evening a bowl of soup with some fresh bread is often all that is called for. This soup from the region of Umbria just north of Rome is typical of the kind that Italians enjoy for their evening meal.

There is another version which uses the same ingredients except that it is a thick mixture which is piled onto hot toast and eaten like a savoury. In Umbria, it is eaten as a first course, but it is quite substantial and so must be followed by something light. Make it exactly as the soup on this page, but omit the stock in step 3, then in step 4 combine the Parmesan cheese with 3 beaten eggs and whisk into the mixture off the heat—it should be rather like scrambled eggs.

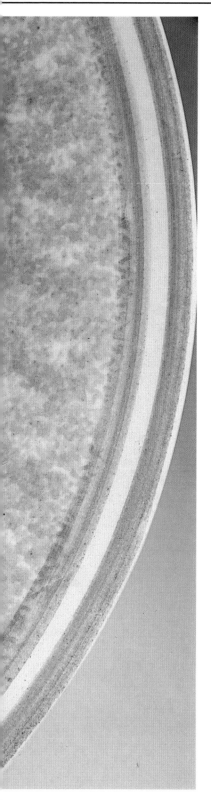

HAM AND BEAN SOUP

2.20* £ ✳ 201 cals

* plus overnight soaking

Serves 4

**225 g (8 oz) dried black beans,
  soaked in cold water overnight**

1 onion, skinned and sliced

**2 celery sticks, trimmed and
  sliced**

1 ham bone

10 ml (2 tsp) mustard powder

juice of $\frac{1}{2}$ a lemon

salt and freshly ground pepper

1 Drain the beans, then place
in a large saucepan with all the
remaining ingredients, except the
lemon juice and salt and pepper.
Add 1.2 litres (2 pints) water.

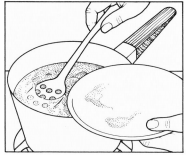

2 Bring to the boil and skim off
any scum with a slotted spoon.
Lower the heat, cover the pan and
simmer for 2 hours or until the
beans are very soft.

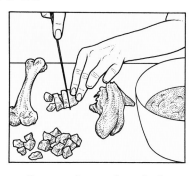

3 Remove the pan from the heat
and lift out the ham bone.
Remove the meat from the bone
and cut into bite-sized pieces. Set
aside.

4 Sieve or purée the soup in a
blender or food processor.
Return to the rinsed-out pan with
the ham and heat through until
bubbling. Adjust the consistency
of the soup with water if it is too
thick and add the lemon juice and
seasoning to taste. Serve when the
soup is piping hot.

Menu Suggestion
This is a hearty American soup,
most suitable for a lunch or
evening meal on its own. Serve
with crusty French bread or hot
garlic bread.

AMERICAN BLACK BEAN SOUP

Black bean soup is something of
an acquired taste. Americans
love it, and you will find recipes
for it in most American cook-
books. Sometimes sherry or rum
is used instead of the lemon
juice suggested here, and sometimes the finished soup is
garnished with slices of hard-
boiled egg and lemon, or with a
sprinkling of hot cooked rice and
finely chopped raw onion.

Black beans, very popular in
South American and Caribbean
cooking, can be found at most
good health food shops. They are
members of the kidney bean
family, and are interchangeable
with red kidney beans in most
recipes.

VEGETABLE SOUP

1.00	£	281 cals

Serves 4

350 g (12 oz) carrot

225 g (8 oz) turnip

175 g (6 oz) onion

225 g (8 oz) celery

5 ml (1 tsp) chopped fresh thyme or 2.5 ml ($\frac{1}{2}$ tsp) dried

5 ml (1 tsp) chopped fresh basil or 2.5 ml ($\frac{1}{2}$ tsp) dried

1 bay leaf

1 garlic clove, skinned and crushed

15 ml (1 tbsp) tomato purée

1.7 litres (3 pints) vegetable stock (see page 350)

salt and freshly ground pepper

125 g (4 oz) macaroni, rigatoni or penne

4 slices of wholemeal bread

50 g (2 oz) Edam cheese, coarsely grated

basil sprigs, to garnish

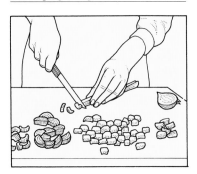

1 Cut the carrot, turnip, onion and celery into large dice.

2 Place the vegetables, thyme, basil, bay leaf and crushed garlic in a large saucepan. Stir over low heat for 2–3 minutes.

3 Stir in the tomato purée, stock and seasoning to taste. Bring to the boil, then lower the heat and simmer for 25–30 minutes.

4 Stir in the pasta. Cover and simmer for a further 12–15 minutes or until the pasta is tender. Taste and adjust the seasoning.

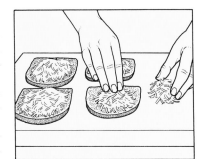

5 Toast the bread lightly on one side. Press a little cheese on to the untoasted side of the bread, dividing it equally between them. Grill until golden. Cut into small triangles.

6 Pour the soup into a warmed serving bowl. Serve immediately, garnished with the sprigs of basil and toasted cheese triangles.

— VARIATION —

Roughly chop 175 g (6 oz) smoked lean bacon and cook with the vegetables at the beginning of the recipe. Proceed as above.

SPINACH SOUP

| 0.30 | 50 cals |

Serves 4

450 g (1 lb) fresh spinach
900 ml (1½ pints) vegetable or
  chicken stock (see page 350)
15 ml (1 tbsp) lemon juice
salt and freshly ground pepper
450 ml (¾ pint) buttermilk
a few drops of Tabasco sauce

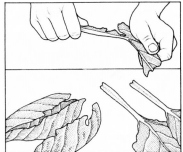

1 Strip the spinach leaves from their stems and wash in several changes of water. Place the spinach, stock, lemon juice and seasoning in a pan. Simmer for 10 minutes.

2 Work the spinach through a sieve, or strain off most of the liquid and reserve, then purée the spinach in a blender or processor.

3 Reheat the spinach purée gently with the cooking liquid, 300 ml (½ pint) of the buttermilk and Tabasco sauce. Swirl in the remaining buttermilk.

Menu Suggestion
Serve with warm wholemeal rolls.

CHEESE AND COURGETTE SOUP

| 0.40 | ✳* | 286 cals |

* freeze at the end of step 2

Serves 4

450 g (1 lb) courgettes, trimmed
   and sliced

1 large onion, skinned and
   chopped

1 litre (1¾ pints) vegetable stock
   (see page 350)

salt and freshly ground pepper

175 g (6 oz) garlic and herb
   cheese

150 ml (¼ pint) single cream

chopped fresh herbs, to garnish

1 Put the courgettes and onion
in a large saucepan with the
stock. Bring to the boil, then lower
the heat, cover the pan and
simmer for 20 minutes or until the
courgettes are really soft.

2 Sieve or purée the soup in a
blender or food processor. Put
the cheese in the rinsed-out pan
and gradually work in the puréed
soup with a wooden spoon.

3 Reheat the soup gently,
stirring constantly, then add
the cream and heat through without boiling. Taste and adjust
seasoning, then pour into 4
warmed soup bowls. Sprinkle
with chopped herbs and serve
immediately.

Menu Suggestion
Serve this French-style soup with
hot garlic or herb bread before a
main course of lamb.

CREAM OF CHICKEN SOUP

0.45 ✳* 120 cals

* freeze without the cream

Serves 4

45 ml (3 tbsp) flour

150 ml (¼ pint) milk

1.1 litres (2 pints) chicken stock (see page 350)

100 g (4 oz) cooked chicken, diced

salt and freshly ground pepper

5 ml (1 tsp) lemon juice

pinch of grated nutmeg

30 ml (2 tbsp) single cream

croûtons and parsley sprigs, to garnish

1 In a large bowl, blend the flour with a little of the milk until it makes a smooth cream.

2 Bring the stock to the boil, then, stir it into the blended mixture. Return to the pan and simmer gently for 20 minutes.

3 Stir in the chicken, seasoning, lemon juice and nutmeg. Mix the rest of the milk with the cream and stir in. Reheat without boiling.

4 Taste and adjust seasoning, then pour into warmed in-dividual soup bowls. Sprinkle with croûtons and parsley sprigs.

Menu Suggestion
Serve this smooth, rich soup with warmed bridge rolls, before a main course of plain roast or grilled meat.

CHICKEN WATERZOOI

2.00 £ ✳* 205 cals

* freeze after step 4

Serves 6

1.4 kg (3 lb) chicken or boiling fowl, with giblets

½ lemon

2 sticks of celery, chopped

2 leeks, trimmed and chopped

1 medium onion, skinned and chopped

2 carrots, peeled and sliced

1 bouquet garni

salt and freshly ground pepper

½ bottle dry white wine

2 egg yolks

90 ml (6 tbsp) single cream

30 ml (2 tbsp) chopped fresh parsley

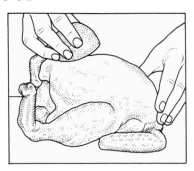

1 Prick the chicken all over with a skewer, then rub with the cut lemon, squeezing the fruit as you do so, to release the juice.

2 Put the chicken in a large saucepan with the giblets, vegetables, bouquet garni and salt and pepper to taste. Pour in the wine, then add enough water to just cover the chicken.

3 Bring the liquid to the boil, then lower the heat and half cover with a lid. Simmer for 1½ hours, or until the meat is tender and beginning to fall away from the bones.

4 Remove the chicken from the liquid. Discard the bouquet garni and the giblets. Cut the chicken flesh into bite-sized pieces, discarding all skin and bones, then return to the liquid.

5 Mix together the egg yolks and cream in a heatproof bowl. Stir in a few ladlefuls of the hot cooking liquid.

6 Return this mixture to the pan. Simmer until thickened, stirring constantly, then add the parsley and taste and adjust seasoning. Serve hot in a warmed soup tureen.

TURKEY AND CHESTNUT SOUP

| 0.45 | ✳ | 156–234 cals |

Serves 4–6

25 g (1 oz) butter or margarine

1 large onion, skinned and chopped

225 g (8 oz) Brussels sprouts

900 ml (1½ pints) turkey stock made from leftover carcass (see page 350) and any leftover turkey meat

439-g (15-oz) can whole chestnuts, drained

10 ml (2 tsp) chopped fresh thyme or 5 ml (1 tsp) dried thyme

salt and freshly ground pepper

stock or milk, to finish

sprigs of thyme, to garnish

1 Melt the fat in a large heavy-based saucepan, add the onion and fry gently for 5 minutes until it has softened.

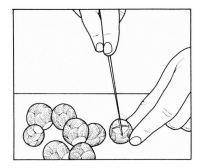

2 Trim the sprouts and cut a cross in the base of each one. Add to the onion, cover the pan with a lid and cook gently for 5 minutes, shaking pan frequently.

3 Pour in the stock and bring to the boil, then add the remaining ingredients, with salt and pepper to taste. Lower the heat, cover and simmer for 30 minutes until the vegetables are tender.

4 Leave to cool slightly, then purée in a blender until smooth. Return to the rinsed-out pan and reheat, then thin down with either stock or milk, according to taste.

5 Taste and adjust seasoning, then pour into warmed individual bowls. Serve hot, garnished with sprigs of thyme.

Menu Suggestion

Serve for an informal family lunch with hot garlic bread, wholemeal toast, cheese on toast or hot sausage rolls.

SOUPE DE POISSONS

| 1.00 | £ £ ✳* | 634 cals |

* freeze at the end of step 3

Serves 4

60 ml (4 tbsp) olive oil

2 onions, skinned and sliced

4 garlic cloves, skinned and chopped

225 g (8 oz) ripe tomatoes, roughly chopped

1.4 litres (2½ pints) fish stock (made from cubes) or water

1 kg (2 lb) mixed fish (see box)

1 bouquet garni

1 strip orange rind

few saffron threads

salt and freshly ground pepper

16 thin slices French bread, from a small loaf

100 g (4 oz) Gruyère, grated

1 Heat the oil in a large saucepan, add the onions and fry gently for 5 minutes or until soft. Add the garlic and tomatoes and continue frying until the juices flow, stirring constantly.

2 Pour in the stock or water and bring to the boil, then add the fish, bouquet garni, orange rind and saffron, with salt and pepper to taste. Lower the heat, cover and simmer for 30 minutes or until the fish starts to disintegrate.

3 Ladle the soup into a fine sieve and work the liquid into a large bowl, pressing down firmly on the bones and shells of the fish to extract as much liquid and flesh as possible.

4 Pour the strained liquid into the rinsed-out pan and reheat until bubbling. Toast the bread on both sides. Place the toast, grated cheese and rouille in bowls.

5 To serve, taste and adjust the seasoning of the soup, then pour into a warmed soup tureen. Guests should help themselves, pouring the hot soup over the bread sprinkled with cheese.

SOUPE DE POISSONS

This kind of fish soup is at its best when made on the Mediterranean coast, where there is such an abundance of interesting fresh fish. For Soupe de Poissons, French cooks use much the same sort of fish as they do when making *bouillabaisse*. Fish with interesting sounding names such as rascasse, gurnard, weever, stargazer and wrasse, plus shellfish such as squille and petite cigale.

Outside Mediterranean waters, it is unlikely that you will be able to find these, but a very good soup can be made with other fresh fish. Choose from monkfish, haddock, cod, whiting, red mullet, brill, sea bass and conger eel, making sure to get a good mixture. For the shellfish, you can use prawns or scampi and mussels, and cook them with their shells for maximum flavour.

CHILLED CUCUMBER SOUP

0.15* £ | 92 cals

* plus 1 hour chilling

Serves 4

1 medium-sized cucumber, trimmed

300 ml ($\frac{1}{2}$ pint) natural yogurt

1 small garlic clove, skinned and crushed

30 ml (2 tbsp) wine vinegar

30 ml (2 tbsp) chopped fresh mint or snipped chives

salt and freshly ground pepper

300 ml ($\frac{1}{2}$ pint) milk

mint sprigs, to garnish

1 Grate the unpeeled cucumber into a bowl, using the finest side of a conical or box grater.

2 Stir in the yogurt, crushed garlic, vinegar and mint or chives. Add seasoning to taste and chill in the refrigerator for 1 hour.

3 Just before serving, stir in the milk, then taste and adjust seasoning. Spoon into individual soup bowls and garnish with sprigs of mint.

Menu Suggestion
This soup can be made in advance and served before the main course of a barbecue.

DEEP-FRIED MUSHROOMS WITH HERBY DRESSING

0.30* ☐ £ 318 cals

* plus 30 minutes cooling and 2 hours chilling

Serves 4

75 ml (5 tbsp) mayonnaise (see page 353)

75 ml (5 tbsp) soured cream

30 ml (2 tbsp) chopped capers

15 ml (1 tbsp) tarragon vinegar

15 ml (1 tbsp) chopped fresh tarragon or 7.5 ml (1½ tsp) dried

15 ml (1 tbsp) snipped fresh chives

salt and freshly ground pepper

50 g (2 oz) plain flour plus a little extra, for coating

30 ml (2 tbsp) maize flour

30 ml (2 tbsp) arrowroot

300 ml (½ pint) iced water

450 g (1 lb) button mushrooms, wiped and trimmed

vegetable oil, for deep-frying

tarragon or parsley sprigs, to garnish

1 Make the herby dressing. Put mayonnaise, soured cream, capers, vinegar, tarragon, chives and seasoning in a bowl and whisk well. Turn into a bowl, cover and refrigerate for at least 2 hours.

2 Make the mushroom batter. Sift flours and arrowroot into bowl; gradually whisk in water. Cover, refrigerate for 30 minutes.

3 Coat the mushrooms lightly in flour; dip into batter. Heat oil in a wok or deep-fat frier, then drop in mushrooms a few at a time.

4 Fry for 1–2 minutes until they rise to the surface of the oil and are golden brown.

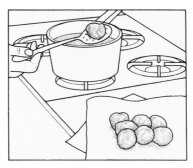

5 Remove the mushrooms from the oil with a slotted spoon and drain on absorbent kitchen paper. Keep hot in the oven while frying the remainder.

6 Pile the mushrooms on four individual serving plates and garnish with tarragon or parsley sprigs. Serve at once, with the dressing handed separately.

SPICY CRAB DIP

0.15* £ £ 136 cals

* plus 2 hours chilling

Serves 4

225 g (8 oz) cottage cheese

225 g (8 oz) frozen white crabmeat, thawed

45 ml (3 tbsp) finely chopped canned pimiento

10 ml (2 tsp) Worcestershire sauce

5 ml (1 tsp) anchovy essence

2.5 ml ($\frac{1}{2}$ tsp) cayenne pepper

juice of $\frac{1}{2}$ lemon

salt and freshly ground pepper

sticks of raw celery, carrot and cucumber, cauliflower florets, spring onions and small whole radishes, to serve

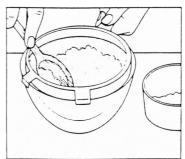

1 Work the cottage cheese through a sieve into a bowl. Flake the crabmeat, then fold into the sieved cottage cheese until evenly mixed.

2 Fold in the pimiento, then stir in the Worcestershire sauce, anchovy essence, half the cayenne, the lemon juice and salt and ground pepper to taste.

3 Turn the dip into a serving bowl, then sprinkle with the remaining cayenne. Chill in the refrigerator for at least 2 hours until serving time. Serve the dip chilled, with a platter of raw vegetables.

MARINATED MUSHROOMS

0.15*	76 cals

* plus 6–8 hours marinating
Serves 4

450 g (1 lb) small button
   mushrooms, wiped

30 ml (2 tbsp) wine vinegar

90 ml (6 tbsp) sunflower oil

pinch of mustard powder

pinch of Barbados sugar

salt and freshly ground pepper

chopped fresh parsley, to garnish

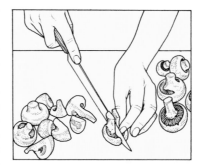

1 Trim the mushrooms. Leave small mushrooms whole and cut larger ones in quarters.

2 Put the vinegar, oil, mustard and sugar in a bowl with seasoning to taste. Whisk together with a fork until well blended.

3 Add the mushrooms and stir to coat in the marinade. Cover and leave to marinate in the refrigerator for 6–8 hours, stirring occasionally.

4 Taste and adjust the seasoning of the mushrooms, then divide equally between 4 individual shallow serving dishes. Sprinkle with chopped parsley and serve immediately.

Menu Suggestion
Marinated mushrooms make a refreshingly light start to a substantial main course. Serve with crusty brown bread to mop up the juices.

BUTTER BEAN PÂTÉ

| 2.30* | £ | ✳ | 151–202 cals |

* plus overnight soaking

Serves 6–8

225 g (8 oz) dried butter beans, soaked in cold water overnight

60 ml (4 tbsp) olive oil

juice of 2 lemons

2 garlic cloves, skinned and crushed

30 ml (2 tbsp) chopped fresh coriander

salt and freshly ground pepper

coriander sprigs and black olives, to garnish

1 Drain the butter beans into a sieve and rinse thoroughly under cold running water. Put in a saucepan, cover with cold water and bring to the boil.

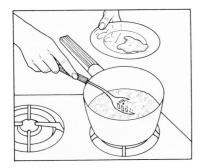

2 With a slotted spoon, skim off any scum that rises to the surface. Half cover the pan with a lid and simmer for 1½–2 hours until the beans are very tender.

3 Drain the beans and rinse under cold running water. Put half of the beans in a blender or food processor with half of the oil, lemon juice, garlic and coriander. Blend to a smooth purée, then transfer to a bowl. Repeat with the remaining beans, oil, lemon juice, garlic and coriander.

4 Beat the 2 batches of purée together until well mixed, then add seasoning to taste.

5 Turn the pâté into a serving bowl and rough up the surface with the prongs of a fork. Garnish with the coriander and black olives. Chill in the refrigerator until serving time.

Menu Suggestion

Serve this creamy dip with fingers of hot wholemeal pitta bread or granary toast for an informal supper party starter.

— VARIATION —

If you want to make this dip really quickly, use two 396 g (14 oz) cans butter beans and start the recipe from the beginning of step 3.

KIPPER MOUSSE

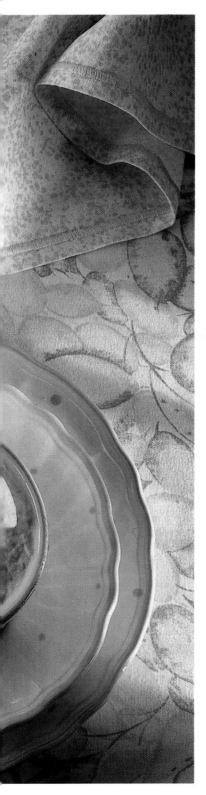

| 0.20* | £ | 192 cals |

* plus 1 hour chilling

Serves 4

350 g (12 oz) kipper fillets
juice of 1 orange
15 ml (1 tbsp) lemon juice
5 ml (1 tsp) gelatine
100 g (4 oz) cottage or curd cheese
150 ml ($\frac{1}{4}$ pint) natural yogurt
1 small garlic clove, skinned and
    crushed
1.25 ml ($\frac{1}{4}$ tsp) ground mace
salt and freshly ground pepper
lemon or orange slices and herb
    sprigs, to garnish

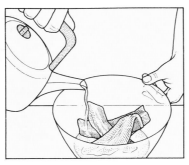

1 Pour boiling water over the kippers and leave to stand for 1 minute. Drain, pat dry and remove the skin. Flake the flesh, discarding any bones, and put into a blender or food processor.

2 In a small heatproof bowl, mix the orange and lemon juices together. Sprinkle on the gelatine and leave to stand for a few minutes until spongy.

3 Meanwhile, add the cottage cheese, yogurt, garlic and mace to the blender or food processor and blend until smooth.

4 Place the bowl of gelatine in a saucepan of hot water and heat gently until dissolved. Add to the kipper mixture and blend until evenly mixed. Season to taste.

5 Divide the kipper mousse equally between 6 oiled individual ramekin dishes. Chill in the refrigerator for at least 1 hour before serving.

6 Turn the mousses out on to individual plates and garnish.

Menu Suggestion
These tangy fish mousses can be served as part of a light lunch, or as a starter to any main meal. Serve with wholemeal toast.

KIPPER MOUSSE
Kippers are herrings which have been split and cold-smoked, that is they need to be cooked before eating—standing them in boiling water for a minute or so is the traditional, and best, method. When buying kippers, check for plump flesh and an oily skin— these are signs of quality. A dark-brown colour does not necessarily mean a good kipper, as this is probably an artificial dye. Some of the best kippers are the undyed Manx variety— available from good fishmongers.

TARAMASALATA

1.30*	£	283 cals

* includes 1 hour chilling

Serves 6

225 g (8 oz) smoked cod's roe

1 garlic clove, skinned

50 g (2 oz) fresh white breadcrumbs

1 small onion, skinned and finely chopped

grated rind and juice of 1 lemon

150 ml (¼ pint) olive oil

90 ml (6 tbsp) hot water

freshly ground pepper

lemon slices, to garnish

pitta bread or toast, to serve (optional)

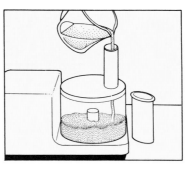

3 Gradually add the oil and blend well after each addition until smooth. Blend in hot water with the pepper.

4 Spoon into a serving dish and chill for at least 1 hour. To serve, garnish with lemon slices. Serve with pitta bread or toast, if liked.

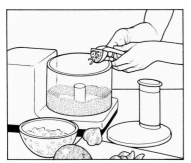

1 Skin the smoked cod's roe and break it up into pieces. Place in a blender or food processor, and blend to form a purée.

2 Crush the garlic, then add to the cod's roe with the breadcrumbs, onion and lemon rind and juice and blend for a few more seconds.

TARAMASALATA
Taramasalata is a creamy dip with a subtle flavour of smoked fish. From the Greek words *tarama*, meaning dried and salted mullet roe, and *salata* meaning salad, it is eaten all over Greece and Turkey as part of the *mezze* before a meal. Salted mullet roe is not so easy to obtain as it was when the recipe was first made, so these days taramasalata is most often made with smoked cod's roe, which is very similar. Many supermarkets and delicatessens sell taramasalata (often labelled 'smoked cod's roe pâté') by the kg (lb) or ready-packed in cartons. Most brands have artificial colouring added to them which gives them an unnatural bright pink colour; they also taste very strongly of fish. Homemade taramasalata tastes so much better than these commercial varieties, and it is very simple and quick to make.

CHICKEN LIVER PÂTÉ

| 0.20* £ ✳ | 201–302 cals |

* plus 3–4 hours chilling

Serves 4–6

100 g (4 oz) unsalted butter
225 g (8 oz) chicken livers
30 ml (2 tbsp) brandy
1 garlic clove, skinned
2.5 ml (½ tsp) dried mixed herbs
salt and freshly ground pepper
bay leaves, to garnish

1 Melt half the butter in a heavy frying pan, add the livers and cook them over moderate heat for 5 minutes, stirring so that they cook evenly. The livers should be brown on the outside, and pink, but set, in the centre.

2 Pour the contents of the frying pan straight into a blender or food processor.

3 Pour the brandy into the pan and bring quickly to the boil, stirring well to incorporate any sediment left on the bottom of the pan. Allow to bubble for 1 minute.

4 Add the brandy and juices to the livers with the garlic and dried herbs and blend until smooth. Blend in the remaining butter and salt and pepper to taste.

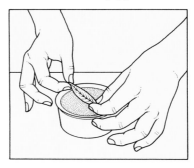

5 Pour the pâté into one terrine, or four to six individual ramekin dishes. Place the bay leaves on top and refrigerate for 3–4 hours before serving.

6 If the pâté is to be kept for several days before serving, pour enough cooled, melted butter over the top to form a complete seal. The pâté will then keep for at least 1 week in the refrigerator.

Menu Suggestion
Serve as a starter with Melba toast or toasted wholemeal or granary bread.

——————— VARIATION ———————

A delicious way of varying this rich and flavoursome dish is by substituting 50 g (2 oz) of the chicken livers with the same weight of **sliced mushrooms**. Choose cap or field mushrooms for a more distinctive flavour, and fry them together with the chicken livers in the pan. Instead of using dried mixed herbs, use the same quantity of **dried thyme**, or **5 ml (1 tsp) chopped fresh thyme**.

Salads and
Cold Dishes

ORIENTAL SALAD

| 0.20 | f | 112 cals |

Serves 8

1 large cucumber
salt and freshly ground pepper
1 small head Chinese leaves
1 red pepper
125 g (4 oz) button mushrooms
225 g (8 oz) beansprouts
30 ml (2 tbsp) soy sauce
15 ml (1 tbsp) peanut butter
30 ml (2 tbsp) sesame oil
30 ml (2 tbsp) rice or wine vinegar
50 g (2 oz) shelled unsalted peanuts

2 Shred the Chinese leaves, wash and drain well. Cut the red pepper in half and remove the core and seeds. Cut the flesh into thin strips. Wipe and slice the mushrooms. Rinse the beansprouts and drain well.

3 Just before serving, mix the soy sauce in a large bowl with the peanut butter, oil, vinegar and salt and pepper to taste. Add the salad ingredients and the peanuts and toss together. Transfer to a serving bowl.

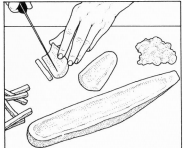

1 Cut the cucumber in half lengthways and scoop out the seeds. Cut the halves into 5 cm (2 inch) sticks, leaving the skin on.

Menu Suggestion
Serve the salad in pockets of pitta bread as an accompaniment to barbecued food or at a picnic.

ORIENTAL SALAD

All the exotic ingredients for this salad can be bought in good supermarkets or health food shops. *Chinese leaves* are an extremely versatile vegetable and can be lightly braised, steamed or served raw in salads. Look for Chinese leaves also under the name of Chinese cabbage or Chinese celery cabbage; it has long white stems and should not be confused with a similar-looking vegetable called 'bok choy', which has dark green stems. *Beansprouts* are the shoots of sprouted mung peas or beans. They are available fresh, and should be eaten as soon as possible after purchase as they quickly discolour and become limp. *Soy sauce* comes in varying strengths, from light to dark brown. For a salad, dark soy sauce is the best one to use because it is fairly mild; light soy sauce can be very salty. *Sesame oil* is made from sesame seeds. It has a rich, golden-brown colour and a nutty aroma and flavour. In Chinese cooking, it is used as a seasoning rather than for cooking, because it burns quickly when heated. *Rice wine vinegar* is available in white, red and black varieties. Each one has a slightly different flavour, from sweet and spicy to rich and pungent. They are cheap, so it is a good idea to try different makes to find which you like best.

WALDORF SALAD

| 0.40 | £ | 402 cals |

Serves 4

450 g (1 lb) eating apples

juice of 1 lemon

5 ml (1 tsp) sugar

150 ml ($\frac{1}{4}$ pint) mayonnaise (see page 353)

$\frac{1}{2}$ head celery, washed, trimmed and sliced

50 g (2 oz) walnuts, chopped

1 lettuce

few walnut halves, to garnish (optional)

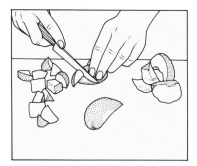

1 Core the apples, slice one and dice the rest. Dip the slices in lemon juice to prevent discoloration of the fruit.

2 Toss the diced apples in 30 ml (2 tbsp) lemon juice, the sugar and 15 ml (1 tbsp) mayonnaise and leave to stand for about 30 minutes.

3 Just before serving, add the sliced celery, chopped walnuts and the remaining mayonnaise, and toss together.

4 Serve in a bowl lined with lettuce leaves and garnish with the apple slices and a few walnut halves, if liked.

PASTA, PRAWN AND APPLE SALAD

$\boxed{0.30^*}$ £ $\boxed{176 \text{ cals}}$

* plus 2–3 hours chilling

Serves 6

175 g (6 oz) pasta shells

150 ml (¼ pint) unsweetened apple juice

5 ml (1 tsp) chopped fresh mint

5 ml (1 tsp) white wine vinegar

salt and freshly ground pepper

225 g (8 oz) peeled prawns

225 g (8 oz) crisp eating apples

lettuce leaves

paprika, to garnish

1 Cook the pasta in boiling salted water for 10–15 minutes until tender. Drain well, rinse in cold running water and drain again.

2 Meanwhile, make the dressing. Whisk together the apple juice, mint, vinegar and seasoning.

3 Dry the prawns with absorbent kitchen paper. Quarter, core and roughly chop the apples. Stir the prawns, apple and cooked pasta into the dressing until well mixed. Cover tightly with cling film and refrigerate for 2–3 hours.

4 Wash the lettuce leaves, dry and shred finely. Place a little lettuce in six individual serving dishes. Spoon the prawn salad on top and dust with paprika.

LEMONY BEAN SALAD

2.00*	312 cals

* plus overnight soaking and 4 hours standing

Serves 4

100 g (4 oz) green flageolet beans (see box), soaked in cold water overnight

90 ml (6 tbsp) olive oil

finely grated rind and juice of 1 lemon

1–2 garlic cloves, skinned and crushed

salt and freshly ground pepper

50 g (2 oz) black olives

30 ml (2 tbsp) chopped mixed fresh herbs, e.g. basil, marjoram, lemon balm, chives

4 large firm tomatoes

about 1.25 ml ($\frac{1}{4}$ tsp) sugar

1 Drain and rinse the beans, then place in a pan with plenty of water. Bring to the boil, then lower the heat, half cover with a lid and simmer for about 1 hour until tender.

2 Drain the beans, transfer to a bowl and immediately add the oil, lemon rind and juice, garlic and seasoning to taste. Stir well to mix, then cover and leave for at least 4 hours to allow the dressing to flavour the beans.

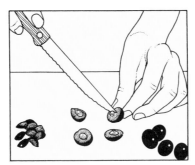

3 Stone the olives, then chop roughly. Add to the salad with the herbs, then taste and adjust seasoning.

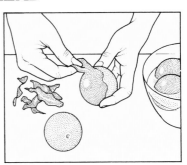

4 Skin the tomatoes. Put them in a bowl, pour over boiling water and leave for 2 minutes. Drain, then plunge into a bowl of cold water. Remove the tomatoes one at a time and peel off the skin with your fingers.

5 Slice the tomatoes thinly, then arrange on 4 serving plates. Sprinkle with sugar and seasoning to taste. Pile the bean salad on top of each plate. Serve chilled.

Menu Suggestion
Fresh and tangy, this summer salad can be served on its own as a starter or light lunch dish, or as an accompaniment to cold meats, especially cold roast chicken or turkey.

LEMONY BEAN SALAD

Green flageolet beans are a very pretty, delicate light green in colour. They are haricot beans which have been removed from their pods when very young and tender, and they get their name from the French word for flute, which they are said to resemble in shape. Most large supermarkets stock green flageolets, but health food shops probably have the fastest turnover. It is important that they have not been stored for too long because, like all dried pulses, they become stale and will not soften, no matter how long you cook them.

INSALATA DI PATATE
(POTATO SALAD)

0.20*	358 cals

* plus 30 minutes cooling

Serves 4

700 g (1½ lb) waxy potatoes, scrubbed not peeled

90 ml (6 tbsp) olive oil

30 ml (2 tbsp) lemon juice

5 ml (1 tsp) anchovy essence

1 small onion, skinned and finely chopped

1 garlic clove, skinned and crushed

15 ml (1 tbsp) capers, chopped

8 anchovy fillets, soaked in milk and finely chopped (optional)

salt and freshly ground pepper

anchovy fillets, to garnish

1 Cook the potatoes gently in their skins in boiling salted water for about 15 minutes, or until just tender.

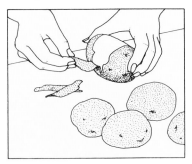

2 Drain the potatoes and leave until just cool enough to handle. Peel off the skins with your fingers.

3 Make the anchovy dressing. In a large bowl, whisk together the oil, lemon juice and anchovy essence until thick. Stir in the onion, garlic, capers and anchovy fillets, if using.

4 Pour the dressing over the potatoes whilst they are still warm. Toss well and leave for about 30 minutes until completely cold. Taste and adjust seasoning before serving. Garnish with anchovy fillets.

Menu Suggestion

With its tangy dressing, this potato salad goes well with salami and rich cold meats such as pork.

INSALATA DI PATATE

The anchovy essence specified in this recipe is available in bottles or tubes at large supermarkets and delicatessens specialising in continental foods. It keeps indefinitely and is a useful store-cupboard ingredient in that it can be used to 'pep up' all kinds of dishes. It is especially good with the rather bland flavours of potatoes and eggs, and is excellent stirred into mayonnaise to give extra zing. Try a teaspoon or two in meat pâtés and loaves, or in home-made hamburgers.

TABOULEH ▶

0.40* £ 181–241 cals

* includes 30 minutes soaking

Serves 6–8

225 g (8 oz) burghul (cracked
   wheat)

4 spring onions, washed and
   trimmed

1 large bunch fresh parsley, total
   weight about 125 g (4 oz)

3 large sprigs fresh mint

60 ml (4 tbsp) olive oil

rind and juice of 1½ lemons

salt and freshly ground pepper

few vine or Cos lettuce leaves

lemon wedges and fresh mint
   sprigs, to garnish

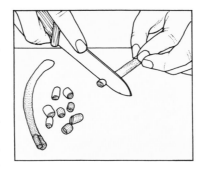

2 Meanwhile, finely chop the
spring onions. Then, using a
blender or food processor, chop
the parsley and mint.

3 Mix the burghul, onion, parsley and mint together in a
bowl, add the olive oil, lemon rind
and juice and season well to taste.

4 To serve, place the salad on a
serving dish lined with lettuce
or vine leaves. Garnish with a few
lemon slices.

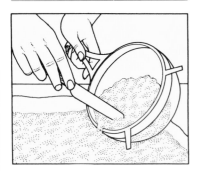

1 Put the burghul in a bowl and
add cold water to cover by
about 2.5 cm (1 inch). Soak for 30
minutes. Drain well in a sieve,
then spread it out on a tea towel
and leave to dry.

MIDDLE EASTERN SALADS

This strange-sounding salad is
Lebanese in origin, and there are
numerous different versions. All
are based on burghul or cracked
wheat and all contain masses of
parsley and mint, with a dressing
of olive oil and lemon juice, although the proportion of these
ingredients varies from one
cook – and one occasion – to another. Some versions even contain
crushed tomatoes, though this is
not traditional.

If you can buy or grow the
frondy, continental-type parsley
for this salad, then so much the
better – this is the type that
would be used in the Middle
East. Curly-leaved English
parsley can be used, but it does
have a different flavour.

Burghul is available at health
food shops – it is whole wheat
grain which has been boiled and
baked then cracked. It does not
need cooking, simply soaking in
cold water for 30 minutes until
the grains swell.

TABOULEH WITH SALAD VEGETABLES AND YOGURT DRESSING

| 0.40* | £ | 108 cals |

* includes 30 minutes soaking

Serves 8

225 g (8 oz) burghul (cracked wheat)

3 spring onions, washed and trimmed

$\frac{1}{2}$ small cucumber

3 tomatoes

1 green pepper

1 large bunch fresh parsley, total weight about 125 g (4 oz)

3 large sprigs fresh mint

60 ml (4 tbsp) natural yogurt

rind and juice of $1\frac{1}{2}$ lemons

salt and freshly ground pepper

1 Cos lettuce

1 Prepare the burghul as in step 1 opposite. Leave to dry out on a clean tea towel.

2 Meanwhile, finely chop the spring onions, tomatoes and cucumber. Core and finely chop the green pepper. Using a blender or food processor, chop the parsley and lemon.

3 Mix the burghul, vegetables, parsley and mint together in a bowl, add the yogurt, lemon rind and juice and season well to taste.

4 Separate the lettuce leaves and wash under cold running water, drain and pat dry on absorbent kitchen paper. Arrange the lettuce leaves around the edge of a serving dish and pile the salad in the centre.

GADO-GADO
(INDONESIAN MIXED VEGETABLE SALAD)

| 1.30 | £ | 275 cals |

Serves 4

vegetable oil, for deep-frying

100 g (4 oz) shelled unsalted peanuts

1 small onion, skinned and very finely chopped

2 garlic cloves, skinned and crushed

2.5–5 ml ($\frac{1}{2}$–1 tsp) chilli powder

5 ml (1 tsp) soft brown sugar

juice of 1 lemon

25 g (1 oz) creamed coconut, roughly chopped (optional)

8 small waxy new potatoes

4 small young carrots

100 g (4 oz) cauliflower florets

100 g (4 oz) green cabbage or spring greens

100 g (4 oz) French beans

100 g (4 oz) beansprouts

lettuce leaves and slices of cucumber and hard-boiled egg, to garnish

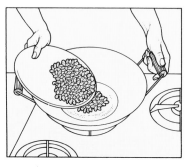

1 Make the peanut sauce. Heat the oil to 190°C (375°F) in a wok or deep-fat frier. Lower the peanuts into the hot oil and deep-fry for about 5 minutes until the skins are well browned. Remove with a slotted spoon and drain on absorbent kitchen paper.

2 If using a wok, pour off all but about 30 ml (2 tbsp) of the oil. (If a deep-fat frier was used to fry the peanuts, pour 30 ml (2 tbsp) of the oil into a heavy-based saucepan.) Reheat the oil, add the onion and garlic and fry gently for about 5 minutes until they are soft and lightly coloured.

3 Add the chilli powder and stir fry for 1–2 minutes, then add 350 ml (12 fl oz) water, the sugar, lemon juice and creamed coconut, if using. Bring to the boil, stirring to combine the ingredients together.

4 Grind the deep-fried peanuts in a food processor or nut mill, or with a pestle and mortar. Add to the sauce and simmer, stirring, until thickened. Remove and set aside until ready to serve.

5 Prepare the vegetables for the salad. Scrub the potatoes and carrots. Slice the carrots thinly. Divide the cauliflower into small sprigs. Cut off any thick, hard stalks from the cabbage and discard. Shred the cabbage leaves. Top and tail the French beans.

6 Boil the potatoes in salted water for about 20 minutes until tender. Remove with a slotted spoon and leave until cool enough to handle. Add the carrots to the water and parboil for 4 minutes. Remove the carrots with a slotted spoon.

7 Blanch the cauliflower and beans in the water for 3 minutes and remove with a slotted spoon. Blanch the cabbage and beansprouts for 1 minute only, then drain and discard the water.

8 Remove the skin from the potatoes, then slice the potatoes into thin rings.

9 Line a large shallow serving dish or platter with lettuce leaves. Arrange the prepared vegetables on top, then garnish with the slices of cucumber and hard-boiled egg.

10 Reheat the sauce, stirring constantly, then pour a little of the sauce over the salad. Serve immediately, with the remaining sauce handed separately in a jug or bowl.

Menu Suggestion
Serve Gado-Gado on its own as a lunch dish, with crisply fried onion rings and prawn crackers.

GADO-GADO
Literally translated, gado-gado means 'a mixture'. Ingredients vary according to availability, since freshness is the keynote to all Indonesian salads—if a particular vegetable is not at its best, it will not be included. Some versions of gado-gado have a fish-flavoured sauce, made by adding a little shrimp paste or *terasi* (available in jars at oriental stores) to the onion and garlic in step 2.

CHICKEN WITH CURRIED LEMON MAYONNAISE

1.30*	871 cals

* plus about 2¼ hours cooling and 30 minutes chilling

Serves 4

1.4 kg (3 lb) chicken
150 ml (¼ pint) dry white wine
1 strip of lemon rind
1 bouquet garni
6 black peppercorns
salt and freshly ground pepper
15 g (½ oz) butter or margarine
1 small onion, skinned and chopped
15 ml (1 tbsp) curry powder
2 sticks of celery, finely chopped
175 ml (6 fl oz) mayonnaise (see page 353)
30 ml (2 tbsp) apricot jam
finely grated rind and juice of 1 lemon
1 red or green pepper, cored, seeded and diced
2 red-skinned eating apples
150 ml (5 fl oz) double or whipping cream
lettuce, to serve

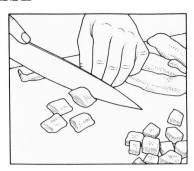

1 Put the chicken in a deep saucepan with the wine, enough water to just cover the bird, lemon rind, bouquet garni, peppercorns and a good pinch of salt. Cover and simmer for 1–1¼ hours until the chicken is tender, then leave for about 2 hours to cool in the liquid.

2 Remove the chicken from the liquid; strain the liquid into a saucepan, then boil until reduced to a few tablespoons. Cool for 5 minutes.

3 Meanwhile, remove the chicken from the bones, and dice the meat, discarding all skin.

4 Melt the fat in a small pan, add the onion and curry powder and fry until soft. Add celery and fry for 2 minutes, stirring. Cool for 10 minutes.

5 Add the onion and celery to the mayonnaise with the apricot jam, lemon rind and juice and the diced pepper. Thin with the reduced cooking liquid. Taste and adjust seasoning.

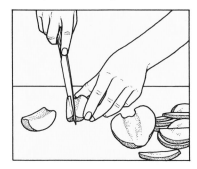

6 Core and dice or slice the apples, but do not peel them. Whip the cream until thick, then fold into the mayonnaise with the apples and chicken. Pile into a salad bowl lined with lettuce leaves. Chill for about 30 minutes before serving.

Menu Suggestion
Serve for a summer lunch with poppadoms or pitta bread.

Beef and Olive Salad

1.40* £ 341 cals

* plus about 2 hours cooling and
30 minutes chilling

Serves 4

450 g (1 lb) rolled lean brisket

1 bay leaf

6 peppercorns

1 large bunch of spring onions

12 black olives

450 g (1 lb) French beans

salt and freshly ground pepper

45 ml (3 tbsp) soy sauce

20 ml (4 tsp) lemon juice

1 Put the beef, bay leaf and
peppercorns in a small
saucepan. Add enough water to
cover. Bring to the boil, cover and
simmer gently for about 1 hour or
until the meat is tender. Leave to
cool in the cooking liquid for
about 2 hours.

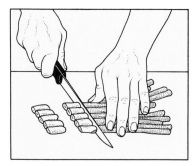

2 Slice the spring onions
diagonally into thick pieces.
Quarter and stone the olives. Trim
and halve the French beans. Cook
the beans in boiling salted water
for 5–10 minutes until just tender.
Drain well, rinse under cold water
and drain again thoroughly.

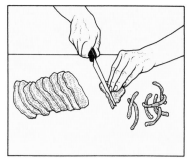

3 Drain the beef and trim off the
fat. Slice thinly and cut into
4 cm (1½ inch) long shreds.

4 Put the beef in a bowl, add
the spring onions, olives,
beans, soy sauce and lemon juice.
Toss well together, then season
with pepper. (The soy sauce
should provide sufficient salt.)
Cover and chill in the refrigerator
for about 30 minutes before
serving.

Menu Suggestion
Beef and Olive Salad is the perfect
main course for an al fresco lunch.
Serve with crusty French bread
and butter.

─────── VARIATION ───────

Slice the beef into about 12 thin
slices. Finely chop **20 stoned
black olives** and mix with **1
crushed garlic clove** and **45 ml
(3 tbsp) olive oil**. Spread the
olive mixture thinly and evenly
over both sides of each slice of
beef. Roll up each slice loosely
from the shortest end and arrange
on a flat serving dish. Cover and
chill in the refrigerator. Trim and
thinly slice **1 large bunch of
radishes**; skin and thinly slice **1
small onion**. Mix in a bowl with
15 ml (1 tbsp) olive oil. Spoon
the radish and onion mixture
around the beef rolls.

CHEF'S SALAD

0.15	£	690 cals

Serves 4

225 g (8 oz) ham

225 g (8 oz) cold cooked chicken

225 g (8 oz) Emmenthal cheese

1 Iceberg or Webb lettuce

2 eggs, hard-boiled, shelled and
    quartered

6 small tomatoes, halved, or 2
    large tomatoes, quartered

3 spring onions, washed, trimmed
    and finely chopped

150 ml ($\frac{1}{4}$ pint) basic vinaigrette
    (see page 352) or blue cheese
    dressing (see page 353), to serve

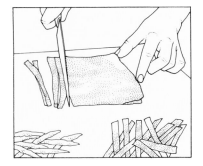

1 Using a sharp knife, cut the ham and the cold cooked chicken into fine strips and set aside.

2 Remove any rind from the cheese. Using a small sharp knife, carefully cut the cheese into small dice. Wash the lettuce under cold running water and pat it dry with absorbent kitchen paper.

3 Finely shred the leaves, or leave them whole, and use to line an oval serving dish.

4 To serve. Arrange the meat and cheese alternately around the edge of the dish. Add egg and tomatoes, sprinkle over the finely chopped spring onions and serve the dressing separately.

SALADE NIÇOISE

| 1.00* | £ | 574 cals |

* includes 30 minutes standing time

Serves 4

198-g (7-oz) can tuna fish, drained

225 g (8 oz) tomatoes, quartered

50 g (2 oz) black olives, stoned

½ small cucumber, thinly sliced

225 g (8 oz) cooked French beans

2 hard-boiled eggs, shelled and quartered

15 ml (1 tbsp) chopped fresh parsley

15 ml (1 tbsp) chopped fresh basil

150 ml (¼ pint) garlic vinaigrette (see page 352)

8 anchovy fillets, halved and drained

French bread, to serve

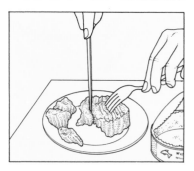

1 Flake the canned tuna into fairly large chunks. Arrange the tuna chunks in a salad bowl with the tomatoes, olives, cucumber slices, beans and eggs.

2 Add the parsley and basil to the garlic vinaigrette, mix well and pour dressing over salad.

3 Arrange the anchovy fillets in a lattice pattern over the salad and allow to stand for 30 minutes before serving. Serve with crusty French bread.

GREEK SALAD

| 0.25 | £ | 511 cals |

Serves 4

2 large tomatoes
1 green pepper
½ medium cucumber
50 g (2 oz) Greek black olives
225 g (8 oz) Feta cheese
120 ml (8 tbsp) olive oil
30–45 ml (2–3 tbsp) lemon juice
salt and freshly ground pepper
large pinch dried oregano
pitta bread, to serve

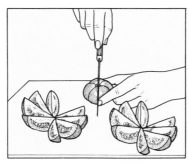

1 Using a sharp knife, cut each tomato in half. Then cut each of the halves into four equal-sized wedges.

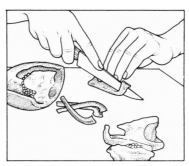

2 Halve, seed and slice the green pepper thinly; then cut the cucumber half into thick slices.

3 Stone the black olives. Arrange the tomato wedges, sliced pepper and cucumber and the olives in a salad bowl.

4 Dice the cheese and add to the bowl, reserving a few dice for garnish. Pour over the olive oil, followed by the lemon juice and season well.

5 Toss the salad well together. Crumble over the remaining cheese cubes, sprinkle with oregano and serve with pitta bread.

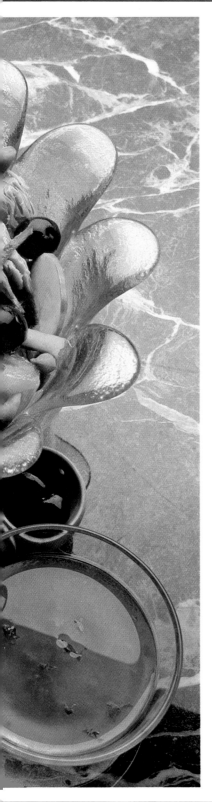

SAUSAGE AND EGG PIE

| 1.30 | 🍴 | £ | 626–939 cals |

Serves 4–6

shortcrust pastry (see page 348)
   made with 275 g (10 oz) plain
   flour

3 eggs, hard-boiled

10 ml (2 tsp) horseradish sauce

225 g (8 oz) sausagemeat

2 eggs, beaten

150 ml ($\frac{1}{4}$ pint) single cream or
   milk

5 ml (1 tsp) chopped fresh sage or
   2.5 ml ($\frac{1}{2}$ tsp) dried

salt and freshly ground pepper

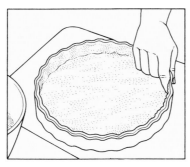

1 Use two-thirds of the pastry to line a 20.5 cm (8 inch) flan ring placed on a baking sheet.

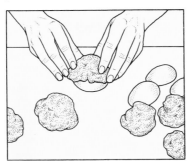

2 Shell the hard-boiled eggs and halve lengthways. Mix the horseradish sauce with the sausagemeat, divide into 6 and mould over the white of each egg half. Place yolk side down in the flan case.

3 Reserve 10 ml (2 tsp) of the beaten eggs for glazing, then mix the remainder with the cream, sage and seasoning to taste. Pour into the flan case.

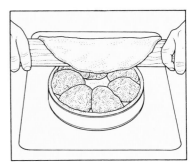

4 Cover with the remaining pastry, sealing the edges well. Decorate with pastry trimmings. Chill in the refrigerator until required.

5 Glaze the pie with the reserved beaten eggs, then bake in the oven at 170°C (325°F) mark 3 for about 1 hour. Serve hot or cold.

Menu Suggestion

Sausage and Egg Pie makes a filling dish for a family supper. Serve hot with French beans tossed in melted herb butter, or baked beans if there are children eating. For a picnic or summer meal in the garden, serve the pie cold with a selection of salads.

SAUSAGE AND EGG PIE

This pie makes a filling family meal from everyday ingredients, yet shows you have gone to a little more trouble than simply giving them sausage and eggs! For best results, choose a good-quality sausagemeat which is not too fatty. Some varieties, especially those that the butcher make himself, have herbs and spices added, which would give the filling a tasty flavour. Served cold, this pie is also excellent for picnics and packed lunches.

MEAT LOAF

1.35*	✳	494–659 cals

* plus cooling and overnight chilling
Serves 6–8

900 g (2 lb) boneless leg or shoulder of pork, minced
225 g (8 oz) mushrooms, finely chopped
225 g (8 oz) streaky bacon, rinded and minced
2 medium onions, skinned and finely chopped
1 large garlic clove, skinned and crushed
125 g (4 oz) fresh breadcrumbs
150 ml ($\frac{1}{4}$ pint) soured cream
45 ml (3 tbsp) dry white wine
5 ml (1 tsp) dried mixed herbs
2.5 ml ($\frac{1}{2}$ tsp) ground allspice
1.25 ml ($\frac{1}{4}$ tsp) grated nutmeg
salt and freshly ground pepper

1 In a large bowl, mix all the ingredients together until evenly combined.

2 Pack the mixture into a 1.4 litre (2$\frac{1}{2}$ pint) loaf tin and cover with foil.

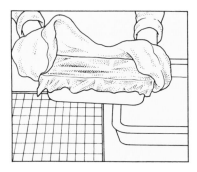

3 Half fill a roasting tin with water and place the loaf tin in the water bath. Cook in the oven at 190°C (375°F) mark 5 for 1 hour.

4 Uncover the tin, increase the oven temperature to 200°C (400°F) mark 6 and cook the meat loaf for a further 30 minutes.

5 Remove the tin from the water bath and leave to cool for 30 minutes. Cover with foil and place heavy weights on top. Chill in the refrigerator overnight.

6 To serve, turn the meat loaf out of the tin and cut into slices for serving.

Menu Suggestion
Thickly sliced Meat Loaf is similar to a pâté or terrine. Serve as a lunch dish with a potato or rice salad, and sprigs of watercress.

SPICY SCOTCH EGGS

0.40*	£	927 cals

* plus 30 minutes chilling

Makes 4

30 ml (2 tbsp) vegetable oil

1 onion, skinned and very finely
   chopped

10 ml (2 tsp) medium-hot curry
   powder

450 g (1 lb) pork sausagemeat

100 g (4 oz) mature Cheddar
   cheese, finely grated

salt and freshly ground pepper

4 eggs, hard-boiled

plain flour, for coating

1 egg, beaten

100–175 g (4–6 oz) dried
   breadcrumbs

vegetable oil, for deep-frying

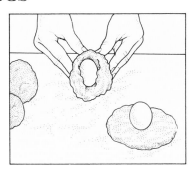

1 Heat the 30 ml (2 tbsp) oil in a
small pan, add the onion and
curry powder and fry gently for 5
minutes until soft.

2 Put the sausagemeat and
cheese in a bowl, add the
onion and salt and pepper to taste.
Mix with your hands to combine
the ingredients well together.

3 Divide the mixture into 4
equal portions and flatten out
on a floured board or work surface.

4 Place an egg in the centre of
each piece. With floured
hands, shape and mould the
sausagemeat around the eggs. Coat
lightly with more flour.

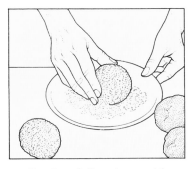

5 Brush each Scotch egg with
beaten egg, then roll in the
breadcrumbs until evenly coated.
Chill for 30 minutes.

6 Heat the oil in a deep-fat
fryer to 170°C (325°F). Carefully lower the Scotch eggs into
the oil with a slotted spoon and
deep-fry for 10 minutes, turning
them occasionally until golden
brown on all sides. Drain and cool
on absorbent kitchen paper.

Menu Suggestion
Home-made Scotch eggs are quite
delicious, with far more flavour
than the commercial varieties.
Serve them cut in halves or
quarters with a mixed salad for
lunch, or wrap them individually
in cling film or foil and pack them
for a picnic or packed lunch —
they are easy to eat with the
fingers. Scotch eggs can also be
served hot for a family meal.

MEAT LOAF
The method of cooking meat
loaves, pâtés and terrines in a
roasting tin half filled with water
is called '*au bain marie*' in
French. It is a very simple
method, but an essential one if
the finished meat mixture is to be
moist in texture. If the loaf tin is
placed directly on the oven shelf,
the mixture will dry out and the
top will form a hard, unpleasant
crust. A *bain marie* creates steam
in the oven, which gives a moist
heat. Special tins called water
baths can be bought at kitchen
shops for cooking '*au bain marie*',
but an ordinary roasting tin does
the job just as well.

LAMB WITH CUCUMBER AND MINT STUFFING

| 1.30 | £ £ ✳ | 695 cals |

Serves 4

½ cucumber, washed

salt and freshly ground pepper

25 g (1 oz) butter or margarine

1 onion, skinned and chopped

30 ml (2 tbsp) chopped fresh mint

50 g (2 oz) fresh white breadcrumbs

1 egg yolk

1.4 kg (3 lb) loin of lamb, boned

mint sprigs, to garnish

soured cream dressing (see page 353), to serve (optional)

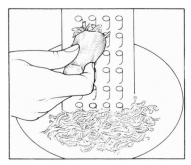

1 Coarsely grate the cucumber, sprinkle with salt and leave to stand for 30 minutes. Drain well. Melt the butter in a frying pan. Add onion and cook gently for about 5 minutes. Stir in the cucumber, mint, breadcrumbs, yolk and seasoning; cool for 30 minutes.

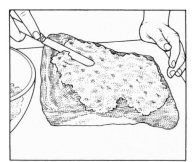

2 Lay the lamb out flat, fat side down, and spread the cold stuffing over the lamb.

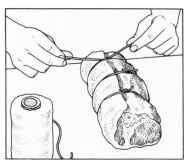

3 Roll up the meat and tie with fine string at regular intervals. Place the joint in a roasting tin and cook in the oven at 180°C (350°F) mark 4 for about 1 hour.

4 To serve, remove the string and carve into thick slices. Garnish with mint sprigs and serve with soured cream dressing if liked. Eat hot or cold.

CORONATION CHICKEN

1.10	£	640 cals

Serves 8

2.3 kg (5 lb) cold cooked chicken
15 ml (1 tbsp) vegetable oil
1 small onion, skinned and chopped
15 ml (1 tbsp) mild curry paste
15 ml (1 tbsp) tomato purée
100 ml (4 fl oz) red wine
1 bay leaf
juice of ½ lemon
4 canned apricot halves, finely chopped
300 ml (½ pint) mayonnaise (see page 353)
100 ml (4 fl oz) whipping cream
salt and freshly ground pepper
watercress sprigs, to garnish

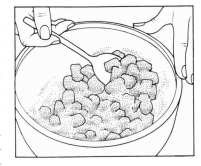

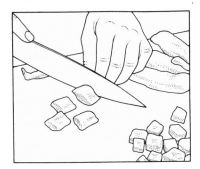

1 Remove the skin from the chicken. Then remove all the meat and dice, making sure to discard all the bones.

2 Make the curry sauce. Heat the oil in a small pan. Add the onion and cook for about 3 minutes, or until softened. Add the curry paste, tomato purée, wine, bay leaf and lemon juice. Simmer, uncovered, for about 10 minutes until well reduced. Strain and leave to cool for 30 minutes.

3 Press the chopped apricots through a sieve or use a blender or food processor to produce a purée. Beat the cooled curry sauce into the mayonnaise with the apricot purée. Lightly whip the cream and fold into the mixture. Season; add extra lemon juice, if necessary.

4 Toss the chicken pieces in the sauce and transfer to a serving dish. To serve, garnish with fresh watercress sprigs.

CORONATION CHICKEN

This delicious recipe – diced cold chicken tossed in a curried apricot mayonnaise – was created in 1953 by the Cordon Bleu School in London, in honour of the coronation of Queen Elizabeth II.

If you prefer, you can garnish the dish with sliced cucumber.

VITELLO TONNATO ▶

1.10* £ £ 722–1083 cals

* plus 2 hours cooling and overnight chilling

Serves 4–6

1 kg (2 lb) boned leg of veal

150 ml (¼ pint) water

75 ml (5 tbsp) dry white wine

75 ml (5 tbsp) white wine vinegar

1 onion, skinned and quartered

1 small carrot, peeled

1 stick of celery, washed and trimmed

sprig of parsley

salt

4 black peppercorns

198-g (7-oz) can tuna, drained

4 anchovy fillets, drained

300 ml (½ pint) lemon mayonnaise (see page 353)

15 ml (1 tbsp) capers

freshly ground pepper

capers, lemon slices and black olives, to garnish

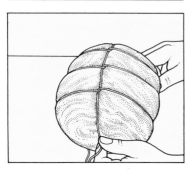

1 Tie the meat securely in a neat roll. Place in a saucepan and add the water, wine, vinegar, onion, carrot, celery, parsley and salt and peppercorns. Bring to the boil, then cover and simmer gently for 1 hour until meat is tender.

2 Remove the meat and leave to cool. Place the cooking liquid and vegetables in a blender or food processor and blend to form a smooth purée.

3 Make the tuna mayonnaise. Mash together the tuna and anchovies with a fork or purée in a blender or food processor.

4 Mix into the mayonnaise. Stir in the capers and pepper (do not add salt—the anchovies and cooking liquid should flavour it enough).

5 Thin the tuna mayonnaise sauce to the consistency of thick cream with the puréed cooking liquid.

6 When the meat is cold, cut into slices and arrange over-lapping on a shallow serving dish. Cover with the sauce.

7 Cover and leave in the refri-gerator overnight. Serve cold, garnished with capers, lemon slices and black olives.

Turkey in Tuna Fish Mayonnaise

| 0.30* | f f | 788–1121 cals |

* plus 2–3 hours chilling

Serves 4–6

6 turkey escalopes (total weight 450–700 g [1–1½ lb])

30 ml (2 tbsp) vegetable oil

25 g (1 oz) butter

198-g (7-oz) can tuna, drained

4 anchovy fillets, drained

300 ml (½ pint) lemon mayonnaise (see page 353)

142 ml (5 fl oz) soured cream

15 ml (1 tbsp) capers

freshly ground pepper

capers, lemon slices and black olives, to garnish

1 Beat out the turkey escalopes between two sheets of damp greaseproof paper or non-stick paper. Cut into thin slices.

2 Heat the oil and butter in a pan and cook the turkey strips for about 5 minutes until lightly browned. Remove from the pan and set aside.

3 Make the tuna mayonnaise. Mash together the tuna and anchovies with a fork or purée in a blender or food processor.

4 Mix into the mayonnaise with the soured cream. Stir in the capers and pepper.

5 When the meat is cold, toss into the tuna mayonnaise and turn into a serving dish. Serve cold, garnished with capers, lemon slices and black olives.

VITELLO TONNATO

A classic Italian dish of cold boned leg of veal coated in a tuna fish mayonnaise, this is the perfect recipe for a hot summer's day, particularly as it must be made the night before to allow the full flavour to develop. Serve outside if possible, with a simple tossed green salad.

OLIVES

Most of the olives we buy come from Spain, Italy and Greece. The olives in this recipe are black, which are simply fully-ripened green olives, preserved in brine. Green olives are mature, but unripe, when they are shaken off the trees onto huge nets on the ground; for black olives, they are left on the trees until they are fully ripe before harvesting.

Greek black olives can be small, with crinkly skins and a sharp, pungent flavour, or they can be succulent and fat, sometimes called 'jumbo' olives – these would be ideal for this recipe.

SMOKED MACKEREL WITH APPLE

| 0.20 | £ | 141 cals |

Serves 8

100 g (4 oz) celery, washed and
    trimmed

100 g (4 oz) cucumber, skinned

100 g (4 oz) red eating apple, cored

350 g (12 oz) smoked mackerel

150 ml ($\frac{1}{4}$ pint) soured cream

30 ml (2 tbsp) lemon juice

paprika pepper

1 small crisp lettuce

lemon wedges, to serve (optional)

1 Finely chop the celery,
cucumber and apple.

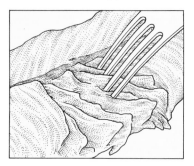

2 Skin the fish, then flake the
flesh roughly with a fork.
Discard the bones.

3 Combine the celery, cucumber,
apple and mackerel in a bowl.
Stir in the soured cream, lemon
juice and paprika to taste.

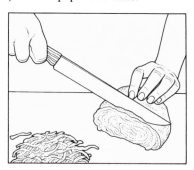

4 Shred the lettuce on a board
with a sharp knife. Place a
little lettuce in the bases of 8
stemmed glasses. Divide the
mackerel equally between them.

5 Garnish each glass with a
lemon wedge if liked, and
sprinkle with paprika. Serve at
room temperature.

Menu Suggestion
Serve with crusty bread as a
starter or as part of a light salad
lunch.

SMOKED MACKEREL WITH APPLE

There are two kinds of smoked
mackerel available: hot-smoked
and cold-smoked. Hot-smoked
mackerel is the one most widely
available, and it does not need
cooking before eating, whereas
cold-smoked mackerel does.
When buying mackerel for this
recipe, check with the
fishmonger or packet
instructions. Smoked fish of all
kinds is first salted or soaked
in a brine solution, and the
length of time it is left at this
stage will affect the flavour of
the fish. Flavour is also affected
by the actual smoking process
itself; traditional methods use
peat, oak chippings or other
similar aromatic woods, but
some modern smoking methods
in factories use synthetic
flavourings—and colourings too.

Cheese and Egg Dishes

FRITTATA
(ITALIAN OMELETTE)

0.20	408 cals

Serves 4

6 eggs

30 ml (2 tbsp) freshly grated Parmesan cheese

salt and freshly ground pepper

25 g (1 oz) butter

15 ml (1 tbsp) olive oil

100 g (4 oz) Mortadella sausage, cut into thin strips

100 g (4 oz) Italian Mozzarella cheese, cut into thin slices

1 Beat the eggs together in a bowl. Add the freshly grated Parmesan cheese and salt and pepper to taste.

2 Melt the butter with the oil in a large, heavy-based frying pan and, when hot, add the eggs. Cook gently for about 5–8 minutes until the mixture is half set underneath and the top of the omelette is still runny.

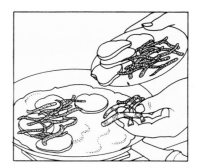

3 Scatter the Mortadella and Mozzarella over the omelette, then cook for 5 minutes until eggs are set.

4 Place pan under heated grill for 2–3 minutes until top of omelette is set. Serve hot, cut into wedges.

Menu Suggestion
Serve for a light lunch with a mixed salad and fresh bread.

VARIATIONS

Omit the Mortadella and Mozzarella, then add one of the following variations.
Vegetable omelette: Fry 1 seeded and finely sliced red pepper in olive oil and butter until lightly coloured. Add 2 thinly sliced courgettes and 2 skinned and roughly chopped tomatoes and cook for 10 minutes until slightly reduced and thickened. Spread this onto omelette after step 2 and cook as above.

Onion omelette: Heat 30 ml (2 tbsp) olive oil in a frying pan, slowly cook 3 finely sliced large onions over low heat until soft and golden. Add this to beaten eggs and cook as above.
Salami omelette: Scatter 100 g (4 oz) diced salami over the omelette at step 3.
Cheese omelette: Add 100 g (4 oz) freshly grated Parmesan cheese to the beaten egg mixture and cook as above.

PEPPER AND TOMATO OMELETTE

| 0.20 | £ | 490 cals |

Serves 2

30 ml (2 tbsp) olive oil

1 onion, skinned and sliced

2 garlic cloves, skinned and crushed

1 green pepper, cored, seeded and sliced

1 red pepper, cored, seeded and sliced

4 tomatoes, skinned and sliced

5 eggs

pinch of dried mixed herbs, or to taste

salt and freshly ground pepper

50 g (2 oz) hard mature cheese (eg Parmesan, Farmhouse Cheddar), grated

1 Heat the olive oil in a non-stick frying pan. Add the onion and garlic and fry gently for 5 minutes until soft.

2 Add the pepper slices and the tomatoes and fry for a further 2–3 minutes, stirring frequently.

3 In a jug, beat the eggs lightly with the herbs and seasoning to taste. Pour into the pan, allowing the egg to run to the sides.

4 Draw in the vegetable mixture with a palette knife so that the mixture runs on to the base of the pan. Cook over moderate heat for 5 minutes until the underside of the omelette is set.

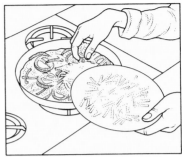

5 Sprinkle the top of the omelette with the grated cheese, then put under a pre-heated hot grill for 2–3 minutes until set and browned. Slide onto a serving plate and cut into wedges to serve.

Menu Suggestion
Pepper and Tomato Omelette can be served hot, straightaway, but it has far more flavour if left to go cold before serving. In this way, it makes the most perfect packed lunch or picnic food.

PEPPER AND TOMATO OMELETTE

This type of omelette is different from the classic French kind, which is cooked for a very short time and served folded over. Pepper and Tomato Omelette is more like the Spanish tortilla, a flat omelette which is cooked for a fairly long time so that the eggs become quite set, then browned under a hot grill so that both sides become firm. Some Spanish cooks turn their tortilla several times during cooking, and there is even a special kind of plate used in Spain which is designed to make the turning easier. Take care when making this kind of omelette that the frying pan you use is not too heavy to lift when you are transferring it to finish off the cooking under the grill. Light, non-stick frying pans are better than the traditional cast iron ones.

DEEP-FRIED MOZZARELLA SANDWICHES

| 0.20 | 🍴 | 268 cals |

Makes 10

| 175 g (6 oz) Italian Mozzarella cheese |
| 10 large slices of white bread, crusts removed |
| salt and freshly ground pepper |
| 2 eggs |
| 175 ml (6 fl oz) milk |
| 75 g (3 oz) plain flour |
| vegetable oil, for frying |

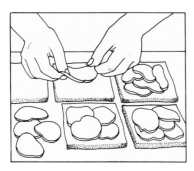

1 Slice the cheese thinly and arrange on five slices of bread, leaving a narrow margin around the edges. Season with salt and pepper and cover with the remaining bread slices. Cut each sandwich in half diagonally or widthways.

2 Beat the eggs in a shallow bowl and add the milk. Season generously with salt and pepper. Spread flour out on a flat plate.

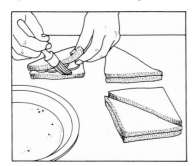

3 Brush a little egg and milk mixture inside edges of sandwiches and press together.

4 Quickly dip each sandwich into the egg mixture, then coat lightly with the flour. Dip again into the egg mixture, shaking off any excess.

5 Pour enough oil into a frying pan to come 1 cm (½ inch) up the sides of the pan and heat until it is hot.

6 Carefully place the sandwiches in the pan, in a single layer. (If your pan is not large enough you may have to use two pans or cook the sandwiches in batches.) Fry for about 3 minutes on each side until brown. Drain on absorbent kitchen paper and serve immediately.

Menu Suggestion
Serve hot as a snack on their own, or as a starter before a light main course.

STUFFED AUBERGINES

1.45	454 cals

Serves 4

4 small aubergines

salt and freshly ground pepper

30 ml (2 tbsp) olive oil

25 g (1 oz) butter

1 small onion, skinned and very finely chopped

4 small ripe tomatoes, skinned and roughly chopped

10 ml (2 tsp) chopped fresh basil or 5 ml (1 tsp) dried

2 hard-boiled eggs, shelled and roughly chopped

15 ml (1 tbsp) capers

225 g (8 oz) Fontina cheese, sliced

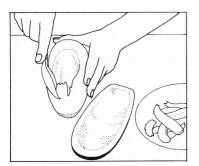

1 Wash and dry the aubergines. Cut each one in half lengthways and scoop out the flesh.

2 Chop the flesh finely, then spread out on a plate and sprinkle with salt. Leave for 20 minutes to remove bitter flavour. Turn aubergine flesh into a colander. Rinse, drain and dry.

3 Heat half of the oil in a pan with the butter, add the onion and fry gently for 5 minutes until soft but not coloured. Add the aubergine flesh, the tomatoes, basil and seasoning to taste.

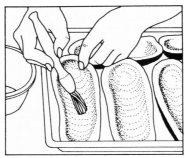

4 Meanwhile, put the aubergines in a single layer in an oiled ovenproof dish. Brush the insides with the remaining oil, then bake in the oven at 180°C (350°F) mark 4 for 10 minutes.

5 Spoon half of the tomato mixture into the base of the aubergine shells. Cover with a layer of chopped eggs, capers, then with a layer of cheese. Spoon the remaining tomato mixture over the top. Return to the oven and bake for a further 15 minutes until sizzling hot. Serve immediately.

69

PANCAKES STUFFED WITH CHEESE AND SPINACH

| 1.00 | ✳︎* | 788 cals |

* freeze after step 8

Serves 4

450 g (1 lb) washed fresh spinach or 226 g (8 oz) packet frozen spinach

50 g (2 oz) butter

1 small onion, skinned and finely chopped

65 g (2½ oz) freshly grated Parmesan cheese

600 ml (1 pint) béchamel sauce (see page 352)

salt and freshly ground pepper

100 g (4 oz) plain flour

1 egg

300 ml (½ pint) milk

oil, for frying

1 Make the filling. Place the spinach in a saucepan without any water and cook gently for 5–10 minutes (or until thawed if using frozen spinach). Drain well and chop finely.

2 Melt the 50 g (2 oz) butter in a saucepan, add the onion and fry gently for 5 minutes until soft but not coloured. Stir in the spinach and cook for a further 2 minutes. Remove from the heat and stir in 50 g (2 oz) Parmesan cheese, 90 ml (6 tbsp) béchamel sauce and seasoning to taste.

3 Make the batter. Place the flour and a pinch of salt in a bowl. Make a well in the centre and add the egg. Beat well with a wooden spoon and gradually beat in the milk.

4 Cook the pancakes. Heat a little oil in an 18-cm (7-inch) heavy-based frying pan until hot, running it round the base and sides of the pan. Pour off any surplus.

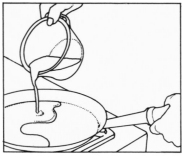

5 Pour in just enough batter to coat the base of pan thinly. Fry for 1–2 minutes until golden brown, turn or toss and cook the second side until golden.

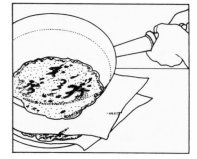

6 Transfer the pancake to a plate. Repeat with the remaining batter to make eight pancakes. Pile the cooked pancakes on top of each other with greaseproof paper in between each one.

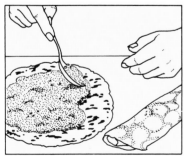

7 Spread an equal amount of the filling on each pancake, leaving a border around the edge. Roll up the pancakes loosely.

8 Arrange the pancakes in a single layer in a buttered oven-proof dish, then pour over the remaining béchamel sauce and sprinkle with the remaining Parmesan cheese.

9 Bake in the oven at 220°C (425°F) mark 7 for about 10 minutes until golden brown. Serve the pancakes hot.

CRESPELLE

Crespelle, sometimes called crespellini, are similar to cannelloni in appearance except that they are made from a pancake batter rather than a pasta dough. Fillings can be as varied as those for cannelloni, so there is no reason to stick to this recipe for cheese and spinach, which comes from Florence. Minced beef, tomato, herbs and garlic would make a tasty alternative filling, so too would minced chicken and béchamel sauce flavoured with freshly grated nutmeg.

SPINACH ROLL

1.20* ⬚ ✳* 653 cals

* plus 2 hours cooling; freeze after step 11

Serves 8

450 g (1 lb) old potatoes, peeled

salt and freshly ground pepper

900 g (2 lb) washed fresh spinach or 450 g (1 lb) packet frozen spinach

30 ml (2 tbsp) olive oil

1 onion, skinned and chopped

100 g (4 oz) curd cheese

50 g (2 oz) Italian salami, finely chopped

50 g (2 oz) freshly grated Parmesan cheese

pinch of freshly grated nutmeg

2 eggs

5 ml (1 tsp) baking powder

about 200 g (7 oz) plain flour

50 g (2 oz) butter

Simple Tomato Sauce to serve (see page 352)

1 Cook the potatoes in a saucepan of boiling salted water for about 20 minutes until tender.

2 Meanwhile, prepare the filling. Place the spinach in a saucepan without any water and cook gently for 5–10 minutes (or until thawed if using frozen spinach). Drain well and chop finely.

3 Heat the oil in a frying pan, add the onion and fry gently for 2–3 minutes until soft but not coloured. Add the spinach and cook for a further 2 minutes.

4 Turn the spinach into a bowl and add the curd cheese, salami, 25 g (1 oz) Parmesan cheese, nutmeg, 1 egg and seasoning. Beat well together.

5 Drain cooked potatoes, then push them through a sieve into a bowl. Make a well in the centre and add the remaining egg, the baking powder and most of the flour. Beat well together.

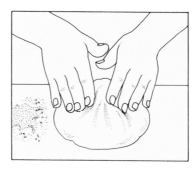

6 Knead on a work surface, adding more flour if necessary, for about 5 minutes. The dough should be smooth and slightly sticky. Shape dough into a ball.

7 Roll out the dough to a rectangle about 35.5 × 30.5 cm (14 × 12 inches). Spread the spinach mixture over the dough, leaving a 2.5 cm (1 inch) border.

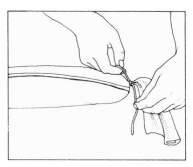

8 Roll the dough into a sausage shape. Wrap tightly in a muslin cloth. Tie ends with string.

9 Bring a large flameproof casserole, roasting tin or fish kettle of salted water to the boil and place the roll in it. Return to the boil then simmer, partially covered, for 30 minutes. Remove the roll from the water, unwrap and leave to cool for 2 hours.

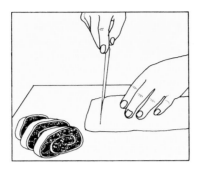

10 Cut the roll into 2.5-cm (1-inch) thick slices and arrange the slices, slightly overlapping, in an ovenproof dish.

11 Melt the butter and pour over the slices. Sprinkle with the remaining Parmesan cheese and bake in the oven at 200°C (400°F) mark 6 for about 15 minutes until golden. Serve hot, with tomato sauce handed separately.

Menu Suggestion
Serve this substantial dish for lunch.

CURRIED EGGS

| 0.40 | £ | 214 cals |

Serves 4

30 ml (2 tbsp) vegetable oil

1 onion, skinned and chopped

1 medium cooking apple, peeled, cored and chopped

10 ml (2 tsp) garam masala

300 ml ($\frac{1}{2}$ pint) vegetable stock (see page 350) or water

225 g (8 oz) can tomatoes

15 ml (1 tbsp) tomato purée

2.5 ml ($\frac{1}{2}$ tsp) chilli powder

salt and freshly ground pepper

300 ml ($\frac{1}{2}$ pint) natural yogurt

4 eggs, hard-boiled

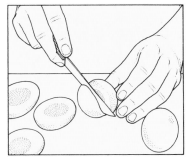

1 Heat the oil in a deep, heavy-based pan. Add the onion, apple and garam masala and fry gently until soft, stirring frequently.

2 Pour in the stock and tomatoes and bring to the boil, stirring to break up the tomatoes as much as possible. Stir in the tomato purée with the chilli powder and seasoning to taste. Lower the heat and simmer, uncovered, for 20 minutes to allow the flavours to develop.

3 Cool the sauce slightly, then pour into a blender or food processor. Add half of the yogurt and work to a purée. Return to the rinsed-out pan.

4 Shell the eggs and cut them in half lengthways. Add them to the sauce, cut side up, then simmer very gently for 10 minutes. Taste the sauce and adjust the seasoning if necessary. Serve hot, with the remaining yogurt drizzled over the top.

Menu Suggestion
Serve in a ring of boiled rice, accompanied by mango chutney and a cucumber salad dressed with natural yogurt and flavoured with fresh mint.

CURRIED EGGS

The Indian spice mixture, garam masala, is available in drums and jars from supermarkets and oriental specialist shops. You can use this ready-made mixture, but you will find your Indian dishes will taste fresher if you make your own garam masala. Ground spices quickly lose their essential oils, and you have no idea how long commercial brands of garam masala have been stored. If you make your own, make it in small quantities to suit your needs and store it in an airtight container. To make garam masala, crush 4 black or 10 green cardamoms, then put them in an electric mill or grinder with 15 ml (1 tablespoon) black peppercorns, 10 ml (2 teaspoons) cumin seeds, 2.5 cm (1 inch) cinnamon stick, 5 ml (1 tsp) cloves and 3 bay leaves. Grind to a fine powder.

EGG MOUSSE

0.45* 🍴 £ 189 cals

* plus 2 hours setting

Serves 10

1 small cucumber

salt

4 hard-boiled eggs, shelled and
finely chopped

1 bunch of spring onions, washed,
trimmed and finely chopped

150 ml ($\frac{1}{4}$ pint) thick mayonnaise

142 ml (5 fl oz) soured cream

finely grated rind of 1 lemon

22.5 ml ($1\frac{1}{2}$ tbsp) chopped fresh dill

freshly ground pepper

15 ml (3 tsp) gelatine

60 ml (4 tbsp) lemon juice

2 egg whites

fresh dill, cucumber and hard-
boiled egg slices, to garnish

3 Meanwhile, put the eggs in a bowl with the spring onions, mayonnaise, soured cream, lemon rind, dill and salt and pepper to taste. Mix well.

4 In a separate heatproof bowl, sprinkle the gelatine over the lemon juice. Leave to soak for 5 minutes until spongy, then stand the bowl over a saucepan of hot water and heat gently until dissolved. Remove from the heat and leave to cool slightly.

5 Pat the cucumber with absorbent kitchen paper. Fold gently into the egg mixture with the dissolved gelatine until evenly mixed.

6 Whisk the egg whites until stiff, then fold into the mousse with a large metal spoon. Turn the mixture into a serving bowl or 1.4-litre (2$\frac{1}{2}$-pint) soufflé dish and level the surface. Chill in the refrigerator for 2 hours before serving garnished with dill sprigs, cucumber and hard-boiled egg slices.

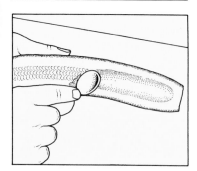

1 Peel the cucumber, cut in half lengthways, then scoop out and discard the seeds.

2 Chop cucumber flesh finely, place in a colander and sprinkle with salt. Cover with a plate, with weights on top; leave for 30 minutes until moisture is removed.

SPICED PEPPER AND ONION FLAN

1.25	530 cals

Serves 4

75 g (3 oz) block margarine

175 g (6 oz) plain flour, plus 30 ml (2 tbsp)

salt

15 ml (1 tbsp) vegetable oil

2 onions, skinned and thinly sliced

1 red pepper, seeded and sliced

25 g (1 oz) butter

5 ml (1 tsp) ground cumin

150 ml ($\frac{1}{4}$ pint) milk

142 g (5 oz) natural yogurt

2 egg yolks

30 ml (2 tbsp) grated Parmesan

1 Make the pastry. Rub the margarine into 175 g (6 oz) flour with a pinch of salt. Bind to a manageable dough with cold water. Knead until smooth.

2 Roll out the dough on a lightly floured surface and use to line a 20.5-cm (8-inch) plain flan ring placed on a baking sheet.

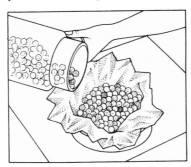

3 Chill for 15–20 minutes, then line with foil and baking beans. Bake blind in the oven at 200°C (400°F) mark 6 for 10–15 minutes until set but not browned.

4 Heat the oil in a frying pan. Sauté the sliced onions and pepper, reserving a few slices to garnish, in the hot oil for 4–5 minutes. Put into the flan case.

5 Melt the butter, stir in 30 ml (2 tbsp) flour and cumin. Cook for 2 minutes before adding the milk and yogurt. Bring to the boil, stirring briskly, simmer for 2–3 minutes. Beat in the egg yolks.

6 Pour over the onion and pepper and sprinkle with Parmesan. Cook in the oven at 190°C (375°F) mark 5 for 35–40 minutes. Serve hot garnished with pepper slices.

Menu Suggestion

Serve as a lunch or supper dish with a green salad tossed in a sharp vinaigrette dressing.

TOMATO AND HERB QUICHE

1.00	✳	423–634 cals

Serves 4–6

225 g (8 oz) packet frozen shortcrust pastry, thawed (or see page 348)

350 g (12 oz) ripe tomatoes

3 eggs

175 g (6 oz) Caerphilly cheese, grated

150 ml ($\frac{1}{4}$ pint) single cream

15 ml (1 tbsp) chopped fresh herbs (eg sage and thyme) or 10 ml (2 tsp) dried mixed herbs

salt and freshly ground pepper

1 Roll out the pastry on a floured surface and use to line a 23.5 cm (9 inch) flan tin or dish placed on a baking sheet. Prick the base with the prongs of a fork, line with foil and baking beans and bake blind in the oven at 200°C (400°F) mark 6 for 15 minutes.

2 Meanwhile, skin the tomatoes. Put them in a heatproof bowl, pour over boiling water and leave to stand for 2–3 minutes. Drain, plunge into ice-cold water, then remove them one at a time and peel off the skin with your fingers.

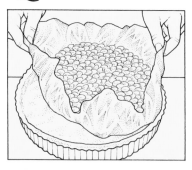

3 Remove the foil and beans from the pastry case and return to the oven for 5 minutes.

4 Meanwhile, break the eggs into a bowl and beat lightly. Add the cheese, cream, herbs and seasoning to taste and beat lightly again to mix.

5 Remove the pastry case from the oven. Slice the tomatoes and arrange half of them in the bottom of the pastry case. Slowly pour the egg and cheese mixture over the tomatoes, then arrange the remaining tomato on top.

6 Bake in the oven for 20–25 minutes until the filling is just set. Remove and leave to stand for 15 minutes before serving.

Menu Suggestion
In late summer when tomatoes are sweet and plentiful, this quiche makes the perfect lunch dish served with a fresh green salad. Cut into thin wedges to serve 8, it also makes a delicious starter.

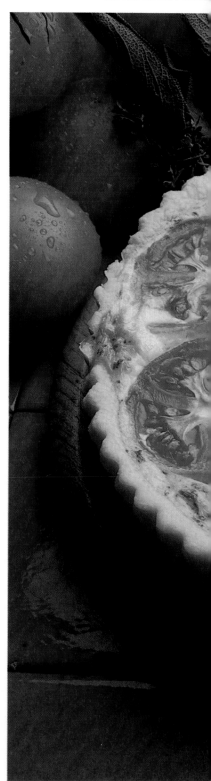

Quick and Light Dishes

STILTON STEAKS

| 0.20 | £ £ | 763 cals |

Serves 4

175 g (6 oz) Blue Stilton cheese

25 g (1 oz) unsalted butter,
    softened

50–75 g (2–3 oz) shelled walnuts,
    finely chopped

salt and freshly ground pepper

4 sirloin or fillet steaks, about
    125–175 g (4–6 oz) each

45 ml (3 tbsp) olive or vegetable oil

10 ml (2 tsp) chopped fresh sage or
    5 ml (1 tsp) dried

1 Put the cheese in a bowl and mash with a fork. Add the butter and walnuts and mix in with salt and pepper to taste. (Add salt sparingly as Stilton cheese tends to be quite salty.)

2 Trim any fat off the steaks, then place on the grill rack. Brush with half of the oil, then sprinkle with half of the sage and plenty of pepper.

3 Put under a preheated hot grill and cook for 2–4 minutes on each side, according to the thickness of the steaks and how well done you like them. When you turn the steaks over to cook the other side, brush with the remaining oil and sprinkle with the remaining sage and pepper.

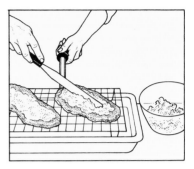

4 Remove the steaks from under the grill, sprinkle the cheese and nut mixture evenly over them and press down with a palette knife. Grill for 1 further minute or until the topping is melted and bubbling. Serve hot.

Menu Suggestion
Succulent Stilton Steaks make a mouthwatering main course with man appeal! Serve with a tossed mixed salad and potatoes cooked in their skins — or with French fries for those who like them.

STILTON STEAKS
Did you know that seventeen gallons of milk are used in the making of each single Stilton cheese, and that only seven dairies in the world, members of the Stilton Cheese Makers' Association, make the authentic, traditional Stilton?

The origins of this famous blue-veined cheese are a little obscure, although it is known that the cheese was sold in the seventeenth century to travellers who stopped at The Bell Inn in the village of Stilton near Melton Mowbray. Legend has it that the first cheese was made by a Mrs Paulet, a local farmer's wife and the sister-in-law of the landlord at The Bell Inn. Nowadays, Stilton is made in the three English counties of Leicestershire, Nottinghamshire and Derbyshire, and is exported all over the world.

BISTECCA ALLA PIZZAIOLA
(STEAK WITH TOMATO SAUCE, GARLIC AND OLIVES)

0.40	£ £	512 cals

Serves 4

4 rump steaks, about 175–225 g (6–8 oz) each

60 ml (4 tbsp) olive oil

4 garlic cloves, skinned and crushed

700 g (1½ lb) ripe tomatoes

10 ml (2 tsp) chopped fresh oregano or 5 ml (1 tsp) dried

2.5 ml (½ tsp) sugar

salt and freshly ground pepper

50 g (2 oz) black olives

30 ml (2 tbsp) finely chopped fresh continental parsley

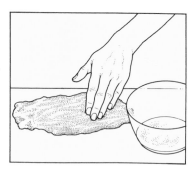

1 Rub each steak on both sides with 30 ml (2 tbsp) of the olive oil and half of the garlic. Place on a plate and set aside while preparing the sauce.

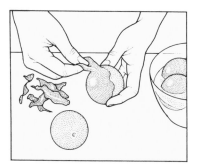

2 Skin the tomatoes. Place them in a bowl, pour over boiling water to cover, then leave to stand for 1 minute. Drain, then cover with fresh cold water. Remove from the water and peel.

3 Chop the tomatoes roughly, then put in a heavy-based saucepan with 15 ml (1 tbsp) of olive oil, the remaining garlic and the rest of the ingredients except the olives and parsley. Bring to the boil, stirring, then lower the heat. Simmer, uncovered, for about 20 minutes until the sauce is thick and reduced, stirring occasionally.

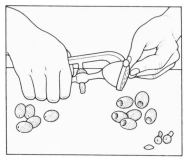

4 Meanwhile, stone the olives, using an olive pitter, if available. Cut each olive in half lengthways.

5 Brush a heavy large sauté or frying pan with the remaining oil and heat until smoking. Add the steaks and fry for 1 minute on each side or until browned.

6 Taste and adjust the seasoning of the sauce, then pour over the steaks. Add the olives and parsley and cover the pan with a lid. Cook for a further 5 minutes, or until the steaks are done to your liking. Transfer to a warmed serving platter and serve immediately.

Menu Suggestion
In Italy, Bistecca alla Pizzaiola would be served as a main course on its own, preceded by a first course of pasta. Spaghetti, penne or macaroni tossed simply in butter and freshly grated Parmesan cheese would go well before the steaks, with their thick and pungent pizzaiola sauce. Finish the main course with a tossed green salad, then follow with fresh fruit.

SMOKED MUSSEL STEAKS

| 0.20 | £ £ | 354 cals |

Serves 4

4 sirloin steaks, about 175 g (6 oz)
   each and 2 cm ($\frac{3}{4}$ inch) thick

105 g ($3\frac{2}{3}$ oz) can smoked mussels

30 ml (2 tbsp) white wine vinegar

1 bunch of watercress, washed

salt and freshly ground pepper

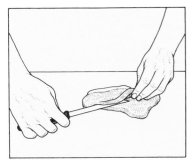

1 Trim the steaks of any excess
fat. With a sharp knife, make a
slit along the length of each steak
to form a pocket.

2 Drain the mussels, reserving
the oil. Chop the mussels
roughly and place in a bowl with
the wine vinegar.

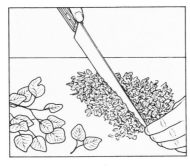

3 Trim the root ends off the
watercress and chop roughly.
Stir into the mussels with plenty
of salt and pepper.

4 Spoon a little of the mussel
mixture into each steak. Place
in a single layer in a shallow
flameproof dish, or on a foil-lined
grill pan. Preheat the grill to hot.

5 Brush the steaks with the
reserved oil from the mussels.
Cook under the preheated grill for
about 3–4 minutes on each side for
a medium steak, about 5–6
minutes for well done. Turn the
steaks over carefully with tongs or
a fish slice to prevent the filling
dropping out. Serve hot.

Menu Suggestion
Serve these steaks for an unusual
main course, accompanied by
creamed potatoes with lemon and
nutmeg.

QUICK BEEF STIR FRY

| 0.40* | 504 cals |

* plus overnight marinating

Serves 4

450 g (1 lb) shin of beef, trimmed
   of fat and sinew

45 ml (3 tbsp) medium sherry

30 ml (2 tbsp) lemon juice

15 ml (1 tbsp) soy sauce

10 ml (2 tsp) paprika

2 medium onions, skinned

125 g (4 oz) button mushrooms

225 g (8 oz) long grain rice

salt and freshly ground pepper

about 45 ml (3 tbsp) peanut or
   vegetable oil

2 Put the sherry in a bowl with the lemon juice, soy sauce and paprika. Whisk together, then add the strips of beef. Stir well, cover and leave to marinate in the refrigerator overnight.

3 The next day, slice the onions and mushrooms thinly. Cook the rice in plenty of boiling salted water for about 12 minutes until just tender. Drain well.

4 Remove the meat from the marinade with a slotted spoon. Heat 45 ml (3 tbsp) oil in a wok or large frying pan until smoky hot.

6 Stir in the sliced onions and mushrooms, adding more oil if necessary. Stir fry for a further 2 minutes, then add the rice and marinade mixture.

7 Reduce the heat and stir fry until the meat is tender and the ingredients are thoroughly combined and heated through. Add salt and pepper to taste. Serve immediately.

Menu Suggestion
Quick Beef Stir Fry contains rice and mushrooms, so it is quite a substantial dish for an everyday meal. Serve with Chinese egg noodles or a little extra boiled rice, if wished.

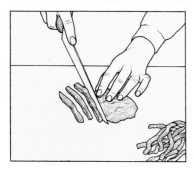

1 Slice the meat wafer thin and shred into matchstick-long strips with a very sharp knife.

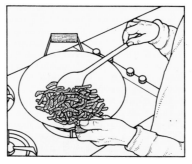

5 Add the meat to the wok and stir fry over high heat for about 2 minutes.

SZECHUAN SHREDDED BEEF

| 1.00 | 🥘 | £ £ | 274 cals |

Serves 4

350 g (12 oz) beef skirt or rump steak
2 fresh red or green chillies
1 large onion
2 garlic cloves
5 cm (1 inch) piece of fresh root ginger
225 g (8 oz) can bamboo shoots, drained
2 medium red peppers
75 ml (5 tbsp) hoisin sauce
60 ml (4 tbsp) dry sherry
30 ml (2 tbsp) corn or vegetable oil
15 ml (1 tbsp) sesame oil

1 Put the steak in the freezer for at least 20 minutes, to make it easier to slice thinly.

2 Meanwhile, prepare the vegetables. Trim the ends off the chillies and slice each one in half lengthways. Hold the chillies under cold running water and remove the seeds. Rinse your hands and pat the chillies dry with absorbent kitchen paper.

3 Chop the chillies finely. Skin the onion and slice thinly. Skin the garlic and crush to a paste.

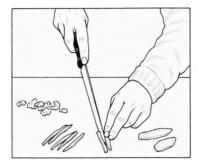

4 Peel the fresh ginger and slice the flesh into thin matchstick strips. Slice the bamboo shoots thinly.

5 Cut the stalk ends off the red peppers and cut out and discard the cores and seeds. Wash the peppers and pat dry with absorbent kitchen paper.

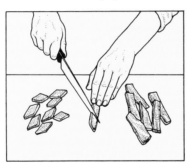

6 Cut the peppers into strips about 5 mm ($\frac{1}{4}$ inch) wide. Cut each strip across diagonally to make 'diamond' shapes.

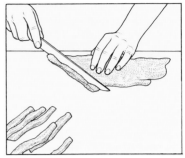

7 Cut the steak into thin slices, then stack several slices one on top of another. With a meat cleaver or very sharp knife, cut lengthways into thin matchstick strips. Put the strips of steak in a bowl, add the hoisin sauce and sherry and stir. Leave to marinate while cooking the vegetables.

8 Heat the oil in a wok until smoking hot. Add the chillies, onion and garlic and stir fry over moderate heat for 3–4 minutes until softened. Remove with a slotted spoon and set aside. Add the red peppers, increase the heat and stir fry for a few seconds. Remove with a slotted spoon and set aside with the chillies.

9 Add the steak and marinade to the wok in batches. Stir fry each batch over high heat for about 2 minutes, removing each batch with a slotted spoon.

10 Return the vegetables to the wok. Add the ginger and bamboo shoots, then the meat and stir fry for a further minute to heat through.

11 Turn the mixture into a warmed serving dish, sprinkle with the sesame oil and serve immediately.

Menu Suggestion
Serve this Chinese stir fry for a quick evening meal. Boiled Chinese egg noodles or rice are the most suitable accompaniments.

TERIYAKI
(JAPANESE SKEWERED BEEF)

| 0.30* | £ £ | 436 cals |

*plus at least 1 hour marinating

Serves 4

90 ml (6 tbsp) mirin (Japanese sweet rice wine) or sweet sherry

120 ml (8 tbsp) shoyu (Japanese soy sauce)

60 ml (4 tbsp) sugar

2.5 cm (1 inch) piece of fresh root ginger, peeled and crushed

1 garlic clove, skinned and crushed

freshly ground pepper

700–900 g (1–1½ lb) fillet steak

12 bamboo skewers, soaked in water for 15 minutes

30 ml (2 tbsp) corn or vegetable oil

1 Put the mirin in a large bowl with the shoyu, sugar, ginger and garlic. Add pepper to taste, then whisk with a fork until well combined.

2 Trim any fat off the steak, then cut into cubes about 0.5 cm (¼ inch) thick. Add to the bowl and coat in the marinade. Cover and marinate at least 1 hour.

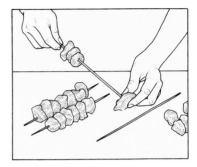

3 Thread the cubes of steak onto the bamboo skewers or 4 oiled flat kebab skewers. Brush the meat with oil, then cook under a preheated hot grill for 4–8 minutes according to how well done you like your steak. Turn the skewers frequently during grilling and brush with more oil and any remaining marinade. Serve immediately.

Menu Suggestion
In Japan, Teriyaki is served together with many other dishes, such as vegetables, fish, soup and rice or noodles—there are no separate courses in a Japanese meal. For a Japanese-style dinner party, however, you can serve a soup to start, with Teriyaki to follow as a main course dish. Boiled rice or noodles and a bowl of stir-fried vegetables would make suitable accompaniments, followed by a refreshing dessert such as a fresh fruit salad or a water ice.

TERIYAKI
Teriyaki sauce—a combination of rice wine, soy sauce, fresh root ginger and garlic—is used extensively in the cooking of Japan. Chicken and prawns are often marinated in teriyaki sauce and cooked on skewers, pork is also sometimes used, and cubes of firm-fleshed white fish. For a special dinner party meal, you could cook a selection of different meats, fish and shellfish in this way, which would look and taste really interesting. Teriyaki is a useful dish to know if you ever have to entertain guests unexpectedly. It can be prepared in 30 minutes, and only needs 1 hour marinating before it can be cooked.

PAN-FRIED VEAL WITH MUSTARD AND CREAM

| 0.20 | £ £ | 358 cals |

Serves 4

4 veal escalopes, about 100–175 g
  (4–6 oz) each

40 g (1½ oz) butter or margarine

150 ml (¼ pint) veal or chicken
  stock

150 ml (¼ pint) single cream

15 ml (1 tbsp) wholegrain mustard

juice of ½ lemon

salt and freshly ground pepper

chopped fresh parsley, to garnish

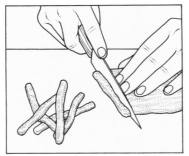

1 Cut the veal into thin, pencil-like strips about 6.5 cm
(2½ inches) long. Melt the butter in
a frying pan and, when foaming,
add the veal. Fry over high heat
for 2–3 minutes, stirring
constantly until lightly browned.

2 Lift the veal out of the pan with a slotted spoon and
transfer to a plate.

3 Add the stock to the pan and boil, until reduced by half,
stirring continuously.

4 Stir in the cream, mustard, the lemon juice and browned veal.
Season to taste with salt and
pepper and simmer for 5 minutes.
Serve immediately, garnished with
plenty of chopped parsley.

Menu Suggestion
These strips of veal escalope pan-
fried with a deliciously creamy
sauce makes a good main course
for a midweek supper when you
are short of time. Serve with
buttered noodles and a tossed
mixed salad.

PAN-FRIED VEAL WITH MUSTARD AND CREAM

The sharp pungency of mustard
is particularly good with the
rather bland flavour of veal.
Wholegrain mustard is specified
in this recipe because it is less
strong than some of the smooth
English and Dijon mustards,
which would completely
overpower the delicate flavour of
the dish. Wholegrain mustards
made from crushed black and
yellow mustard seeds are usually
French and vinegar-based, with
a seasoning of pimentos, cloves
and cinnamon. Look for the
famous Moutarde de Meaux in
delicatessens and good
supermarkets; its granular
texture adds interest to the sauce
in this recipe, and it has just the
right degree of 'hotness'.

LAMB CUTLETS WITH LEMON AND GARLIC

| 0.35 | £ £ | 502 cals |

Serves 4

2 lemons

3 small garlic cloves, skinned and crushed

salt and freshly ground pepper

8 lamb cutlets

30 ml (2 tbsp) vegetable oil

25 g (1 oz) margarine or butter

1 medium onion, skinned and finely chopped

175 ml (6 fl oz) natural yogurt

150 ml ($\frac{1}{4}$ pint) chicken stock

5 ml (1 tsp) chopped fresh basil or 2.5 ml ($\frac{1}{2}$ tsp) dried

parsley or basil sprigs, to garnish

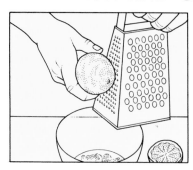

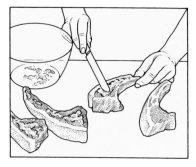

1 On the finest side of a conical or box grater, grate the rind of 1$\frac{1}{2}$ lemons into a bowl. Add the garlic and freshly ground pepper to taste and blend together.

2 Place the cutlets on a board and spread the lemon rind and garlic evenly over the meat. Leave for 15 minutes.

3 Heat the oil and margarine in a pan, add the cutlets and fry for about 3 minutes each side or until tender. Drain and keep warm on a serving dish.

4 Pour off all but 30 ml (2 tbsp) fat from the pan, add the onion and fry gently for 5 minutes until soft but not coloured. Stir in the yogurt and stock with the squeezed juice of the 1$\frac{1}{2}$ lemons and the basil. Bring to the boil and simmer for 2–3 minutes. Add salt and freshly ground pepper to taste.

5 Spoon the juices over the meat and garnish with the parsley or basil sprigs and the remaining $\frac{1}{2}$ lemon, cut into wedges, if liked. Serve immediately.

Menu Suggestion
Serve with French beans topped with grilled almonds and new potatoes in their skins.

CRUMB TOPPED PORK CHOPS

| 1.00 | £ | 408 cals |

Serves 4

4 lean pork loin chops

50 g (2 oz) fresh white breadcrumbs

15 ml (1 tbsp) chopped fresh parsley or 5 ml (1 tsp) dried parsley

5 ml (1 tsp) chopped fresh mint or 2.5 ml ($\frac{1}{2}$ tsp) dried mint

pinch of dried thyme

finely grated rind of 1 lemon

2.5 ml ($\frac{1}{2}$ tsp) coriander seeds, crushed

1 egg, beaten

salt and freshly ground pepper

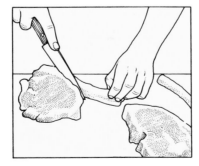

1 Cut the rind off the chops and put them in one layer in a baking tin.

2 Mix the remaining ingredients together with seasoning to taste. Spread this mixture evenly over the chops with a palette knife.

3 Bake in the oven at 200°C (400°F) mark 6 for about 45–50 minutes, or until golden. Serve hot, on a warmed dish.

Menu Suggestion
Serve with jacket-baked potatoes (cooked in the oven at the same time) and a vegetable dish which has its own sauce such as ratatouille or tomatoes in cream.

KIDNEYS PROVENÇAL

0.35	211 cals

Serves 4

12–16 lambs' kidneys

30 ml (2 tbsp) olive oil

1 large onion, skinned and
  chopped

1–2 garlic cloves, skinned and
  crushed

3 medium courgettes, trimmed
  and sliced

4 large tomatoes, skinned and
  roughly chopped

100 ml (4 fl oz) red wine or stock

10 ml (2 tsp) chopped fresh basil
  or 5 ml (1 tsp) dried basil

salt and freshly ground pepper

12 black olives

sprigs of chervil, to garnish

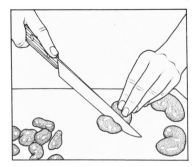

1 Skin the kidneys, then cut
each one in half. Snip out the
cores with kitchen scissors. Cut
each half into two.

2 Heat the oil in a large heavy-
based frying pan, add the onion
and garlic to the pan and fry
gently for 5 minutes until soft but
not coloured.

3 Add the kidneys and fry over
low heat for 3 minutes until
they change colour. Shake the pan
and toss the kidneys frequently
during frying.

4 Add the courgettes, tomatoes
and wine or stock and bring to
the boil, stirring constantly. Lower
the heat and add half the basil
with seasoning to taste. Simmer
gently for 8 minutes until the
kidneys are tender.

5 Add the olives to the pan and
heat through for 1–2
minutes. Taste and adjust the
seasoning. Sprinkle with the
remaining basil and chervil just
before serving. Serve very hot.

Menu Suggestion
This strongly flavoured dish needs
a contrasting bland accompaniment such as plain boiled rice.
Follow with a simple green salad,
cheese and fresh fruit for a
complete, well-balanced meal.

LIVER WITH VERMOUTH

0.35	£	319 cals

Serves 4

450 g (1 lb) lamb's liver, sliced

15 ml (1 tbsp) wholewheat flour

30 ml (2 tbsp) vegetable oil

1 onion, skinned and chopped

1 garlic clove, skinned and crushed

finely grated rind and juice of 1 orange

finely grated rind and juice of 1 lemon

60 ml (4 tbsp) sweet vermouth or sherry

30 ml (2 tbsp) chopped fresh parsley

salt and freshly ground pepper

few orange and lemon slices, to garnish

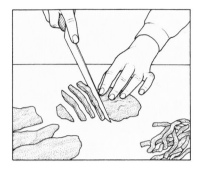

1 Cut the liver into thin strips, trimming away all ducts and gristle. Coat in the flour.

2 Heat the oil in a flameproof casserole, add the onion and garlic to the casserole and fry gently for 5 minutes until soft but not coloured.

3 Add the liver strips and cook over high heat until browned on all sides.

4 Add the orange and lemon rind and juices and the vermouth and bring to the boil. Stir constantly with a wooden spoon to scrape up any sediment and juices from the base of the casserole, and continue boiling until the sauce reduces.

5 Lower the heat and add half the parsley and salt and freshly ground pepper to taste.

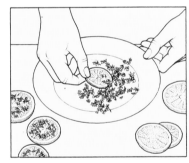

6 Dip the orange and lemon slices in the remaining chopped parsley. Transfer the liver and sauce to a warmed serving dish. Garnish with the orange and lemon slices and serve immediately, while piping hot.

Menu Suggestion
Serve this tangy liver dish on a bed of brown rice or with wholewheat noodles. Stir-fried beansprouts, mushrooms or spinach would make a good vegetable accompaniment.

CROSTINI

| 0.30 | 380 cals |

Serves 4

225 g (8 oz) chicken livers

65 g (2½ oz) butter

30 ml (2 tbsp) olive oil

1 small onion, skinned and
finely chopped

1 garlic clove, skinned and
crushed

2 celery sticks, trimmed and
finely chopped

10 ml (2 tsp) tomato purée

10 ml (2 tsp) chopped fresh sage or
5 ml (1 tsp) dried, or 10 ml (2 tsp)
chopped fresh parsley

salt and freshly ground pepper

15 ml (1 tbsp) capers (optional)

about 60 ml (4 tbsp) dry white wine
or vermouth, to moisten

½ large loaf of French bread

extra fresh sage or parsley,
to garnish

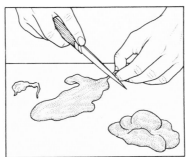

1 Trim the chicken livers,
cutting away any ducts and
gristle. Cut the livers into small
bite-sized pieces.

2 Melt 25 g (1 oz) of the butter
in a frying pan with the oil.
Add the chicken livers and fry
over brisk heat until just changing
in colour, shaking the pan and
tossing the livers constantly.
Remove with a slotted spoon and
set aside.

3 Add the onion, garlic and
celery to the pan and fry
gently for 7–10 minutes until
softened.

4 Add the tomato purée, sage
and salt and pepper to taste
and stir well to mix. Return the
chicken livers to the pan and add
the capers with enough wine or
vermouth to moisten. Cook over
gentle heat for about 5 minutes,
stirring frequently, until just
tender.

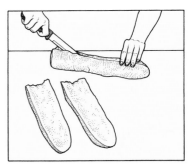

5 Meanwhile, cut the loaf of
French bread in half, then
slice through each half to make 4
'boat' shapes.

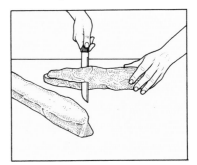

6 Cut the bottom crusts off the
bread. Toast the bread on 1
side only, then spread the toasted
side with the remaining butter.

7 Pile the chicken liver mixture
on the hot toasted bread and
sprinkle with sage and parsley.
Serve immediately.

STIR-FRIED CHICKEN WITH VEGETABLES AND CASHEW NUTS

| 0.40 | 335 cals |

Serves 4

1 bunch spring onions
3 celery sticks
1 green pepper
100 g (4 oz) cauliflower florets
2 carrots
175 g (6 oz) button mushrooms
4 boneless chicken breasts
30 ml (2 tbsp) sesame or vegetable oil
10 ml (2 tsp) cornflour
30 ml (2 tbsp) dry sherry
15 ml (1 tbsp) soy sauce
15 ml (1 tbsp) hoisin sauce (see box)
5 ml (1 tsp) soft brown sugar
150 ml ($\frac{1}{4}$ pint) water
75 g (3 oz) unsalted cashew nuts
salt and freshly ground pepper

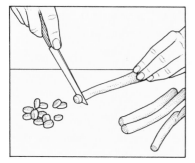

1 Prepare the vegetables. Trim the spring onions and slice them into thin rings. Trim the celery and slice finely.

2 Halve the green pepper, remove the core and seeds and slice the flesh into thin strips. Divide the cauliflower florets into tiny sprigs.

3 Peel the carrots, then grate into thin slivers using the coarse side of a conical or box grater or cut into matchsticks. Wipe the mushrooms and slice them finely.

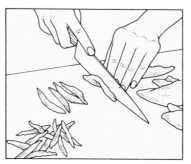

4 Skin the chicken and cut into bite-sized strips about 4 cm (1$\frac{1}{2}$ inches) long with a sharp knife.

5 Heat the oil in a wok or deep frying pan, add the prepared vegetables and stir-fry over brisk heat for 3 minutes. Remove with a slotted spoon and set aside.

6 In a jug, mix the cornflour to a paste with the sherry, soy sauce and hoisin sauce, then add the sugar and water.

7 Add the chicken strips to the pan and stir-fry over moderate heat until lightly coloured on all sides. Pour the cornflour mixture into the pan and bring to the boil, stirring constantly until thickened.

8 Return the vegetables to the pan. Add the cashew nuts and seasoning to taste, and stir-fry for a few minutes more. Serve immediately.

Menu Suggestion

With meat and vegetables cooked together, this Chinese-style dish is quite substantial. Serve with small bowls of rice—and chopsticks! Provide extra soy sauce for those who like it.

STIR-FRIED CHICKEN WITH VEGETABLES AND CASHEW NUTS

The hoisin sauce used in this Chinese-style recipe is just one of the many bottled and canned sauces which are used frequently in Chinese cookery. Look for them in oriental specialist shops and some large supermarkets — they will give an 'authentic' touch to your oriental dishes.

Chinese cooks use commercial sauces all the time. Hoisin sauce is made from soya bean flour, sugar, spices and food colouring; it is thick and pungent, a reddish-brown in colour. Add it to any stir-fried dish for extra body and flavour, and use it in sweet and sour dishes.

CHEESE AND ANCHOVY GRILLED CHICKEN BREASTS

1.00	£ £	511 cals

Serves 6

50 g (2 oz) can anchovy fillets in oil

30 ml (2 tbsp) finely chopped onion

5 ml (1 tsp) lemon juice

6 chicken breasts

vegetable oil, for brushing

225 g (8 oz) Mozzarella cheese, sliced

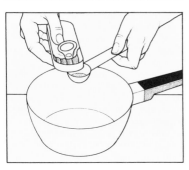

1 Drain 15 ml (1 tbsp) of the oil from the anchovy can into a small saucepan. Chop the anchovies finely.

2 Heat the anchovy oil, add the anchovies and onion and cook for about 5 minutes, until a paste forms. Stir in the lemon juice, then remove from the heat and leave to cool.

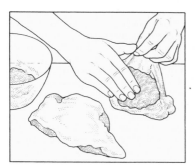

3 Lift the skin from each chicken breast and rub 5 ml (1 tsp) of the anchovy mixture on the flesh underneath the skin.

4 Put the chicken pieces, skin side down, on to a rack placed over the grill pan. Grill under moderate heat for 35–45 minutes until tender, turning once. Brush with oil occasionally during cooking, to moisten.

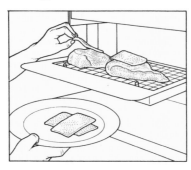

5 Cover the chicken breasts with slices of cheese and grill for a further 5 minutes, or until the cheese begins to bubble.

CHEESE AND ANCHOVY GRILLED CHICKEN BREASTS

Anchovies tend to be rather salty. If you have the time when preparing this dish, it helps to soak the anchovies first, to remove excess salt. Simply drain the oil from the can, then place the anchovy fillets in a shallow dish. Pour over just enough milk to cover, then leave to soak for 20–30 minutes. Drain thoroughly and pat dry. The anchovies are now ready for use.

DUCK WITH MANGO

0.35	£ £	683 cals

Serves 4

1 ripe, but still firm mango

4 duck portions, about 275 g (10 oz) each

60 ml (4 tbsp) peanut oil

2.5 ml ($\frac{1}{2}$ tsp) ground allspice

45 ml (3 tbsp) plum jam

20 ml (4 tsp) wine vinegar

salt and freshly ground pepper

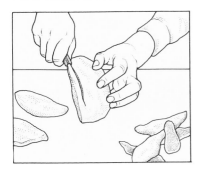

1 Skin and thickly slice the mango on either side of the large central stone.

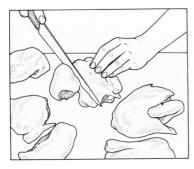

2 Remove any excess fat from the duck portions. Divide each portion into three and place in a saucepan. Cover with cold water and bring to the boil. Lower the heat and simmer gently for 15–20 minutes. Drain well and pat dry with absorbent kitchen paper. Trim bones.

3 Heat the oil in a wok or large frying pan until hot and smoking. Add the duck pieces and allspice. Brown well on all sides.

4 Stir in the plum jam and wine vinegar. Cook for a further 2–3 minutes, stirring constantly, until well glazed. Stir in the mango slices with seasoning to taste. Heat through, then turn into a warmed serving dish and serve immediately.

CHICKEN TACOS

0.15	297 cals

Serves 6

6 Mexican taco shells

25 g (1 oz) butter or margarine

1 medium onion, skinned and chopped

450 g (1 lb) cooked chicken, diced

4 tomatoes, skinned and chopped

salt and freshly ground pepper

shredded lettuce

100 g (4 oz) Cheddar cheese, grated

Tabasco sauce

1 Put the taco shells in the oven to warm according to the instructions on the packet.

2 Make the filling. Melt the fat in a frying pan and fry the onion until soft but not coloured. Stir in the chicken, half the tomatoes and seasoning and heat through.

3 Spoon 15–30 ml (1–2 tbsp) filling into each shell. Add a little lettuce, the remaining tomatoes and the cheese with a few drops of Tabasco sauce; serve the filled tacos immediately.

Menu Suggestion

Serve spicy hot tacos as a snack to be eaten with the fingers. Ice-cold lager is the only accompaniment needed, and maybe some fresh fruit such as pineapple to refresh the palate afterwards.

101

MAIN COURSES
Meat and Poultry

MINTED LAMB GRILL

0.25*	✳*	255 cals

* plus 1 hour marinating; freeze in the marinade

Serves 4

4 lamb chump chops

30 ml (2 tbsp) chopped fresh mint
  or 15 ml (1 tbsp) dried

20 ml (4 tsp) white wine vinegar

30 ml (2 tbsp) clear honey

salt and freshly ground pepper

fresh mint sprigs, to garnish

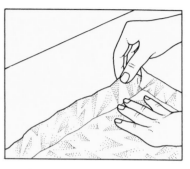

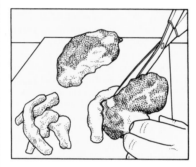

1 Trim any excess fat off the chump chops using a pair of sharp kitchen scissors.

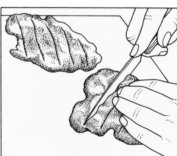

2 With a knife, slash both sides of the chops to a depth of about 5 mm ($\frac{1}{4}$ inch).

3 Make the marinade. Mix the chopped fresh mint, vinegar, honey and seasonings together, stirring well.

4 Place a sheet of foil in the grill pan and turn up the edges to prevent marinade running into pan.

5 Place the chops side by side on the foil and spoon over the marinade. Leave in a cool place for about 1 hour, basting occasionally.

6 Grill under a moderate heat for 5–6 minutes on each side, turning once only. Baste with the marinade during the cooking time. Garnish with mint before serving.

MINT
This herb has a natural affinity with lamb, but did you know there are many different kinds? *Spearmint* is perhaps the best known, and is a well-known cure for indigestion as well as being used as a culinary herb. *Applemint* is woolly in appearance compared with spearmint, and has the flavour of apples and spearmint combined together. It goes particularly well with lamb, and is excellent for making mint sauce and mint jelly. *Peppermint* is yet another kind of mint; it has a strong scent and flavour—its oil is used in the making of sweets—and is also sometimes called brandy mint.

SHEPHERD'S PIE

| 1.00 | £ | ✳ | 524 cals |

Serves 4

700 g (1½ lb) potatoes, peeled

salt and freshly ground pepper

450 g (1 lb) cooked lamb

30 ml (2 tbsp) vegetable oil

1 medium onion, skinned and chopped

30 ml (2 tbsp) plain flour

300 ml (½ pint) lamb or beef stock

15 ml (1 tbsp) Worcestershire sauce

90 ml (6 tbsp) chopped fresh parsley

5 ml (1 tsp) dried marjoram

50 g (2 oz) Cheddar cheese, grated

chopped fresh parsley, to garnish

1 Cook the potatoes in a saucepan of boiling salted water for about 20 minutes until tender.

2 Meanwhile, trim the excess fat from the lamb and discard. Chop finely or mince coarsely.

3 Heat the oil in a frying pan, add the onion and fry for about 5 minutes until lightly browned. Stir in the flour and fry for 2–3 minutes. Add the stock and simmer, stirring, until thickened.

4 Stir in the lamb, Worcestershire sauce, parsley, marjoram and salt and pepper. Spoon into a 1.1 litre (2 pint) shallow pie dish.

5 Drain the potatoes. Mash well, then gradually beat in the cheese and salt and pepper. Spoon or pipe over the lamb.

6 Bake in the oven at 200°C (400°F) mark 6 for 30 minutes until well browned. Serve hot, sprinkled with chopped parsley.

Menu Suggestion

Traditional vegetables to serve with Shepherd's Pie are cabbage or spring greens. To ensure that the nutrients are retained, shred the leaves, blanch and stir-fry rather than boiling.

SHEPHERD'S PIE

Although not traditional, Shepherd's Pie tastes extra good if you add mashed carrots or swedes to the potato topping. You can add as many or as few as you like, but a good proportion is half the weight of root vegetable to potato. Carrots and swedes not only add flavour, they also give the topping a warming golden-yellow colour.

IRISH STEW

3.15*	£	367–550 cals

Serves 4–6

900 g (2 lb) scrag end of neck of lamb

1 kg (2¼ lb) potatoes, peeled and sliced

2 large onions, skinned and sliced

salt and freshly ground pepper

15 ml (1 tbsp) pearl barley

about 450 ml (¾ pint) chicken stock (see page 350)

chopped fresh parsley, to garnish

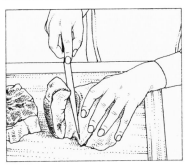

1 Using a sharp knife, divide meat into 8, then trim.

2 Place alternate layers of vegetables and meat in a saucepan, seasoning with salt and pepper. Finish with the pearl barley sprinkled over and a final layer of potatoes. Add sufficient stock to half cover.

3 Cover with a lid and simmer very slowly for about 3 hours. (Alternatively, cook the stew in a casserole in the oven at 190°C (375°F) mark 5 for 2½–3 hours.) Serve sprinkled with parsley.

Menu Suggestion

Traditional Irish stew, with meat and potatoes cooked together in the same pot, should be served with a simple vegetable such as carrots, peas or cabbage.

IRISH STEW

This recipe was originally intended for the toughest cuts of mutton and goat—the long, slow cooking made them tender and palatable, and their strong flavours mingled with herbs, onions and potatoes to produce a wonderfully aromatic dish. Nowadays, lamb is most often used—either scrag end as in this recipe, or best end, which is slightly more expensive but not quite so fatty. If using scrag end, ask the butcher to chop it into serving pieces for you if you wish, as the bones are quite difficult to cut yourself at home. Best end is sold as chops, therefore no cutting is required.

SPICED LAMB WITH SPINACH

1.20* | 533 cals

* plus 4 hours marinating
Serves 4

900 g (2 lb) boned leg or shoulder of lamb, trimmed of fat and cubed

90 ml (6 tbsp) natural yogurt

1 cm ($\frac{1}{2}$ inch) piece fresh root ginger, peeled and chopped

2 garlic cloves, skinned and chopped

2.5 cm (1 inch) cinnamon stick

2 bay leaves

2 green cardamoms

4 black peppercorns

3 whole cloves

5 ml (1 tsp) ground cumin

5 ml (1 tsp) garam masala

1.25–2.5 ml ($\frac{1}{4}$–$\frac{1}{2}$ tsp) chilli powder

5 ml (1 tsp) ground coriander

5 ml (1 tsp) salt

450 g (1 lb) fresh or 225 g (8 oz) frozen spinach

sprig of mint and lemon slices, to garnish

1 Place the cubes of meat in a bowl. Then, in a separate bowl, mix together the yogurt, ginger, garlic, whole and ground spices and the salt.

2 Spoon the mixture over the meat and mix thoroughly. Cover and leave to marinate at room temperature for about 4 hours.

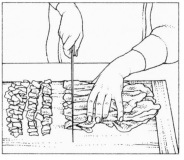

3 Meanwhile, thoroughly wash and chop the fresh spinach. Thaw frozen spinach in a pan.

4 Put the marinated meat in a heavy-based saucepan and cook over a low heat for about 1 hour, stirring occasionally, until all the moisture has evaporated and the meat is tender.

5 Stir in the spinach and cook over low heat for a further 10 minutes. Serve garnished with mint and lemon slices.

Menu Suggestion
Spicy and rich, this Indian dish of lamb and spinach goes well with plain boiled basmati rice. Serve cucumber raita and mango chutney as side dishes.

POT ROAST LAMB WITH WINTER VEGETABLES

3.00	442–590 cals

Serves 6–8

15 ml (1 tbsp) vegetable oil
1.6 kg (3½ lb) leg of lamb
3 onions, skinned and quartered
4 carrots, peeled and thickly sliced
2 leeks, sliced and washed
30 ml (2 tbsp) tomato purée
396 g (14 oz) can tomatoes
1 garlic clove, skinned and crushed
bouquet garni
salt and freshly ground pepper

1 Heat the oil in a large frying pan and fry the joint of meat on all sides for about 10 minutes until browned. Remove meat and place in a large casserole.

2 Add the onions, carrots and leeks to frying pan and fry for 5 minutes, stirring occasionally. Remove from pan, then arrange around the lamb. Stir in the tomato purée with the tomatoes and their juice. Add the garlic, bouquet garni and seasoning.

3 Cover and cook in the oven at 170°C (325°F) mark 3 for about 2½ hours or until the meat is tender.

4 Discard the bouquet garni. Transfer the lamb to a warmed serving dish and surround with the vegetables.

5 Skim as much fat as possible from the liquid in the casserole, and serve separately in a sauceboat.

Menu Suggestion
An unusual alternative to roast lamb for Sunday lunch. Serve with jacket baked potatoes and a seasonal green vegetable.

MARINATED LAMB KEBABS

| 0.30* | 412 cals |

* plus 1–2 days marinating

Serves 4

150 ml ($\frac{1}{4}$ pint) natural yogurt

2.5 cm (1 inch) piece fresh root ginger, peeled and grated

2 garlic cloves, skinned and crushed

30 ml (2 tbsp) chopped fresh mint

10 ml (2 tsp) crushed cumin seeds

5 ml (1 tsp) ground turmeric

5 ml (1 tsp) salt

2.5 ml ($\frac{1}{2}$ tsp) chilli powder

700 g (1$\frac{1}{2}$ lb) lean lamb shoulder, trimmed of excess fat and cut into cubes

2 medium onions

fresh mint sprigs and lemon wedges, to garnish

1 Put the yogurt in a large bowl and add the ginger, garlic, mint, cumin, turmeric, salt and chilli powder. Stir well to mix.

2 Add the cubes of lamb to the bowl and stir to coat in the marinade. Cover and refrigerate for 1–2 days, turning occasionally.

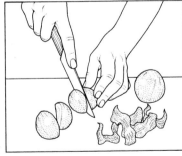

3 When ready to cook, skin the onions and cut into quarters with a sharp knife.

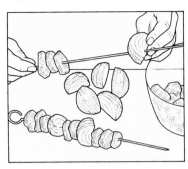

4 Thread the lamb and onion quarters alternately on to 4 oiled kebab skewers, pressing the pieces as close together as possible. Reserve any leftover marinade.

5 Grill the kebabs under moderate heat for 10 minutes until the lamb is browned on the outside and pink in the centre. Turn frequently during grilling and brush with the reserved marinade. Serve hot, garnished with mint and lemon wedges.

Menu Suggestion

Serve on a bed of brown rice with a Middle Eastern style salad of tomatoes, cucumber, chopped fresh mint and black olives.

MARINATED LAMB KEBABS

The marinating of the lamb in yogurt is an important stage, in this kebab recipe, so don't be tempted to skimp on the length of marinating time recommended. Natural yogurt contains a special bacteria which has the effect of tenderising meat and making it more succulent when cooked. The longer the meat is left in a yogurt marinade the more tender it will be—in the cookery of the Middle East, yogurt is frequently used for this purpose, especially with tough, sinewy cuts of meat.

MIDDLE EASTERN MEATBALLS WITH AUBERGINE AND TOMATO

| 1.30* | ⬚ | ✳ | 415 cals |

* plus 30 minutes degorging
aubergines and 1 hour chilling

Serves 6

2 medium aubergines, about 450 g
   (1 lb) total weight, sliced

salt and freshly ground pepper

150 ml (¼ pint) vegetable oil

450 g (1 lb) boneless lamb

2 thick slices of white bread,
   crusts removed

1 small onion, skinned

10 ml (2 tsp) ground cumin

450 g (1 lb) tomatoes, skinned and
   chopped

15 ml (1 tbsp) tomato purée

450 ml (¾ pint) chicken stock (see
   page 350) or dry white wine and
   water, mixed

2.5 ml (½ tsp) ground allspice

450 ml (¾ pint) vegetable oil, for
   deep-frying

chopped fresh parsley, to serve

1 Layer the aubergine slices in a
colander, sprinkling each layer
with salt. Cover with a plate,
weight down and leave for 30
minutes to draw out moisture.

2 Drain the aubergine slices,
rinse and dry well. In a large
frying pan, fry for 4–5 minutes in
batches in the oil, turning once.
Drain the fried aubergines on
absorbent kitchen paper.

3 Put the lamb through the
blades of a mincer twice with
the fried aubergines, bread and
onion. (Or work the ingredients in
a food processor.)

4 In a bowl, mix the minced
meat with the cumin and
seasoning to taste, then chill in the
refrigerator for about 30 minutes,
until firm.

5 Meanwhile, put the tomatoes,
tomato purée, stock and
allspice in a large flameproof
casserole with seasoning to taste.
Bring to the boil, stirring to break
up the tomatoes, then lower the
heat and simmer while making
the meatballs.

6 With floured hands, form the
mixture into 30 walnut-sized
balls. Chill in the refrigerator for
30 minutes to firm.

7 Heat the oil for deep-frying to
190°C (375°F). Add the meatballs in batches and fry until
browned on all sides. Remove
with a slotted spoon and drain on
absorbent kitchen paper.

8 Add the drained meatballs to
the tomato sauce then cover
and simmer gently for 30 minutes,
shaking the casserole frequently
so that the meatballs become
saturated in the sauce.

9 Taste and, if necessary, adjust
the seasoning of the tomato
sauce before serving. Garnish with
chopped fresh parsley.

Menu Suggestion
Serve with boiled basmati rice as
part of a Middle Eastern style
meal. Start with hot pitta bread
and taramasalata or houmos, and
finish with a fresh fruit salad.

MIDDLE EASTERN MEATBALLS

Lamb, aubergines and tomatoes
are a popular combination of
ingredients in Middle Eastern
cookery. Here the lamb and
aubergines are minced together
to make meatballs, an unusual
method, but one which gives a
tasty, moist result. To save time,
buy ready-minced lamb, but
make sure it is fairly lean, or
the fat will run out into the sauce
and make the dish unpalatable.

ROAST BEEF WITH YORKSHIRE PUDDING

| 1.35 | 🍴 £ £ | 617 cals |

Serves 6

1.4 kg (3 lb) boned and rolled
sirloin, rib, rump or topside

50 g (2 oz) beef dripping (optional)

freshly ground pepper

5 ml (1 tsp) mustard powder
(optional)

125 g (4 oz) plain flour

pinch of salt

1 egg

200 ml (7 fl oz) milk

25 g (1 oz) lard or dripping or 30 ml
(2 tbsp) vegetable oil

Thin Gravy, to serve (page 350)

1 Weigh the meat and calculate the cooking time, allowing 15 minutes per 450 g (1 lb) plus 15 minutes for rare beef, 20 minutes per 450 g (1 lb) plus 20 minutes for medium beef or 25 minutes per 450 g (1 lb) plus 25 minutes for well-done.

2 Put the meat into a shallow roasting tin, preferably on a grid, with the thickest layer of fat uppermost and the cut sides exposed to the heat. Smear with dripping if the meat is lean. Grind pepper all over and sprinkle with mustard, if wished.

3 Roast the joint in the oven at 180°C (350°F) mark 4 for the calculated time, basting occasionally with the juices from the tin. Forty-five minutes before the end of the cooking time, cover the joint with foil and place on the bottom shelf of the oven. Increase the oven temperature to 220°C (425°F) mark 7.

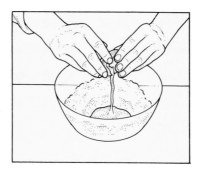

4 Make the Yorkshire pudding. Mix the flour and salt in a bowl, make a well in the centre and break in the egg.

5 Add half of the milk and, using a wooden spoon, gradually work in the flour. Beat the mixture until smooth, then add the remaining milk and 100 ml (3½ fl oz) water. Beat until well mixed and the surface is covered with tiny bubbles.

6 Put the fat in a small roasting or other baking tin and place in the oven for about 5 minutes until the fat shows a haze.

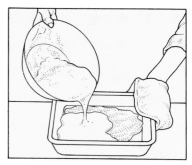

7 Pour in the batter and return to the oven to cook for 40–45 minutes, until risen and golden brown. Do not open the oven door for 30 minutes.

8 After 30 minutes, transfer the meat to a serving dish, cover and place on the lowest shelf in the oven. Use the juices in the roasting tin to make Thin Gravy.

Menu Suggestion
Serve with Roast Potatoes (page 355), a green vegetable such as broccoli or cabbage, carrots or parsnips and Horseradish Sauce (page 352).

——————— VARIATION ———————

For individual Yorkshire Puddings or Popovers, use **50 g (2 oz) plain flour,** a pinch of **salt, 1 egg, 150 ml (¼ pint) milk** and **water** mixed. Pour into 12 patty tins and cook for 15–20 minutes.

ROAST BEEF WITH YORKSHIRE PUDDING

In Yorkshire, 'batter pudding' was traditionally served as a first course with gravy, then the beef and vegetables followed on as a separate course. The idea behind this was to fill hungry stomachs before the beef was served.

There are many theories about making light, fluffy Yorkshire puddings. Yorkshire cooks maintain that the batter should be made with half milk and half water rather than all milk, but what is certain is that the batter should be well beaten and the fat sizzling hot before it is poured in.

BRAISED BRISKET WITH RED WINE

| 2.45 | £ | 529 cals |

Serves 6

1.1 kg (2¼ lb) boned and rolled lean brisket

15 ml (1 tbsp) plain flour

15 ml (1 tbsp) vegetable oil

2 medium carrots, peeled and cut into chunks

2 medium parsnips, peeled and cut into chunks

2 medium onions, skinned and diced

150 ml (¼ pint) beef stock

15 ml (1 tbsp) tomato purée

60 ml (4 tbsp) red wine

5 ml (1 tsp) chopped fresh thyme or 2.5 ml (½ tsp) dried

1 bay leaf

salt and freshly ground pepper

10 ml (2 tsp) cornflour

1 Roll the joint in the flour until well coated. Heat the oil in a 2.3 litre (4 pint) flameproof casserole, add the joint and fry until well browned all over. Remove from the casserole and set aside while frying the vegetables.

2 Stir the vegetables into the fat remaining in the pan and fry gently for 2 minutes. Add the stock, tomato purée, wine, thyme and bay leaf, with salt and pepper to taste. Bring to the boil.

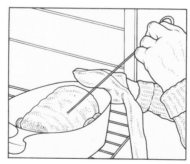

3 Place the meat in the centre of the vegetables, cover the casserole tightly and cook in the oven at 170°C (325°F) mark 3 for about 2¼ hours, until the meat is tender when pierced with a skewer.

4 Remove the meat from the casserole and carve into slices. Arrange on a warmed serving dish with the vegetables, cover and keep warm.

5 Mix the cornflour to a smooth paste with 30 ml (2 tbsp) water. Stir into the meat juices, then bring slowly to the boil. Boil for 1 minute, then taste and adjust seasoning. Pour into a sauceboat and serve separately.

Menu Suggestion
This French-style dish of braised beef has its own root vegetables. Serve with steamed or boiled new potatoes tossed in parsley butter, and a green vegetable or salad.

MEDITERRANEAN POT ROAST

3.45	923 cals

Serves 6

45 ml (3 tbsp) olive oil

1.8 kg (4 lb) boned and rolled brisket

1 medium Spanish onion, skinned and finely chopped

1–2 garlic cloves, skinned and finely chopped

2 celery sticks, trimmed and finely chopped

2 carrots, peeled and finely chopped

450 g (1 lb) ripe tomatoes, skinned and roughly chopped

150 ml ($\frac{1}{4}$ pint) full-bodied red wine, e.g. Côtes du Rhône, Chianti, Rioja

300–450 ml ($\frac{1}{2}$–$\frac{3}{4}$ pint) beef stock (see page 350) or water

10 ml (2 tsp) chopped fresh mixed herbs or 5 ml (1 tsp) dried

salt and freshly ground pepper

185 g ($6\frac{1}{2}$ oz) can pimientos, drained and sliced

15 g ($\frac{1}{2}$ oz) butter or margarine

25 g (1 oz) plain flour

extra chopped herbs, to garnish

1 Heat 30 ml (2 tbsp) of the oil in a large flameproof casserole. Add the brisket and fry over moderate heat, turning constantly until well browned on all sides.

2 Remove the beef with 2 slotted spoons and drain on absorbent kitchen paper while frying the vegetables.

3 Heat the remaining oil in the casserole, add the chopped onion, garlic, celery and carrots and fry over moderate heat for 10–15 minutes until softened and lightly coloured, stirring frequently.

4 Add the tomatoes and mix with the fried vegetables, then pour in the wine and stock or water. Bring to the boil, stirring to help break up the tomatoes, then sprinkle in the herbs and salt and pepper to taste.

5 Return the beef to the casserole, adding more stock or water, if necessary, to almost cover the beef. Cover and cook in the oven at 150°C (300°F) mark 2 for 3 hours, or until the beef is very tender. Remove the beef from the casserole and place on a warmed serving platter. Set aside to 'rest' in a warm place.

6 Meanwhile, transfer the casserole to the top of the cooker and skim the excess fat off the surface of the cooking liquid. Add the pimientos and heat through gently.

7 On a small plate, work the butter and flour together to form a paste (beurre manié). Add to the simmering liquid a little at a time, whisking vigorously after each addition. Simmer until the sauce thickens, then taste and adjust seasoning.

8 Carve the beef into neat slices and arrange on a warmed serving platter. Pour over a little sauce and sprinkle with the herbs. Hand the remaining sauce separately.

Menu Suggestion

Serve for a family supper or weekend lunch dish, with steamed potatoes or jacket baked potatoes. Follow with a crisp salad.

PAPRIKA BEEF

| 2.15 | £ | ✳ | 213 cals |

Serves 4

450 g (1 lb) lean shin of beef

15 ml (1 tbsp) plain wholewheat
  flour

7.5 ml (1½ tsp) mild paprika

1.25 ml (¼ tsp) caraway seeds

1.25 ml (¼ tsp) dried marjoram

salt and freshly ground pepper

175 g (6 oz) onion, skinned and
  sliced

225 g (8 oz) carrots, peeled and
  sliced

200 ml (7 fl oz) beef stock

15 ml (1 tbsp) tomato purée

1 garlic clove, skinned and crushed

1 whole clove

100 g (4 oz) button mushrooms,
  wiped and sliced

chopped fresh parsley, to garnish

1 Trim the fat from the beef.
Cut the meat into chunky
cubes. Mix together the flour,
paprika, caraway seeds, marjoram
and seasoning to taste. Toss the
beef in the seasoned flour.

2 Layer the meat, onion and
carrots in a 2 litre (3½ pint)
flameproof casserole.

3 Whisk together the stock,
tomato purée, crushed garlic
and clove. Pour into the casserole.
Bring to the boil and simmer,
uncovered, for 3–4 minutes.

4 Cover the casserole tightly and
cook in the oven at 180°C
(350°F) mark 4 for about 1½ hours,
stirring occasionally.

5 Remove the casserole from the
oven and stir in the mushrooms.
Cover again and return to the oven
for a further 15 minutes or until
the meat is tender. Taste and
adjust seasoning. Garnish.

Menu Suggestion
Serve with layered sliced potatoes
and onions, moistened with stock
and baked in the oven.

ALMOND BEEF WITH CELERY

| 2.00 | £ ✳* | 476 cals |

* freeze at the end of step 3

Serves 6

| 900 g (2 lb) shin of beef |
| 45 ml (3 tbsp) vegetable oil |
| 15 ml (1 tbsp) plain flour |
| 90 ml (6 tbsp) ground almonds |
| 1 garlic clove, skinned and crushed |
| 300 ml ($\frac{1}{2}$ pint) beef stock |
| salt and freshly ground pepper |
| 4 celery sticks |
| 25 g (1 oz) butter |
| 50 g (2 oz) flaked almonds |

1 Cut the beef into 2.5 cm (1 inch) pieces. Heat the oil in a flameproof casserole, add the meat a few pieces at a time and brown well, removing each batch with a slotted spoon.

2 Return all the meat to the pan. Stir in the flour, ground almonds and crushed garlic. Stir over the heat for 1 minute, then pour in the beef stock. Bring to the boil and season to taste with salt and pepper.

3 Cover the casserole and cook in the oven at 180°C (350°F) mark 4 for about 1$\frac{1}{2}$ hours or until the meat is tender.

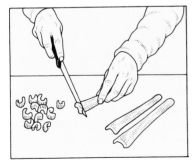

4 Ten minutes before the end of cooking time, slice the celery. Melt the butter in a large frying pan, add the celery and flaked almonds and sauté for about 6 minutes or until golden brown.

5 Taste and adjust the seasoning of the beef. Sprinkle with the celery and almond mixture and serve at once.

Menu Suggestion

Serve this unusual casserole with jacket baked potatoes, which can be cooked in the oven at the same time. Carrots tossed in plenty of chopped fresh parsley will help give the meal colour.

ALMOND BEEF

The almonds in this casserole help increase its nutritional value—something to bear in mind when preparing everyday meals, especially if there are growing children in the family. Almonds are a good source of protein, B vitamins and unsaturated fats, so try to use them regularly.

STEAK AND KIDNEY PUDDING

5.45	🍳	£	536 cals

Serves 6

550 g (1¼ lb) stewing steak in a piece, trimmed and cut into 1 cm (½ inch) cubes

225 g (8 oz) ox kidney, cut into small pieces

1 medium onion, skinned and finely chopped

30 ml (2 tbsp) chopped fresh parsley

45 ml (3 tbsp) plain flour

finely grated rind of 1 lemon

salt and freshly ground pepper

275 g (10 oz) self-raising flour

150 g (5 oz) shredded suet

butter or margarine, for greasing

1 Place the beef and kidney in a bowl with the onion and the parsley. Sprinkle in the plain flour and lemon rind and season well with salt and pepper.

2 In a separate bowl, mix together the self-raising flour, suet and a good pinch of salt. Stir in about 200 ml (7 fl oz) cold water, until a soft dough is formed. Knead lightly.

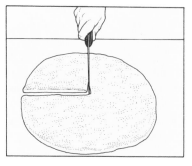

3 Roll out the dough on a lightly floured surface to a circle about 35 cm (14 inches) in diameter. Cut one-quarter of the dough in a fan shape to within 2.5 cm (1 inch) of the centre.

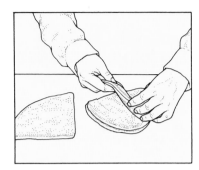

4 Lightly grease a 1.7 litre (3 pint) pudding basin. Dust the top surface of the large piece of dough with flour. Fold in half, then in half again.

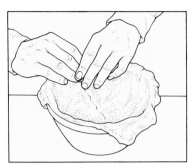

5 Lift the dough into the basin, unfold and press into the base and up the sides, taking care to seal the join well. The pastry should overlap the basin top by about 2.5 cm (1 inch).

6 Spoon the meat mixture into the lined pudding basin. Spread the meat out evenly. Add about 120 ml (8 tbsp) water. This should come about two-thirds of the way up the meat mixture.

7 Roll out the remaining piece of dough to a round 2.5 cm (1 inch) larger than the top of the basin. Dampen the exposed edge of the dough lining the basin.

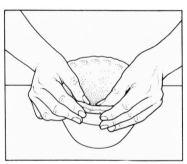

8 Lift the round of dough on top of the filling and push the pastry edges together to seal. Trim around the top of the basin to neaten. Roll the sealed edges inwards around top of basin.

9 Cut a piece of greaseproof paper and a piece of foil large enough to form a hat over the top of the basin. Place them together and pleat across the middle. Lightly butter the greaseproof side and put them over the pudding, greaseproof-side down. Tie securely on to the basin with string, running the string just under the lip.

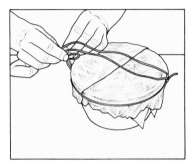

10 Make a string handle across the basin top. Place the basin in a large saucepan and pour in enough boiling water to come halfway up the basin.

11 Bring to the boil, half cover with a lid and steam for about 5 hours. Top up with boiling water as necessary and do not let the water go off the boil.

12 To serve, remove the basin from the pan, discard the string, greaseproof and foil. Wrap the basin with a folded napkin and place on a serving plate. Serve hot. (Alternatively, the pudding can be turned out on to the plate.)

Menu Suggestion
Serve this filling meat pudding for a family meal with seasonal vegetables.

CHILLI CON CARNE (SPICED BEEF AND BEANS)

2.45* £ ✳ 409 cals

* plus overnight soaking of dried beans

Serves 6

225 g (8 oz) dried red kidney beans, soaked overnight

30 ml (2 tbsp) vegetable oil

2 onions, skinned and chopped

900 g (2 lb) chuck steak, cubed

1 large garlic clove, skinned and crushed

1 bay leaf

1 green chilli, seeded and chopped

5 cm (2 inch) stick cinnamon

4 whole cloves

1.25 ml ($\frac{1}{4}$ tsp) dried oregano

1.25 ml ($\frac{1}{4}$ tsp) dried marjoram

2.5 ml ($\frac{1}{2}$ tsp) cayenne pepper

1.25 ml ($\frac{1}{4}$ tsp) sesame seeds

15 ml (1 tbsp) salt

freshly ground pepper

30–45 ml (2–3 tbsp) chilli seasoning or 2.5 ml ($\frac{1}{2}$ tsp) chilli powder

30 ml (2 tbsp) tomato purée

793 g (28 oz) can tomatoes

pinch of sugar

5 ml (1 tsp) malt vinegar

2 coriander sprigs

1 Drain the soaked beans and place in a saucepan of cold water. Bring to the boil and boil rapidly for 10 minutes, then drain.

2 Meanwhile, heat the oil in a flameproof casserole and fry the onions for 5 minutes until softened. Add the meat and cook for about 8 minutes until browned.

3 Add the next twelve ingredients to the meat and continue to fry for 2 minutes, stirring constantly. Add the tomato purée, tomatoes with their juice, sugar, vinegar, coriander and the boiled and drained beans.

4 Bring to the boil, cover and cook in the oven at 170°C (325°F) mark 3 for about $2\frac{1}{4}$ hours until the meat is tender.

Menu Suggestion
Chilli con Carne is traditionally eaten with plain boiled rice. If you find it hot, serve it with natural yogurt and sliced cucumber to cool the palate.

CHILLI CON CARNE

If you forget to soak the red kidney beans overnight for this dish, there is still no reason why it shouldn't be made on the day. One short-cut method is to make the casserole without the beans altogether, then 10 minutes before serving, simply stir in a can of ready-cooked red kidney beans (drained and rinsed) and heat through. Another alternative is the hot-soak method for dried beans: put the beans in a pan, cover with cold water and bring to the boil. Boil for 10 minutes, then turn off the heat, cover the pan and leave to soak for 1 hour. Continue from step 1 of the recipe.

BOBOTIE
(CURRIED MINCE AND APPLE BAKE)

1.10	£	695 cals

Serves 4

50 g (2 oz) slice of bread, crusts removed

300 ml (½ pint) milk

40 g (1½ oz) butter or margarine

2 medium onions, skinned and finely chopped

1 cooking apple, cored and chopped

15 ml (1 tbsp) mild curry powder

700 g (1½ lb) minced beef

30 ml (2 tbsp) raisins

25 g (1 oz) flaked almonds

15 ml (1 tbsp) lemon juice

salt and freshly ground pepper

2 bay leaves

3 eggs

1 Put the bread in a bowl, pour in the milk and leave to soak. Meanwhile, melt the butter in a saucepan, add the onions and fry for about 5 minutes until beginning to soften. Add the apple and curry powder and fry, stirring, for a further 2–3 minutes.

2 Turn the onion mixture into a bowl, add the meat, raisins, almonds, lemon juice and salt and pepper to taste. Mix until well combined.

3 Squeeze the milk from the bread, reserving the milk, and stir the bread into the meat mixture.

4 Place the bay leaves on the bottom of a 1.1 litre (2 pint) pie dish. Fill with the meat mixture and then cover with foil. Bake in the oven at 180°C (350°F) mark 4 for 35 minutes, then remove the foil and break up the meat mixture with a fork.

5 Whisk the eggs together with the reserved milk and pour over the meat, stirring gently to distribute the custard mixture.

6 Return the dish to the oven and cook for a further 35 minutes, or until the custard has set and the top browned. Serve hot, straight from the dish.

Menu Suggestion

Serve with boiled rice and crisp poppadoms. Mango chutney and lime pickle also go well with Bobotie, and ice-cold beer or lager is the ideal drink.

BOBOTIE

This South African dish is sometimes made with minced lamb and sometimes with cooked minced meat, but whichever you use, the end result is just as good. The recipe originates from the time when the Dutch founded the Cape in the seventeenth century, bringing with them their Malay cooks from the Dutch colonies in the Far East. Many South African dishes like Bobotie have spicy ingredients, which is the Malay influence.

KEEMA CURRY WITH PEAS

| 1.00 | £ | ✳ | 615 cals |

Serves 4

45 ml (3 tbsp) ghee or butter

1 medium onion, skinned and finely chopped

1–2 garlic cloves, skinned and crushed

700 g (1½ lb) minced beef

4 medium tomatoes, skinned and roughly chopped

15 ml (1 tbsp) tomato purée

20 ml (4 tsp) ground coriander

10 ml (2 tsp) ground cumin

7.5 ml (1½ tsp) ground fenugreek

2.5 ml (½ tsp) chilli powder

5 ml (1 tsp) salt

350 g (12 oz) frozen peas

juice of ½ lemon

45 ml (3 tbsp) chopped fresh coriander

10 ml (2 tsp) garam masala

150 ml (¼ pint) natural yogurt

1 Heat the ghee in a heavy-based saucepan, add the onion and garlic and fry gently for about 5 minutes until soft and lightly coloured.

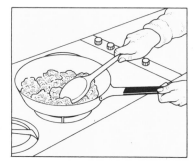

2 Add the minced beef in batches and fry until browned, pressing the meat with a wooden spoon to remove any lumps.

3 Add the tomatoes, tomato purée, coriander, cumin, fenugreek, chilli powder and salt and stir well to mix. Pour in 300 ml (½ pint) water and bring to the boil, stirring. Lower the heat, cover and simmer for 30 minutes.

4 Pour 150 ml (¼ pint) water into the pan and bring to the boil. Add the peas, cover the pan and simmer for a further 10 minutes, or until the peas are just tender.

5 Remove the curry mixture from the heat and stir in the lemon juice, fresh coriander and garam masala. Cover the pan and leave to stand for 5 minutes. Stir the yogurt into the curry and serve immediately.

Menu Suggestion
This simple curry is very quick to prepare. Serve it for supper with parathas or puris (there are excellent packet mixes available), mango chutney and lime pickle.

BEEFBURGERS
(HAMBURGERS)

| 0.15 | £ | ✳* | 473 cals |

* freeze before greasing in step 2

Serves 4

450 g (1 lb) lean beef, e.g. chuck, shoulder or rump steak, minced

½ small onion, skinned and grated (optional)

salt and freshly ground pepper

melted butter or vegetable oil, for grilling, or vegetable oil, for shallow frying

4 large soft buns

butter or margarine, for spreading

lettuce and onion rings, to serve (optional)

Menu Suggestion
Homemade Beefburgers taste so much better than the commercial varieties—and you know exactly what is in them. Serve them for the children's tea or for a quick family supper, with a colourful mixed salad.

——— VARIATIONS ———

CHEESEBURGERS
Top the cooked beefburgers with a slice of **Cheddar or Gruyère cheese** and cook under the grill for a further minute or until the cheese has melted.

CHILLIBURGERS
Add **15 ml (1 tbsp) chilli seasoning** when mixing the beefburgers.

PEPPERCORNBURGERS
Crush **15 ml (1 tbsp) green peppercorns** and add when mixing the beefburgers.

1 Mix the minced beef well with the onion (if using) and plenty of salt and pepper.

2 Shape the mixture lightly into 4 round, flat patties. Brush sparingly with melted butter or vegetable oil.

3 Grill the burgers for 8–10 minutes until cooked according to taste, turning once, or fry in a little oil in a frying pan, turning them once and allowing the same amount of time.

4 Meanwhile, split the buns in half and spread with a little butter. Put 1 beefburger inside each bun. Add a lettuce leaf and some onion rings, if liked, and serve immediately.

BITKIS

2.00* £ 637 cals

* plus overnight soaking and 2–3
hours cooling

Serves 6

100 g (4 oz) medium oatmeal

300 ml (½ pint) milk

2 medium onions, roughly chopped

900 g (2 lb) lean minced beef

salt and freshly ground pepper

15 ml (3 tsp) caraway seeds
   (optional)

75 ml (5 tbsp) seasoned flour

60 ml (4 tbsp) vegetable oil

25 g (1 oz) butter

25 g (1 oz) plain flour

450 ml (¾ pint) beef or chicken
   stock (see page 350)

30 ml (2 tbsp) tomato purée

300 ml (½ pint) soured cream

parsley sprigs, to garnish

1 Soak the oatmeal in the milk
overnight. Squeeze out excess
milk and mix the oatmeal with the
onions, minced beef and seasoning
to taste.

2 Put this mixture twice through
a mincer or mix in a food
processor until smooth. Beat in
10 ml (2 tsp) of the caraway seeds,
if using.

3 Shape into 18 round flat cakes,
or bitkis. Coat with seasoned
flour.

4 Heat the oil in a large frying
pan and brown the bitkis well.
Place in a single layer in a large
shallow ovenproof dish.

5 Melt the butter in a saucepan,
add the flour and cook over
low heat, stirring with a wooden
spoon, for 2 minutes. Gradually
blend in the stock, stirring after
each addition to prevent lumps
forming. Bring to the boil slowly,
then simmer for 2–3 minutes,
stirring. Stir in the tomato purée,
soured cream and remaining
caraway seeds, if using.

6 Pour the sauce over the bitkis
and cool for 2–3 hours. Cover
with foil and chill in the
refrigerator until required.

7 Bake in the oven at 180°C
(350°F) mark 4 for about
1¼ hours or until the juices run
clear when the bitkis are pierced.
Garnish with parsley just before
serving.

Menu Suggestion
Serve these Russian beef patties
for a family meal with noodles
and a mixed salad which includes
grated or chopped beetroot.

BEEF KABOBS WITH HORSERADISH RELISH

| 0.45 | £ | ✳ | 399 cals |

Serves 6

700 g (1½ lb) lean minced beef

250 g (9 oz) grated onion

135 ml (9 tbsp) horseradish sauce

45 ml (3 tbsp) chopped fresh thyme

250 g (9 oz) fresh white
  breadcrumbs

salt and freshly ground pepper

1 egg, beaten

plain flour, for coating

150 ml (¼ pint) natural yogurt

120 ml (8 tbsp) finely chopped fresh
  parsley

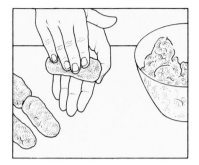

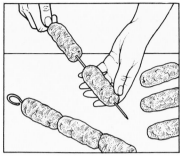

1 Place the minced beef in a large bowl and mix in the onion, 90 ml (6 tbsp) of the horseradish, thyme, breadcrumbs and seasoning to taste.

2 Add enough egg to bind the mixture together and, with well-floured hands, shape into 18 even-sized sausages. Cover and chill in the refrigerator until required.

3 Thread the kabobs lengthways on to 6 oiled skewers. Place under a pre-heated grill and grill for about 20 minutes, turning frequently.

4 Meanwhile, mix the yogurt with the remaining horse-radish and parsley. Serve the kabobs hot, with the sauce handed separately.

BEEF KABOBS WITH HORSERADISH RELISH

Kabobs—or kebabs as we also call them—are very popular in Indian cookery, and this method of threading minced meat kebabs on skewers is a very common one. In India, such kabobs are cooked on the street, and passers-by stop to buy them and eat them as they are going along. A charcoal grill is used for cooking, which gives them such a wonderful aroma that they are hard to resist if you are hungry when walking by a kabob stall. If you have a barbecue, then cook the kabobs on it, and you will understand why!

SPICED VEAL WITH PEPPERS

| 1.30 | £ | 250 cals |

Serves 4

550 g (1¼ lb) pie veal

2 medium onions, skinned

2 small red peppers, cored and seeded

225 g (8 oz) tomatoes

15 ml (1 tbsp) vegetable oil

1 garlic clove, skinned

2.5 ml (½ tsp) ground ginger

2.5 ml (½ tsp) turmeric

2.5 ml (½ tsp) ground cumin

2.5 ml (½ tsp) chilli powder

1.25 ml (¼ tsp) ground cloves

300 ml (½ pint) natural yogurt

salt and freshly ground pepper

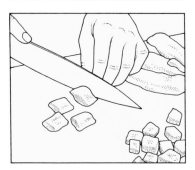

1 Trim the veal of fat and cut into chunky cubes. Slice the onions and peppers thinly. Skin the tomatoes and chop roughly.

2 Heat the oil in a large saucepan. Add the onions, peppers, crushed garlic and spices and fry for 1 minute. Stir in the chopped tomatoes.

3 Turn the heat to very low and add the yogurt very gradually, stirring well between each addition.

4 Add the veal, with salt and pepper to taste. Cover and simmer gently for 30 minutes.

5 Uncover the pan and cook the veal for a further 30 minutes or until it is tender and the liquid has reduced. Stir occasionally to prevent the meat sticking to the pan. Taste and adjust seasoning before serving.

Menu Suggestion
Serve this spicy veal casserole with boiled rice and a tossed green salad for a tasty midweek family meal.

SPICED VEAL WITH PEPPERS

Pie veal is one of the most economical cuts of veal, widely available in both supermarkets and butchers shops, and ideal for everyday meals. The name 'pie veal' comes from the fact that the meat was traditionally used in the making of veal and ham pie, but nowadays pie veal is also used in stews and casseroles, and in French blanquettes.

The actual cut varies from one butcher and one region to another, but it is usually from the shin, leg and neck of the calf. Pie veal is normally sold boned and cubed, which makes it a most convenient cut, but always check the meat before using as some pie veal can be very fatty. For this particular recipe, you will have to trim off as much of the fat as possible, or it will spoil the yogurt sauce.

ROAST STUFFED BREAST OF VEAL

3.00	🍳	£ £	335 cals

Serves 8

40 g (1½ oz) butter or margarine

50 g (2 oz) bacon, rinded and chopped

100 g (4 oz) fresh breadcrumbs

15 ml (1 tbsp) chopped fresh parsley

30 ml (2 tbsp) chopped fresh herbs such as thyme, rosemary, marjoram

finely grated rind and juice of ½ lemon

1 egg, beaten

salt and freshly ground pepper

milk or stock, to moisten

1.6 kg (3½ lb) boned lean breast of veal

1 Melt the butter in a frying pan, add the bacon and fry gently for 2–3 minutes without browning.

2 Put the breadcrumbs in a bowl with the parsley, herbs, lemon rind and juice. Mix well together. Stir in the cooked bacon and butter and bind together with the beaten egg. Season to taste with salt and pepper. Moisten with a little milk or stock if the stuffing looks dry.

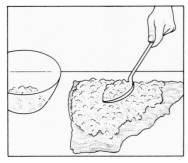

3 Lay the veal, boned side uppermost, on a board and remove any fat or gristle. Spread the stuffing evenly over the meat.

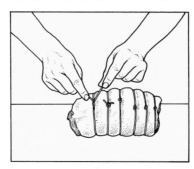

4 Roll up the joint and tie neatly with string. Weigh the rolled joint and calculate the cooking time, allowing 25 minutes per 450 g (1 lb) plus 25 minutes. Wrap in foil and place in a roasting tin.

5 Roast the joint in the oven at 180°C (350°F) mark 4 for the calculated cooking time, uncovering the roast for the last hour.

6 Turn the oven off and leave the meat to rest for 15 minutes. Remove the string and carve the meat into thick slices. Serve hot.

Menu Suggestion

Breast of veal can be served simply with the pan juices poured over, or with Thin Gravy (page 350). Courgettes or ratatouille go well with veal, so too do Château Potatoes (page 355) which can be cooked in the oven at the same time.

ROAST STUFFED BREAST OF VEAL

Breast of veal is an economical cut, and one that is full of flavour. Not all butchers stock it, however, so it is worth checking as you may have to order in advance.

To make the breast easier to stuff, it is a good idea to cut a 'pocket' between the two layers of muscle. This will also help contain the stuffing during roasting and ensure a neat-looking joint.

PORK IN CIDER

2.15	580–870 cals

Serves 4–6

1.1 kg (2½ lb) boned and rolled lean shoulder or hand of pork, rind and excess fat removed

2 garlic cloves, skinned and cut into slivers

30 ml (2 tbsp) vegetable oil

salt and freshly ground pepper

300 ml (½ pint) dry cider

about 350 g (12 oz) white cabbage

1 large cooking apple

25 g (1 oz) butter

1 onion, skinned and sliced

5 ml (1 tsp) caraway seeds

paprika, to garnish (optional)

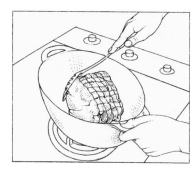

1 With a sharp, pointed knife, make deep incisions in the pork. Insert the garlic slivers, pushing them down into the meat.

2 Heat the oil in a large flame-proof casserole, add the pork and fry over moderate heat until browned on all sides. Sprinkle with salt and pepper, then pour in the cider and bring very slowly to boiling point.

3 Cover the casserole and cook in the oven at 170°C (325°F) mark 3 for 1½ hours.

4 Meanwhile, shred the cabbage, cutting away all thick, coarse stalks. Peel and core the apple, then slice it thickly.

5 Melt the butter in a saucepan, add the cabbage and apple and fry gently for 5 minutes, tossing the mixture constantly. Stir in the caraway seeds.

6 Add the cabbage mixture to the casserole, stirring it into the cooking liquid around the pork. Continue cooking for a further 30 minutes or until the pork is tender. Taste and adjust the seasoning of the cabbage and sauce before serving. Garnish the cabbage with paprika, if liked.

Menu Suggestion
Pork in Cider is ideal for a family weekend lunch. Serve with contrasting colourful vegetables such as carrots and broccoli. Roast potatoes can also be served if liked.

PORK IN CIDER
This combination of pork, apples, cider and cabbage is popular in the Alsace region of north-eastern France, where it is simply called Porc Alsacienne. Alsatian cider is strong and dry and gives this dish a unique, heady flavour. French dry cider is now available in many supermarkets and off licences, and is well worth seeking out if you are keen for this dish to have an authentic flavour.

ITALIAN-STYLE BRAISED PORK

| 2.00 | 450 cals |

Serves 6

15 ml (1 tbsp) vegetable oil

25 g (1 oz) butter

1 kg (2¼ lb) loin of pork, rinded

2 garlic cloves, skinned

1 large onion, skinned and chopped

568 ml (1 pint) milk

5 juniper berries

2 rosemary sprigs, plus extra for garnish

salt and freshly ground pepper

1 Heat the oil and the butter in a large saucepan or flameproof casserole into which the meat will just fit and fry the pork, garlic and onion for about 15 minutes until the pork is browned on all sides. Add the milk, juniper berries, rosemary and seasoning.

2 Bring to the boil, cover, turn the heat down and cook for 1½–2 hours until the pork is tender, turning and basting from time to time.

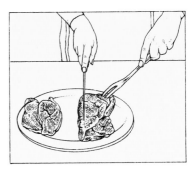

3 Transfer the pork to a warmed serving dish and carve into thick slices. Discard the garlic, juniper berries and rosemary. The milky cooking juices will look curdled, so rub the sauce through a sieve or liquidise in a blender or food processor until smooth. Taste and adjust the seasoning. Pour a little of the sauce over the slices and serve the remaining sauce separately. Garnish with sprigs of rosemary.

Menu Suggestion
Rich and tender, this casserole of pork braised in milk tastes good with steamed or boiled new potatoes, and a green salad tossed in a sharp oil and vinegar dressing.

ITALIAN-STYLE BRAISED PORK

Cooking pork in milk may seem a very strange combination at first, but it is very popular in Italy. The milk and the long, slow cooking produce the most tender results, making Arrosto di Maiale al Latte, as the Italians call this dish, a firm favourite for Sunday lunches, even with the less tender cuts of pork. The loin used in this recipe is a tender, expensive, cut of pork, but it can be rather dry if roasted in the normal way, because it is so lean. Braising loin of pork in milk ensures that the meat will be moist and succulent, and the flavour of garlic, juniper and rosemary gives the dish a unique aromatic taste.

133

HUNGARIAN PORK

2.45* £ £ ✳* 770 cals

* plus overnight chilling; freeze at the end of step 7

Serves 4

700 g (1½ lb) pork shoulder

1 medium onion, skinned and roughly chopped

1 large garlic clove, skinned and roughly chopped

50 g (2 oz) stuffed green olives

100 g (4 oz) fresh white breadcrumbs

salt and freshly ground pepper

1 egg, beaten

30 ml (2 tbsp) flour

700 g (1½ lb) fresh spinach, trimmed and washed (see box)

1.25 ml (¼ tsp) grated nutmeg

50 g (2 oz) butter

450 g (1 lb) ripe tomatoes, skinned and sliced

30 ml (2 tbsp) vegetable oil

200 ml (7 fl oz) chicken stock (see page 350)

200 ml (7 fl oz) dry white wine

7.5 ml (1½ tsp) paprika

150 ml (¼ pint) soured cream

extra paprika, to garnish

1 Trim the fat off the pork, then put through the mincer twice with the onion, garlic and olives. Turn into a bowl, add the breadcrumbs and seasoning to taste and mix well. Bind with the beaten egg.

2 With floured hands, roll the mixture into 36 small balls. Coat in the remaining flour, then chill for 30 minutes.

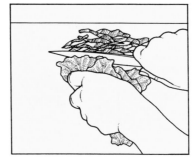

3 Meanwhile cook the spinach in a large saucepan with only the water that clings to the leaves. Drain well, then chop finely. Add the nutmeg and seasoning to taste.

4 Melt half the butter in a large frying pan, add the tomatoes and fry for 1–2 minutes. Transfer to an ovenproof casserole. Place the spinach on top.

5 Melt the remaining butter with the oil in the frying pan, add the meatballs in batches and fry over moderate heat until lightly coloured on all sides. Remove from the pan with a slotted spoon and drain on absorbent kitchen paper.

6 Add the stock and wine to the frying pan and bring to the boil, stirring to scrape up the sediment from the base and sides of the pan. Add the paprika and seasoning to taste, then remove from the heat. Cool for 5 minutes, then stir in 45 ml (3 tbsp) of the soured cream.

7 Put the meatballs on top of the spinach in the casserole, then pour over the sauce. Leave until cold, then cover and chill overnight.

8 Cook in the oven at 200°C (400°F) mark 6 for 1¼ hours. Serve hot straight from the casserole or transfer to a serving dish. Drizzle with the remaining soured cream and the extra paprika.

HUNGARIAN PORK

It is not always possible to buy fresh spinach exactly when you want it, but frozen spinach can be used in this recipe with almost equal success. If you can, buy the frozen whole leaf spinach, as it tends to have more body than the chopped varieties. To make up the equivalent of 700 g (1½ lb) fresh spinach for this recipe, you will need 350–450 g (12 oz–1 lb) frozen. Thaw the spinach in step 3 by heating it gently in a heavy saucepan for about 10 minutes, stirring and breaking up any lumps with a spoon. If using leaf spinach, do not chop it or it will go too limp.

CHILLI PORK

1.00* £ £ ✳* 879 cals

* plus at least 4 hours marinating;
freeze after step 4

Serves 4

900 g (2 lb) pork fillets (tenderloin)
45 ml (3 tbsp) soy sauce
15 ml (1 tbsp) hoisin sauce (see box)
15 ml (1 tbsp) soft brown sugar
30 ml (2 tbsp) crushed fresh root ginger or 10 ml (2 tsp) ground
60 ml (4 tbsp) vegetable oil
15 ml (1 tbsp) crushed dried red chillies, or less, according to taste
150 ml (¼ pint) chicken stock (see page 350) or water
10 ml (2 tsp) cornflour
350 g (12 oz) long-grain rice, boiled, to serve
few sliced red chillies, to garnish

1 Place the pork fillets in a shallow dish. Mix together the next four ingredients with half of the oil and pour over the pork. Cover and leave to marinate for at least 4 hours.

2 Heat the remaining oil in a flameproof casserole, add crushed chillies to taste and fry gently for 5 minutes, stirring all the time.

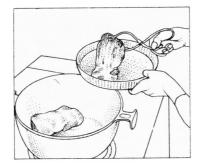

3 Remove the pork fillets from the marinade and add to the casserole. Fry over moderate heat, turning constantly until browned on all sides.

4 Mix the marinade with the stock or water, then pour over the pork. Bring slowly to boiling point, then lower the heat, cover and simmer for 45 minutes or until the pork is tender. Baste the pork frequently during the cooking time.

5 To serve, remove the pork from the cooking liquid and place on a board. Mix the cornflour to a paste with a little water, then stir into the cooking liquid and bring to the boil. Simmer, stirring, until the sauce thickens.

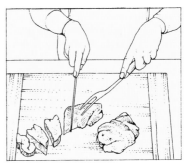

6 Carve the pork neatly into thin diagonal slices. Spread the hot boiled rice out on a warmed serving platter, arrange the pork slices on top and spoon over some of the sauce. Garnish with sliced chillies and serve, with the remaining sauce handed separately.

Menu Suggestion
Spicy and hot, Chilli Pork is served with boiled rice. Follow with a cooling green salad of shredded lettuce, cucumber and celery.

CHILLI PORK

This recipe for Chilli Pork is similar to the Chinese 'Red-Cooked Pork' and the Burmese 'Red Pork' or 'Wet-thani'. Such dishes are immensely popular in Eastern and Oriental cookery, where chillies are used both as a flavouring and colouring. Dried red chillies are easy to obtain in Oriental and Asian stores, but if you are unable to buy them, then you can use chilli powder instead. For this recipe, use 5 ml (1 tsp) chilli powder, as the flavour should be hot and strong, although different brands of chilli powder vary in their strength, so it is best to taste before serving in case more needs to be added. Hoisin sauce, also called hosin sauce and sometimes Chinese barbecue sauce, is sold in Chinese supermarkets. Available in cans and jars, it keeps for months in the refrigerator once opened, and can be used in numerous Chinese dishes. Made from soya beans, flour, sugar and spices, it helps give this dish its characteristic red colour.

BRACIOLE DI MAIALE
(PORK CHOPS WITH HERBS)

| 0.50 | 691 cals |

Serves 4

15 ml (1 tbsp) plain flour

5 ml (1 tsp) chopped fresh sage or
2.5 ml ($\frac{1}{2}$ tsp) dried

5 ml (1 tsp) chopped fresh
marjoram or 2.5 ml (1 tsp) dried

salt and freshly ground pepper

4 pork loin chops, trimmed of
excess fat

30 ml (2 tbsp) olive oil

15 g ($\frac{1}{2}$ oz) butter

300 ml ($\frac{1}{2}$ pint) Simple Tomato
Sauce (see page 352)

350 g (12 oz) spaghetti or other long
thin pasta, to serve

fresh sage and marjoram sprigs,
to garnish

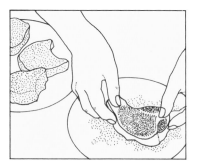

1 On a flat plate, mix together
the flour and herbs with a
liberal sprinkling of salt and
pepper. Coat the chops in the
flour mixture.

2 Heat the oil with the butter
in a heavy-based frying pan.
Add the chops and fry over
moderate heat for a few minutes
on each side until golden.

3 Pour the tomato sauce into the
base of an ovenproof serving
dish. Transfer the chops to the
serving dish.

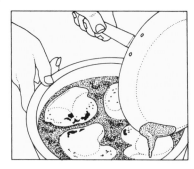

4 Pour over the cooking juices
from the frying pan. Cover the
dish with a lid or foil and bake in
the oven at 180°C (350°F) mark 4
for 30 minutes.

5 Meanwhile, cook the spaghetti
in boiling salted water for 8–
12 minutes until just tender.

6 Drain the spaghetti well. To
serve, arrange the chops at
one end of the serving dish and
garnish with the sprigs of herbs.
Arrange the spaghetti at the other
end. Serve immediately.

Menu Suggestion
Serve for a family meal followed
by a crisp green salad and some
fresh fruit.

BRACIOLE DI MAIALE
This tasty dish of pork chops
served with spaghetti and tomato
sauce would be served differ-
ently in Italy. The spaghetti and
tomato sauce would be eaten
separately as a first course, then
the chops would follow on their
own, with maybe a green or
mixed salad to refresh the palate
afterwards. Italians never eat the
pasta and meat course together,
but it is a matter of personal
preference how you serve them.

BACON HOT POT

2.45	£	335–502 cals

Serves 4–6

700 g (1½ lb) unsmoked collar or
   slipper joint of bacon

900 g (2 lb) potatoes

1 small onion, skinned and thinly
   sliced

2 cooking apples, peeled, cored and
   thickly sliced

10 ml (2 tsp) chopped fresh sage or
   5 ml (1 tsp) dried

salt and freshly ground pepper

150 ml (¼ pint) natural
   unsweetened apple juice

150 ml (¼ pint) water

15 g (½ oz) unsalted butter

15 ml (1 tbsp) vegetable oil

1 Remove the rind and excess fat
from the bacon and cut the
bacon into bite-sized pieces. Put
the pieces in a saucepan, cover
with cold water and bring to the
boil. Drain thoroughly.

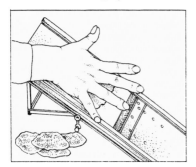

2 Peel the potatoes and slice
them thinly, using a mandolin
slicer if available.

3 Put the bacon, potatoes, onion
and apples in a shallow ovenproof casserole, sprinkling each
layer with sage and seasoning to
taste. (Take care not to add too
much salt because the bacon is
already salty.) Finish with a layer
of potatoes.

4 Mix together the apple juice
and water, then pour slowly
into the casserole. Cover and cook
in the oven at 180°C (350°F) mark
4 for 1½ hours.

5 Melt the butter with the oil in
a small pan. Uncover the
casserole and brush the top potato
layer with the melted fat. Return
to the oven and cook uncovered
for a further 30 minutes or until
the potatoes are golden brown.
Serve hot.

Menu Suggestion
Serve for a midweek supper with a
seasonal vegetable such as spinach,
peas or carrots.

CASSOULET

| 3.30 | 🍲 | £ £ | 508 cals |

Serves 12

700 g (1½ lb) dried white haricot
   beans

225 g (8 oz) salt pork or bacon, in
   one piece

450 g (1 lb) loin or shoulder of pork,
   boned

30 ml (2 tbsp) vegetable oil or fat
   from preserved goose

2 medium onions, skinned and
   thinly sliced

3 garlic cloves, skinned and finely
   chopped

1.4 kg (3 lb) shoulder of lamb
   (or ½ large shoulder), boned

1 piece of preserved goose

450 g (1 lb) piece coarse pork and
   garlic sausage

60 ml (4 tbsp) tomato purée

1.7 litres (3 pints) water

salt and freshly ground pepper

1 bouquet garni

100 g (4 oz) fresh breadcrumbs (see
   step 8 of method)

1 Rinse the beans in cold water, then put into a large saucepan. Cover with cold water, bring slowly to the boil and simmer for 5 minutes. Remove from the heat, cover and leave to soak in the water while you prepare the remaining ingredients.

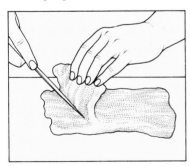

2 Remove the rind from the salt pork or bacon, and from the pork, and cut it into small squares.

3 Heat the oil or goose fat in a large frying pan and fry the onions and garlic for 5 minutes until softened. Add the pieces of pork rind and fry gently for 5 minutes. Raise the heat and brown on all sides, in turn, the pork and salt pork, the shoulder of lamb, the piece of goose and the sausage. Remove each from the pan when it is browned and set aside.

4 Add the tomato purée to the pan with a little of the water, stir well to amalgamate any sediment and bring quickly to the boil.

5 Drain the beans, rinse them and put them in a clean saucepan with the remaining cold water. Bring to the boil, then pour the beans and water into a cassoulet pot or large flameproof casserole.

6 Add the contents of the frying pan, salt and pepper to taste and stir well. Bury the salt pork or bacon, the pork, the shoulder of lamb, the preserved goose and the sausage among the beans, add the bouquet garni, and bring to simmering point on top of the stove.

7 Sprinkle on a thick layer of breadcrumbs. Cook in the oven at 150°C (300°F) mark 2 for 2–3 hours, until the meat and beans are tender.

8 From time to time press down the crust which will have formed on top and sprinkle on a further layer of breadcrumbs. Tradition has it that the crust must be pressed down and re-newed seven times, but three times should give an attractive golden crust. Cut up larger pieces of meat before serving.

Menu Suggestion
In France, Cassoulet is served on its own, with only chunks of fresh *baguette* (French stick) to accompany it. Follow with a crisp green salad tossed in a sharp vinaigrette dressing for a very filling meal.

CASSOULET
Cassoulet is a hearty peasant dish which originates from the Languedoc region of southern France. There are, of course, many different variations, but the central theme is a casserole of haricot beans, flavoured with tomato and cooked for several hours with a mixture of fresh and preserved meats and poultry until they are all completely tender and the flavoursome juices amalgamated. A bread-crumb topping acts as a seal on top, conserving all the goodness in the casserole and acting as a deliciously crunchy contrast to the meat and beans below.

   Preserved goose, a traditional ingredient of cassoulet, is avail-able canned from most good grocers.

BACON AND MUSHROOM PANCAKES

| 1.30 | 🍴 £ ✳* | 625 cals |

* freeze before baking at step 7

Serves 4

vegetable oil, for frying

one quantity pancake batter
  (page 349)

50 g (2 oz) butter or margarine

2 medium onions, skinned and
  roughly chopped

225 g (8 oz) cooked boiled bacon,
  finely chopped

175 g (6 oz) mushrooms, roughly
  chopped

30 ml (2 tbsp) plain flour

300 ml (½ pint) milk

125 g (4 oz) Cheddar cheese, grated

pinch of mustard powder

salt and freshly ground pepper

1 To make the pancakes, heat a little oil in an 18 cm (7 inch) heavy-based pancake or frying pan until very hot, running it around to coat the sides of the pan. Pour off any surplus.

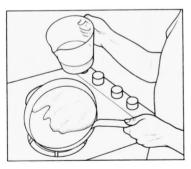

2 Ladle or pour in a little batter, rotating the pan at the same time, until enough batter is added to give a thin coating.

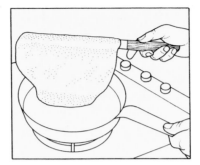

3 Cook until the pancake begins to brown underneath. Ease a palette knife under the centre and flip over. Fry the other side until golden brown, then turn on to a warmed plate, cover with a sheet of greaseproof paper and keep hot. Continue cooking the batter to make 8 pancakes, adding a little oil to the pan each time. Stack the pancakes up on the plate, inter-leaving each one with a sheet of greaseproof paper.

4 Melt 25 g (1 oz) of the butter in a deep frying pan, add the onions and fry for about 5 minutes until softened. Stir in the bacon and mushrooms and fry 2–3 minutes until the mushrooms are soft. Remove from the heat.

5 Melt the remaining 25 g (1 oz) butter in a saucepan, add the flour and cook gently, stirring, for 1–2 minutes. Remove from the heat and gradually blend in the milk. Bring to the boil, stirring constantly, then simmer for 3 minutes until thick and smooth. Add the cheese, mustard and salt and pepper to taste and stir until the cheese has melted. Remove from the heat.

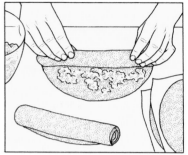

6 Fill the pancakes with the bacon and mushroom filling and roll or fold up. Place side by side, seam side downwards, in a buttered ovenproof dish.

7 Pour over the cheese sauce and bake in the oven at 180°C (350°F) mark 4 for 25–30 minutes. Serve hot, straight from the dish.

Menu Suggestion

Serve these savoury pancakes for a filling family supper dish. Accompany them with a crisply cooked green vegetable to give contrast in texture and colour, or with a mixed salad of grated raw vegetables.

BACON AND MUSHROOM PANCAKES

This dish is an excellent way to make a meal out of a small quantity of bacon leftover from a joint which you have boiled yourself. Alternatively, you can use boiled ham, but do not buy the ready-sliced variety as this will be too thin. Ask for 'ham on the bone' and get the shopkeeper to carve a thick slice so that you can chop it at home. If you prefer to buy bacon especially to make this dish, then the most convenient way to buy it is in a 'boil-in-the-bag' vacuum pack.

SALSICCIE CON PEPERONI
(ITALIAN SAUSAGE AND SWEET PEPPER CASSEROLE)

| 0.45 | 510 cals |

Serves 4

450 g (1 lb) Italian frying sausages
 (*salsiccia*)

45 ml (3 tbsp) olive oil

25 g (1 oz) butter

1 large onion, skinned and chopped

3 peppers (1 green, 1 red, 1 yellow),
 cored, seeded and sliced

225 g (8 oz) can tomatoes

90 ml (6 tbsp) chicken or beef stock

60 ml (4 tbsp) dry white wine or
 water

5 ml (1 tsp) dried sage

5 ml (1 tsp) dried rosemary

salt and freshly ground pepper

chopped fresh parsley, to garnish

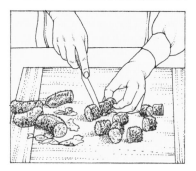

1 Plunge the sausages into a
 large pan of boiling water and
simmer for 10 minutes. Drain,
leave until cool enough to handle,
then remove the skin and cut the
sausages into bite-sized pieces.

2 Heat the oil with the butter in
 a flameproof casserole, add the
onion and fry gently for 5 minutes
until soft but not coloured.

3 Add the sausage and peppers
 and fry for a further 5
minutes, stirring constantly.

4 Mash the tomatoes with their
 juice in a bowl, then add to the
casserole with the stock and wine.
Bring slowly to boiling point, then
lower the heat, add the herbs and
seasoning to taste and simmer uncovered for 10–15 minutes. Taste
and adjust seasoning, then garnish
with parsley before serving.

Menu Suggestion
Serve this colourful Italian dish
with a risotto for supper. A salad
of fennel and cucumber tossed in a
minty olive oil and lemon juice
dressing may be served afterwards
to complete the meal.

SALSICCIE CON PEPERONI

Italian frying sausage sold in
specialist delicatessens is available
as individual sausages, usually
called *salamelle*, or in one long
piece called *luganega* or *salsiccia
a metro*, which is cut and sold by
the kg (lb). Both types are suitable for this recipe, but check
with the shopkeeper before buying as some varieties are peppery
hot and may not be to your taste.
Italians eat a lot of this kind of
sausage, which they either fry or
grill, or sometimes boil. It is also
used frequently in stuffings, and
you may like to use it in recipes
calling for sausagemeat — with its
tasty herbs and spices, it is far
less bland than most traditional
pork or beef sausagemeats.

FEGATO ALLA VENEZIANA
(CALF'S LIVER WITH ONIONS AND SAGE)

0.35	285 cals

Serves 6

50 g (2 oz) butter

45 ml (3 tbsp) olive or vegetable oil

2 large onions, skinned and sliced

6 fresh sage leaves

12 slices of calf's liver

salt and freshly ground pepper

15 ml (1 tbsp) white wine vinegar

fresh sage leaves and lemon
   wedges, to garnish

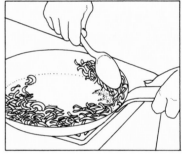

1 Heat the butter and oil in a
frying pan. Add the onions
and cook very gently for 20
minutes, stirring occasionally,
until soft. Stir in sage and cook
for 2–3 minutes.

2 Add the liver to the pan. Raise
heat and fry for 2–3 minutes
on each side.

3 Season the liver, then transfer
to a warmed serving dish with
the onions. Cover and keep hot.
Add the vinegar to the pan and
boil briskly for 1–2 minutes,
stirring in sediment from pan.

4 To serve. Pour the vinegar
mixture over the liver and
garnish with sage and lemon.

LIVER WITH ORANGE

| 0.40 | £ | 470 cals |

Serves 4

3 oranges
300 ml (½ pint) boiling water
45 ml (3 tbsp) vegetable oil
1 onion, skinned and chopped
1 garlic clove, skinned and crushed
700 g (1½ lb) lamb's liver
salt and freshly ground pepper
45 ml (3 tbsp) plain flour
175 g (6 oz) mushrooms, sliced
fresh chervil, to garnish

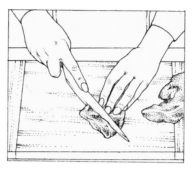

1 Thinly peel one of the oranges. Cut peel into thin strips and blanch in the 300 ml (½ pint) boiling water for 1 minute. Drain, reserving the peel and water. Squeeze the juice from the remaining oranges.

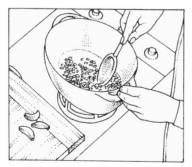

2 Heat the oil in a flameproof casserole and fry the onion and garlic for 5 minutes until golden.

3 Slice the liver and coat in seasoned flour. Add to the casserole and fry for 3 minutes until browned.

4 Make up the squeezed orange juice to 425 ml (14 fl oz) with the reserved blanching water. Add to the casserole with the mushrooms and seasoning.

5 Bring to the boil, stirring. Cover, reduce the heat and simmer gently for 20 minutes until tender. Garnish the liver with the blanched peel and chervil just before serving.

Menu Suggestion
Serve Liver with Orange for a family meal with creamed potatoes and a green vegetable such as petits pois or sliced courgettes.

LIVER WITH ORANGE
There are two reasons for blanching the orange peel in this recipe. The obvious reason is that the peel softens and therefore becomes more palatable as a garnish; blanching also helps retain the colour of citrus peel, especially if it is plunged into ice-cold water immediately after draining. Take care not to include any of the white pith when removing the peel from the orange as it tastes bitter.

ORANGE OXTAIL STEW

| 3.45* | £ | 433 cals |

* plus cooling and overnight chilling

Serves 4

2 oranges

30 ml (2 tbsp) plain flour

10 ml (2 tsp) dried mixed herbs

salt and freshly ground pepper

1.4 kg (3 lb) oxtail, jointed into
    serving pieces

30 ml (2 tbsp) corn or vegetable oil

1 onion, skinned and roughly
    chopped

2 celery sticks, trimmed and sliced

3 medium carrots, peeled and
    sliced

300 ml ($\frac{1}{2}$ pint) dry cider

2 bay leaves

1 Cut the rind of 1 orange into thin matchstick strips with a cannelle knife. Blanch in boiling water for 2 minutes, then drain and reserve. Finely grate the rind of the remaining orange. Squeeze the juice from both of the oranges and set aside.

2 Put the flour in a large polythene bag with the herbs and salt and pepper to taste. Shake well to mix.

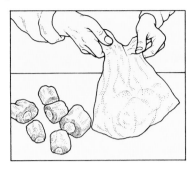

3 Add the oxtail to the bag a few pieces at a time and shake the pieces until evenly coated in the flour mixture.

4 Heat the oil in a large flameproof casserole, add as many pieces of oxtail as will fit on the base of the pan and fry over moderate heat until well browned. Remove with a slotted spoon and drain on absorbent kitchen paper while frying the remainder.

5 Add the onion, celery and carrots to the oil remaining in the casserole and fry gently for about 10 minutes, stirring frequently, until softened. Pour in the cider, add the grated orange zest and the orange juice and bring to the boil.

6 Return the oxtail pieces to the casserole and pour in water to cover. Add the bay leaves, bring to the boil, then cover and cook in the oven at 150°C (300°F) mark 2 for 3 hours. Leave until cold, then chill in the refrigerator overnight.

7 The next day, skim off the fat and remove the bay leaves. Simmer the casserole on top of the cooker for 10 minutes until thoroughly heated through, then taste and adjust the seasoning of the sauce. Serve hot, garnished with the reserved orange rind.

Menu Suggestion
Oxtail Stew is traditionally served with creamed or mashed potatoes and buttered cabbage.

STUFFED HEARTS

2.40 | f | 363 cals

Serves 8

8 lamb's hearts, each weighing about 175 g (6 oz)

50 g (2 oz) butter or margarine

1 small onion, skinned and chopped

100 g (4 oz) fresh breadcrumbs

10 ml (2 tsp) grated lemon rind

30 ml (2 tbsp) chopped fresh sage

salt and freshly ground pepper

pinch of grated nutmeg

1 egg, beaten

60 ml (4 tbsp) plain flour

30 ml (2 tbsp) vegetable oil

300 ml ($\frac{1}{2}$ pint) chicken stock (see page 350)

chopped fresh sage and grated lemon rind, to garnish

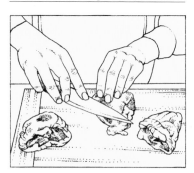

1 Wash the hearts thoroughly under cold running water. Trim them and remove any ducts.

2 Melt 25 g (1 oz) of the fat in a frying pan and lightly fry the onion for about 5 minutes until softened. Remove from the heat and stir in the breadcrumbs, lemon rind, parsley and seasonings. Bind with egg and mix well.

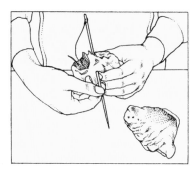

3 Fill the hearts with the stuffing and sew up neatly. Coat the hearts in the flour.

4 Heat the remaining fat and the oil in a flameproof casserole and brown the hearts well. Pour over the stock, season well and bring to the boil.

5 Cover and cook in the oven at 150°C (300°F) mark 2 for about 2 hours or until tender. Serve the hearts whole or sliced and pour the skimmed juices over. Garnish with sage and grated lemon rind.

Menu Suggestion
Serve with creamed potatoes and a dish of braised red cabbage, onion and apple, which can be cooked in the oven at the same time as the stuffed hearts.

STUFFED HEARTS

Hearts are inexpensive to buy, yet ideal for casseroling. Their dense, muscular tissue benefits from long, slow cooking, resulting in tender, moist meat which is amazingly lean. Lamb's hearts are the best size for stuffing, because one heart is just about the right quantity for one serving. Calf's and pig's hearts are larger, serving two to three; ox heart is larger still, and so tough that it is best chopped or thinly sliced rather than stuffed.

POLLO AL FINOCCHIO
(STUFFED ROAST CHICKEN WITH FENNEL)

| 2.15 | 376–564 cals |

Serves 4–6

| 1.8 kg (4 lb) oven-ready chicken |
| 60 ml (4 tbsp) vegetable oil |
| 1 small onion, skinned and finely chopped |
| 1 garlic clove, skinned and crushed |
| 1 small bulb of fennel |
| 4 slices of pancetta or unsmoked streaky bacon, diced |
| 100 g (4 oz) fresh white breadcrumbs |
| 25 g (1 oz) freshly grated Parmesan cheese |
| 1 egg, beaten |
| salt and freshly ground pepper |
| 25 g (1 oz) butter |
| 150 ml ($\frac{1}{4}$ pint) dry white wine |

1 Remove the giblets from the chicken and chop the heart and liver finely. Wash the chicken inside and out, then dry thoroughly.

2 Make the stuffing. Heat half the oil in a small pan, add the onion and garlic and fry gently for 5 minutes until soft but not coloured.

3 Chop the fennel finely, reserving the feathery tops for the garnish.

4 Add the fennel to the onion and continue frying for 5 minutes, stirring constantly. Add the pancetta and fry 5 minutes more until changing colour.

5 Turn the fried mixture into a bowl. Add the breadcrumbs, Parmesan, egg and salt and pepper to taste. Mix well to combine.

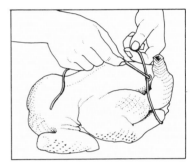

6 Fill the neck end of the chicken with the stuffing, then truss with string.

7 Heat the remaining oil with the butter in a large flame-proof casserole, then brown the chicken lightly on all sides. Turn the right way up, pour in the wine and bring to boiling point. Add salt and pepper to taste.

8 Transfer the casserole to the oven and cook the chicken at 180°C (350°F) mark 4 for $1\frac{3}{4}$ hours, or until the juices run clear when the thickest part of the thigh is pierced with a skewer. Turn the chicken frequently during cooking.

9 To serve. Remove the trussing string and carve the chicken into neat slices. Garnish each serving with a little of the reserved fennel tops. Hand the cooking liquid separately, if liked, or make a gravy in the usual way.

CHICKEN POT PIES

3.00* ✳* 847 cals

* plus cooling overnight; freeze
without pastry glaze in step 10

Serves 4

1.1 kg (2½ lb) chicken, giblets removed
1 lemon
few sprigs of fresh tarragon or 2.5 ml (½ tsp) dried
1 bay leaf
salt and freshly ground pepper
2 leeks, trimmed and sliced
2 large carrots, peeled and thinly sliced
175 g (6 oz) button onions, topped and tailed
40 g (1½ oz) butter or margarine
175 g (6 oz) button mushrooms, wiped and halved or sliced if large
45 ml (3 tbsp) plain flour
60 ml (4 tbsp) double cream
368 g (13 oz) packet frozen puff pastry, thawed
a little beaten egg, to glaze

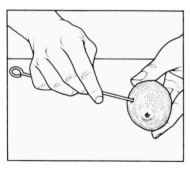

1 Wash the chicken inside and out. Prick the lemon all over with a skewer, then place inside the chicken.

2 Put the chicken in a large saucepan with the tarragon, bay leaf and seasoning to taste. Add the giblets (except the liver), then pour in just enough water to cover the chicken and bring slowly to the boil. Lower the heat, half cover with a lid and simmer for 1¼ hours or until tender.

3 Add the leeks and carrots for the last 30 minutes of the cooking time. Remove the pan from the heat and leave the chicken and vegetables to cool in the liquid.

4 Remove the chicken from the cooking liquid. Cut the flesh from the bird, discarding all skin and bones. Dice the flesh into bite-sized pieces. Set aside.

5 Place the button onions in a bowl, pour in boiling water to cover and leave for 2–3 minutes. Drain and plunge into cold water, then remove the onions one at a time and peel off the skins with your fingers.

6 Melt the butter or margarine in a clean saucepan, add the onions and fry gently for 5 minutes until lightly coloured.

7 Strain the cooking liquid from the chicken, measure and reserve 300 ml (½ pint). Add the mushrooms to the onions, together with the leeks and carrots, discarding the tarragon sprigs, if used, and the bay leaf. Fry the vegetables gently for 1–2 minutes, then add the chicken pieces and fry for a few minutes more.

8 Mix the flour to a paste with the cream. Gradually blend in the measured cooking liquid, then pour into the pan of chicken and vegetables. Add seasoning to taste. Simmer, stirring, for 2–3 minutes, then turn into four 300 ml (½ pint) ovenproof pie dishes. Cover and leave until completely cold, overnight if convenient.

9 Roll out the pastry on a floured surface and cut out four circles or ovals to make lids. Cut four strips of pastry long enough to go around the rims of the dishes.

10 Dampen the rims of the pie dishes then place the strips of pastry around them. Dampen the pastry strips, then place the circles of pastry on top. Press firmly to seal, then knock up and flute. Make a hole in the centre of each pie and decorate with pastry trimmings if liked. Glaze with beaten egg.

11 Bake the pies in the oven at 200°C (400°F) mark 6 for 25 minutes or until the pastry is golden brown and the filling heated through. Serve hot.

Menu Suggestion
These individual pies are perfect for supper, served simply with a tossed mixed salad. Follow with a selection of different cheeses and fresh fruit.

CHICKEN AND SPINACH PIE WITH MUSHROOMS

| 1.10 | ✳* | 538 cals |

* freeze at step 6, before baking

Serves 4

4 cooked chicken portions

900 g (2 lb) fresh spinach or 450 g (1 lb) frozen leaf spinach

1.25 ml ($\frac{1}{4}$ tsp) grated nutmeg

salt and freshly ground pepper

568 ml (1 pint) milk

45 ml (3 tbsp) wholewheat flour

5 ml (1 tsp) dried tarragon

225 g (8 oz) button mushrooms, wiped and roughly chopped

1 egg, beaten

50 g (2 oz) Gruyère cheese

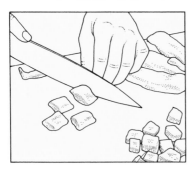

1 Skin the chicken portions and then remove the meat from the bones. Cut the meat into bite-sized pieces.

2 Trim the fresh spinach, discarding any thick stalks. Wash the leaves thoroughly, then place in a saucepan with only the water that clings to them. Cover the pan and cook for about 5 minutes until tender. Drain and chop roughly. If using frozen spinach, put in a heavy-based saucepan and heat gently for 7–10 minutes until defrosted. Season the spinach with the nutmeg and plenty of salt and freshly ground pepper.

3 Put the milk and flour in a blender or food processor. Blend until evenly mixed, then pour into a heavy-based saucepan. Bring slowly to boiling point, then simmer for 5 minutes, stirring frequently, until thickened.

4 Remove the sauce from the heat, reserve one third and stir the chicken, tarragon and seasoning to taste into the remaining sauce.

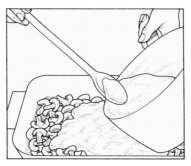

5 Spread one-third of the spinach over the bottom of a lightly greased ovenproof dish. Arrange half of the mushrooms on top of the spinach then pour over half of the chicken sauce. Repeat these layers once more, then spread over the remaining spinach.

6 Stir the egg into the reserved sauce, then pour over the spinach. Grate the cheese over the top. Bake in the oven at 190°C (375°F) mark 5 for about 30 minutes or until the topping is bubbling. Serve hot.

Menu Suggestion
Serve with creamed potatoes and braised leeks.

CHICKEN MARYLAND

0.30	679 cals

Serves 4

1.4 kg (3 lb) chicken, jointed into 8 pieces

45 ml (3 tbsp) flour

salt and freshly ground pepper

1 egg, beaten

100 g (4 oz) dried breadcrumbs

50 g (2 oz) butter

15–30 ml (1–2 tbsp) vegetable oil

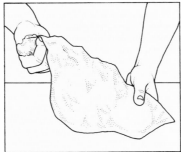

1 Put the chicken portions in a large polythene bag with the flour and salt and pepper to taste. Shake well to coat the chicken in the flour.

2 Dip the chicken first in the beaten egg and then roll in the breadcrumbs to coat.

3 Heat the butter and oil together in a large frying pan, add the coated chicken and fry for 2–3 minutes until lightly browned on all sides.

4 Continue frying gently, turning the pieces once, for about 20 minutes, or until tender. Alternatively, deep-fry the chicken in hot oil, 170°C (325°F), for 5–10 minutes. Serve the chicken hot and crisp, with fried bananas and corn fritters (see above right).

Fried bananas
Peel and slice 4 bananas lengthways. Fry gently in a little hot butter or chicken fat for about 3 minutes until lightly browned.

Corn fritters
Sift 100 g (4 oz) plain flour and a pinch of salt into a bowl. Break in 1 egg and add 75 ml (3 fl oz) milk and beat until smooth. Gradually beat in a further 75 ml (3 fl oz) milk. Fold in a 312-g (11-oz) can sweetcorn kernels, drained. Fry

spoonfuls of the mixture in a little hot fat for 5 minutes until crisp and golden, turning once. Drain well on absorbent kitchen paper.

Menu Suggestion
With its own accompaniments of fried bananas and corn fritters, Chicken Maryland needs nothing further to serve, apart from a crisp green salad to refresh the palate afterwards.

SESAME OVEN-FRIED DRUMSTICKS

0.50*	✳✳	350 cals

* plus 1 hour marinating; freeze after step 3

Serves 4

8 even-sized chicken drumsticks, skinned

45 ml (3 tbsp) lemon juice

50 g (2 oz) flour

salt and freshly ground pepper

1 egg, beaten

about 125 g (4 oz) sesame seeds

finely grated rind of ½ a lemon

125 g (4 oz) butter, melted

lemon wedges and green salad, to serve

1 Prick the skinned drumsticks all over with a fork. Place in a shallow dish with the lemon juice and marinate for 1 hour, turning from time to time.

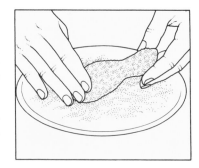

2 Remove the drumsticks from the marinade, coat in the flour seasoned with salt and pepper, then in beaten egg.

3 Mix together the sesame seeds and grated lemon rind, then use to coat the drumsticks.

4 Put into a roasting tin with the melted butter and marinade juices and cook in the oven at 190°C (375°F) mark 5 for 40–45 minutes, until tender, basting frequently. Serve hot, with lemon wedges and a green salad.

Menu Suggestion

Serve these crisp and crunchy chicken drumsticks with a mixed salad for a light lunch, or with a salad such as coleslaw and French fries for a more substantial evening meal.

SPANISH CHICKEN AND RICE

1.30	✳	654 cals

Serves 4

1.4 kg (3 lb) chicken, jointed into 8 pieces

30 ml (2 tbsp) flour

salt and freshly ground pepper

60 ml (4 tbsp) vegetable oil

1 medium onion, skinned and chopped

396-g (14-oz) can tomatoes

170-g (6-oz) can pimientoes, drained and sliced

2 chicken stock cubes, crumbled

8 stuffed olives

175 g (6 oz) long grain rice

225 g (8 oz) chorizo sausages, cut into 1-cm (½-inch) slices

100 g (4 oz) frozen peas

watercress sprigs, to garnish

1 Toss the chicken joints in the flour seasoned with salt and pepper. Heat the oil in a large saucepan, brown the chicken on all sides and remove. Add the onion and fry until golden brown.

2 Drain the tomatoes and add enough water to make the juice up to 450 ml (¾ pint).

3 Return the chicken to the pan. Add the tomato juice, the tomatoes and the next five ingredients. Season to taste.

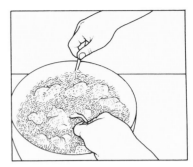

4 Cover the pan tightly and simmer gently for 45 minutes, forking carefully through the rice occasionally to prevent it sticking.

5 Add the peas to the pan, cover again and simmer for a further 30 minutes until the chicken is tender. Before serving, taste and adjust seasoning and garnish with the sprigs of watercress.

Menu Suggestion
A substantial main course dish needing no further accompaniment.

CHICKEN PAPRIKASH

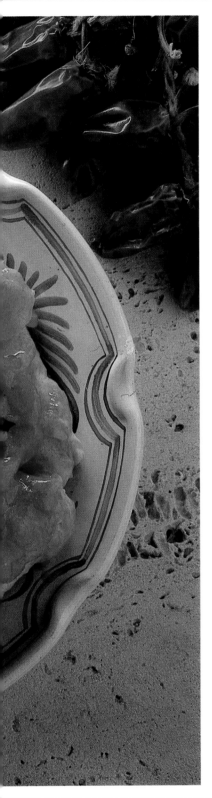

| 1.30 | ✳* | 398 cals |

* freeze after step 5

Serves 4

1.4 kg (3 lb) chicken, jointed into 8 pieces

50 g (2 oz) flour

salt and freshly ground pepper

50 g (2 oz) butter or chicken fat

450 g (1 lb) onions, skinned and sliced

1 red pepper, cored, seeded and sliced

15 ml (1 tbsp) paprika

1 garlic clove, skinned and crushed

397-g (14-oz) can tomatoes

300 ml ($\frac{1}{2}$ pint) chicken stock

1 bay leaf

142 ml (5 fl oz) soured cream

1 Toss the chicken joints in the flour, liberally seasoned with salt and pepper, to coat.

2 Melt the fat in a frying pan and fry the chicken joints until golden brown. Transfer the joints to a casserole large enough to take them in a single layer.

3 Add the onions and red pepper to the frying pan and fry gently for 5 minutes until soft. Stir in the paprika, garlic and any remaining flour. Cook gently, stirring, for a few minutes.

4 Add the tomatoes with their juice, the stock and bay leaf. Season and bring to the boil. Pour over the chicken.

5 Cover tightly and cook in the oven at 170°C (325°F) mark 3 for about 1 hour until the chicken is tender. Discard the bay leaf.

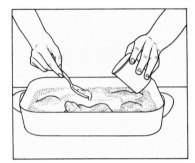

6 Stir half the soured cream into the casserole. Spoon the remaining soured cream over the top and serve immediately.

Menu Suggestion
This main course chicken dish, with its rich and pungent sauce, needs plain accompaniments such as jacket baked potatoes or boiled rice, and a green salad tossed in vinaigrette dressing.

CHICKEN PAPRIKASH

There often seems to be some confusion over the difference between paprika, which is used in this dish, and cayenne pepper. The reason for this is probably because in the dried powdered form they look very similar, but in fact, they are derived from different sources.

Cayenne pepper is made from ground dried chillies (from which Tabasco sauce is also made), and it has a pungent, hot flavour. Paprika is made from sweet red peppers. Probably the best type to choose is the mild Hungarian paprika, sometimes described as sweet paprika.

CHICKEN AND REDCURRANT CURRY

| 1.30* | ✳ | 441 cals |

* plus 2–3 hours cooling

Serves 4

4 chicken leg joints

350 g (12 oz) onions, skinned and roughly chopped

2.5 cm (1 inch) piece fresh root ginger, peeled and finely chopped

2 garlic cloves, skinned and crushed

30 ml (2 tbsp) vegetable oil

10 ml (2 tsp) ground cumin

10 ml (2 tsp) ground coriander

5 ml (1 tsp) chilli powder

2.5 ml ($\frac{1}{2}$ tsp) ground turmeric

30 ml (2 tbsp) lemon juice

100 g (4 oz) redcurrant jelly

200 ml ($\frac{1}{3}$ pint) chicken stock (see page 350)

salt and freshly ground pepper

2 bay leaves

coriander sprigs, to garnish

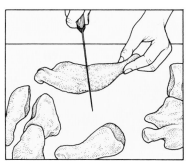

1 Cut the chicken legs into thighs and drumsticks; remove skin and fat.

2 In a blender or food processor, work the onions, ginger and garlic together until fairly smooth.

3 Heat the oil in large heavy-based pan, add the onion paste and fry gently until golden. Add the chicken joints and fry until golden on all sides.

4 Add the cumin, coriander, chilli, turmeric and lemon juice. Cook for 5 minutes until the chicken pieces are evenly coated with spices, then stir in the redcurrant jelly, stock and seasoning to taste. Bring to the boil, add the bay leaves, cover and simmer for 45–50 minutes or until the chicken is tender.

5 Remove from the heat, leave to cool for 2–3 hours, then cover and chill in the refrigerator until required.

6 Bring to the boil on top of the cooker, then lower the heat and simmer gently for 10–15 minutes to heat through. Taste and adjust seasoning and garnish with coriander just before serving.

Menu Suggestion

This curry is best served with plain boiled rice and side dishes of sliced banana and coconut, yogurt and cucumber, mango chutney and lime pickle.

CHICKEN AND REDCURRANT CURRY

If you have time, the chicken in this recipe would benefit from being marinated in the onion, ginger and garlic paste. After skinning the chicken, make a few slashes in the flesh with the tip of a sharp knife, then place in a bowl and spread with the paste. If you like, you can add the juice of 1 lime or $\frac{1}{2}$ a lemon. Leave for at least 1 hour, or overnight in the refrigerator if possible. Fry the paste and chicken together in step 3, then continue as in the recipe above.

CHICKEN KORMA

| 1.20 | ⏢ | £ £ | ✳ | 408 cals |

Serves 4

50 g (2 oz) blanched almonds

50 g (2 oz) poppy seeds

50 g (2 oz) fresh coconut flesh

4 medium onions, skinned and roughly chopped

2.5-cm (1-inch) piece of fresh root ginger, peeled and roughly chopped

2 garlic cloves, skinned

45 ml (3 tbsp) ghee or 40 g (1½ oz) butter, melted

1.1 kg (2½ lb) chicken, skinned and cut into 8 joints

60 ml (4 tbsp) coarsely chopped coriander leaves

15 ml (1 tbsp) chopped fresh mint leaves or 10 ml (2 tsp) dried mint

30 ml (2 tbsp) ground coriander

2.5 ml (½ tsp) chilli powder

5 ml (1 tsp) salt

45 ml (3 tbsp) lemon juice

120 ml (8 tbsp) natural yogurt

about 450 ml (¾ pint) water

1 Dry-roast the almonds and the poppy seeds in a frying pan or under a grill until the nuts are a pale golden, then transfer to a blender or food processor.

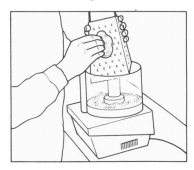

2 Grate the coconut into a blender or processor, then blend to a paste. Remove and set aside.

3 Place the onions, ginger and garlic in the blender or food processor and blend to a paste. Heat the ghee or butter in a large, heavy-based saucepan, add the onion paste and fry until golden, stirring frequently. Add the chicken and fry to a golden colour or until all the moisture in the pan has evaporated.

4 Meanwhile, blend the coriander leaves and mint to a smooth paste. Add all the spices, the salt and the lemon juice and blend together. Add this mixture to the chicken in the pan and fry, stirring frequently, for about 10 minutes so that the chicken is well coated with the spices. Add the coconut mixture and stir in well.

5 Add the yogurt a little at a time to the chicken, stirring continuously to blend it into the mixture. Continue stirring for 3–5 minutes and fry until the ghee begins to separate.

6 Pour in just enough water to cover the chicken, cover the pan, reduce the heat and allow to cook for another 20–30 minutes or until the chicken is really tender. Transfer to a warmed serving dish and serve hot.

Menu Suggestion
Although a mild Indian curry, Chicken Korma is spicily rich. Serve with boiled or pilau rice and the usual accompaniments of chutney, pickle and poppadoms. A spinach curry *(sag bhaji)* also goes well with Chicken Korma.

CHICKEN KORMA
Indian cooking is famed for its korma dishes—chicken or lamb being the most popularly used meats. The meat is simmered in a mixture of pungent spices and herbs which are counterbalanced by the addition of cool, creamy coconut and yogurt—the resultant mixture is irresistibly delicious!

CHICKEN AND CAPER CROQUETTES

1.00* 🔲 £ **302 cals**

* plus 30 minutes cooling and several hours chilling

Makes 12

1.4 kg (3 lb) chicken, poached
100 g (4 oz) butter
100 g (4 oz) plain flour
568 ml (1 pint) milk
30 ml (2 tbsp) chopped fresh tarragon or 10 ml (2 tsp) dried
15 ml (1 tbsp) chopped fresh parsley
30 ml (2 tbsp) chopped capers
salt and freshly ground pepper
2 eggs, beaten
50 g (2 oz) fresh white breadcrumbs
25 g (1 oz) chopped almonds
vegetable oil, for frying

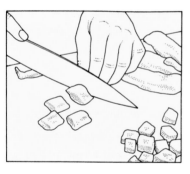

1 Remove the flesh from the cold chicken and dice roughly.

2 Melt the butter in a saucepan, add the flour and cook over low heat, stirring with a wooden spoon, for 2 minutes. Gradually blend in the milk, stirring after each addition to prevent lumps forming. Bring to the boil slowly, then simmer for at least 10 minutes, until very thick. Stir in the tarragon, parsley and capers. Season well and leave to cool for 30 minutes.

3 Stir in the chicken and spread the mixture out on a large flat plate. Chill in the refrigerator for several hours.

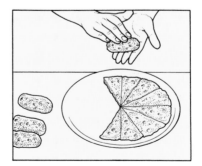

4 Divide the mixture into 12 equal sections. Shape each into a croquette 6.5 cm (2½ inch) long, using floured hands.

5 Brush each croquette evenly with beaten egg. Mix the breadcrumbs and almonds together and use to coat the croquettes. Pat well in, to coat thoroughly and evenly. Chill in the refrigerator until required.

6 Deep fry in oil at 180°C (350°F) for 4–5 minutes or shallow fry for about 6–7 minutes until golden brown. Drain well on absorbent kitchen paper before serving.

Menu Suggestion
These croquettes make a tasty everyday main course for the family. Serve with a mixed salad tossed in lots of blue cheese dressing, or with coleslaw. Children will probably enjoy them best with French fries.

QUICK TURKEY CURRY

| 0.45 | ✳ | 288–433 cals |

Serves 4–6

| 30 ml (2 tbsp) vegetable oil |
| 3 bay leaves |
| 2 cardamom pods, crushed |
| 1 cinnamon stick, broken into short lengths |
| 1 medium onion, skinned and thinly sliced |
| 1 green pepper, cored, seeded and chopped (optional) |
| 10 ml (2 tsp) paprika |
| 7.5 ml (1½ tsp) garam masala |
| 2.5 ml (½ tsp) turmeric |
| 2.5 ml (½ tsp) chilli powder |
| salt and freshly ground pepper |
| 50 g (2 oz) unsalted cashew nuts |
| 700 g (1½ lb) turkey fillets, skinned and cut into bite-size pieces |
| 2 medium potatoes, blanched, peeled and cut into chunks |
| 4 tomatoes, skinned and chopped, or 225-g (8-oz) can tomatoes |
| bay leaves, to garnish |

1 Heat the oil in a flameproof casserole, add the bay leaves, cardamom and cinnamon and fry over moderate heat for 1–2 minutes. Add the onion and green pepper (if using), with the spices and salt and pepper to taste. Pour in enough water to moisten, then stir to mix for 1 minute.

2 Add the cashews and turkey, cover and simmer for 20 minutes. Turn the turkey occasionally during this time to ensure even cooking.

3 Add the potatoes and tomatoes and continue cooking a further 20 minutes until the turkey and potatoes are tender. Taste and adjust seasoning before serving. Garnish with bay leaves.

Menu Suggestion
Serve with boiled rice, poppadoms, mango chutney and a yogurt and cucumber salad (raita).

QUICK TURKEY CURRY
The subtle blend of spices gives this a medium hot taste, without being too fiery! Chilli powder should be used with caution, since it is intensely hot.

Garam masala is readily available from Indian shops, specialist stores and some supermarkets. However, if you'd like to make your own, you will need about 100 g (4 oz) mixed large and small green cardamoms, 50 g (2 oz) cumin seeds, 15 g (½ oz) each black peppercorns, cloves and stick cinnamon and a little grated nutmeg. Dry-fry the whole spices for a few minutes, then grind together, mix in the nutmeg and store in an airtight container.

TURKEY ESCALOPES EN PAPILLOTE

1.00	£ £	230–260 cals

Serves 4

4 turkey breasts, total weight 550–700 g (1¼–1½ lb), boned

15 ml (1 tbsp) corn oil

1 small red pepper, cored, seeded and thinly sliced

225 g (8 oz) tomatoes, skinned and sliced

30 ml (2 tbsp) chopped fresh parsley

salt and freshly ground pepper

60 ml (4 tbsp) medium dry sherry

40 g (1½ oz) fresh wholewheat breadcrumbs, toasted

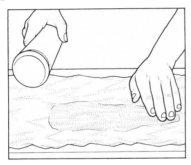

1 Split each turkey breast through its thickness with a sharp knife, then bat out between 2 sheets of greaseproof paper to make 8 thin escalopes.

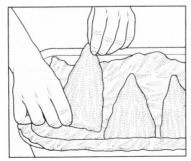

2 Place a large sheet of foil on a baking sheet and brush lightly with the oil. Put half of the turkey escalopes side by side on the foil.

3 Blanch the pepper slices for 1 minute in boiling water, drain and refresh under cold running water. Pat dry with absorbent kitchen paper.

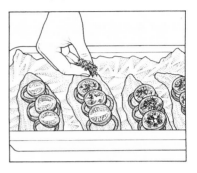

4 Layer the pepper and tomato slices on top of the escalopes with half of the parsley and seasoning to taste.

5 Cover with the remaining escalopes, spoon 15 ml (1 tbsp) sherry over each and close up the foil like a parcel.

6 Bake in the oven at 180°C (350°F) mark 4 for 35–40 minutes or until the meat is tender when pierced with a fork or skewer.

7 Arrange the escalopes on a warmed serving dish, cover and keep warm in the oven turned to its lowest setting. Transfer the juices to a pan and reduce to 60 ml (4 tbsp), then spoon over the turkey. Sprinkle with the freshly toasted breadcrumbs and the remaining parsley and serve immediately.

Menu Suggestion
Serve Turkey Escalopes en Papillote with new potatoes and tiny fresh green peas.

MAIN COURSES
Fish and
Shellfish

LA BOURRIDE
(MEDITERRANEAN FISH STEW WITH AÏOLI)

1.00* 🍴 £ £ 984 cals

* plus extra time for making fish stock

Serves 4

1 egg yolk

10 garlic cloves, skinned

300 ml (½ pint) olive oil

juice of 1 lemon

5 ml (1 tsp) lukewarm water

salt and freshly ground pepper

900 g (2 lb) firm white fish fillets (e.g. bass, turbot, whiting, monkfish or halibut), skinned

1.1 litres (2 pints) homemade fish stock (see page 350)

1 small onion, skinned and thinly sliced

1 leek, trimmed and thinly sliced

1–2 parsley sprigs

1 bay leaf

1 thin strip of orange rind

1 small baguette (French stick), sliced, to serve

chopped fresh parsley, to garnish

1 First make the aïoli. Put the egg yolk and 8 roughly chopped garlic cloves in a mortar and crush with a pestle. Add the oil a drop at a time and work until ingredients emulsify and thicken.

2 Continue adding the oil in a thin, steady stream, beating vigorously until the mayonnaise is very thick and smooth.

3 Beat in the lemon juice and water, and salt and pepper to taste. Set aside in a cool place.

4 Cut the fish into thick chunks and place in a large saucepan. Pour in the stock, then add the next five ingredients, with the remaining garlic, halved, and salt and pepper to taste. Cover and simmer for 15 minutes until tender.

5 Transfer the fish and vegetables with a slotted spoon to a warmed serving dish. Keep warm.

6 Strain cooking liquid into a jug and blend a few spoonfuls into the aïoli. Toast the sliced baguette and keep warm.

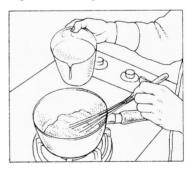

7 Put the aïoli in a heavy-based pan, then gradually whisk in the remaining cooking liquid. Heat through gently, stirring constantly. Adjust seasoning. Pour over the fish and sprinkle with parsley. Serve at once, with the toast.

Menu Suggestion
La Bourride needs no accompaniment other than the toasted baguette in the recipe.

Summer Fish Hot Pot

1.10* £ 459 cals

* plus 30 minutes cooling

Serves 4

4 sticks of celery, washed and
    trimmed

50 g (2 oz) butter

50 g (2 oz) plain flour

450 ml ($\frac{3}{4}$ pint) milk

salt and freshly ground pepper

700 g (1$\frac{1}{2}$ lb) firm white fish fillets
    (cod, haddock or monkfish)

275 g (10 oz) Florence fennel,
    untrimmed weight

60 ml (4 tbsp) chopped parsley

10 ml (2 tsp) lemon juice

450 g (1 lb) new potatoes, boiled

chopped fresh parsley, to garnish

1 Slice the celery finely. Melt
the butter in a flameproof
casserole, add the celery and cook
gently for 5 minutes until soft.
Add the flour and cook over low
heat, stirring with a wooden
spoon, for 2 minutes. Remove
from the heat and gradually blend
in the milk, stirring after each
addition to prevent lumps
forming. Bring to the boil slowly,
then simmer for 2–3 minutes,
stirring. Add seasoning to taste
and remove from the heat.

2 Place the fish in a saucepan
and just cover with water.
Bring to the boil, remove from the
heat and drain. Cut into fork-size
pieces, discarding the skin and any
bones.

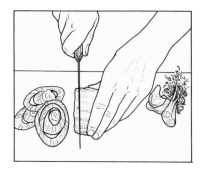

3 Trim the fennel and cut into
thin slices. Blanch in boiling
salted water for 2 minutes and
drain.

4 Add the fennel, parsley and
lemon juice to the sauce; mix
well. Stir in the fish, taking care
not to break up the flesh; cool for
30 minutes.

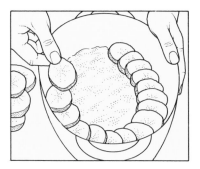

5 Slice the cooked potatoes and
arrange on top of the fish.
Cover the dish with buttered foil
and chill in the refrigerator until
required.

6 Bake in the oven, with foil
covering, at 180°C (350°F)
mark 4 for about 50 minutes or
until the fish is cooked. Sprinkle
with chopped parsley before
serving.

Menu Suggestion
This Mediterranean style fish stew
contains fennel and potatoes, and
so does not need a vegetable
accompaniment. Serve for a family
meal with crusty fresh bread or
bread rolls.

CREAMY COD BAKE

0.45	586 cals

Serves 4

454 g (1 lb) packet frozen leaf
   spinach

50 g (2 oz) butter or margarine

4 frozen cod steaks

2.5 ml (½ tsp) freshly grated nutmeg

salt and freshly ground pepper

450 ml (¾ pint) cheese sauce (see
   page 351)

100 g (4 oz) Cheddar cheese, grated

two 25 g (0.88 oz) packets cheese
   and onion crisps, finely crushed

1 Put the frozen spinach in a
heavy-based saucepan and
thaw over low heat, adding a few
spoonfuls of water if necessary to
prevent the spinach from sticking
to the bottom of the pan.

2 Meanwhile, melt half the fat in
a separate frying pan and fry
the cod steaks for a few minutes
on each side until golden.

3 Transfer the spinach to the
base of an ovenproof dish and
mix in the remaining fat with half
the nutmeg and seasoning to taste.

4 Arrange the steaks in a single
layer on top of the spinach and
pour over any cooking juices.

5 Stir the remaining nutmeg
into the cheese sauce, then
pour the sauce evenly over the fish
to cover it completely. Mix the
grated cheese with the crushed
crisps and sprinkle over the top.

6 Bake in the oven at 190°C
(375°F) mark 5 for 30 minutes
until golden brown and bubbling.
Serve hot, straight from the dish.

Menu Suggestion
Serve with plain boiled or
creamed potatoes. A few baked or
grilled tomatoes as a vegetable
accompaniment would add extra
colour to the meal.

CREAMY COD BAKE

This is the perfect dish to
serve for the children's lunch or
supper—they will love the soft
combination of spinach, fish and
cheese sauce and its crunchy,
crisp topping. Even if you
normally find it difficult to
persuade them to eat fish and
spinach—with this dish they
won't realise what they are
eating!

Spinach is a nutritious vegetable. It is a valuable source of
vitamins A and C, and has a
high iron and calcium content.
The frozen spinach used in this
recipe is just as good as fresh
and much quicker to prepare,
but if you prefer to use the fresh
vegetable, you will need double
the quantity. Wash it thoroughly
in several changes of water, discarding any yellow or damaged
leaves and thick stalks. Place the
leaves in a large saucepan with
only the water that clings to
them. Cook gently for about 7
minutes until tender, then drain
very thoroughly and chop
roughly. Continue with the
recipe as for frozen spinach.

STUFFED PLAICE FILLETS WITH MUSHROOM SAUCE

| 1.10 | 🖾 | 185 cals |

Serves 4

4 double plaice fillets

salt and freshly ground pepper

**225 g (8 oz) cottage cheese with
prawns (see box)**

**1.25 ml ($\frac{1}{4}$ tsp) Tabasco sauce, or
less according to taste**

**finely grated rind and juice of 1
lemon**

**225 g (8 oz) button mushrooms,
wiped and thinly sliced**

90 ml (6 tbsp) dry white wine

**5 ml (1 tsp) chopped fresh tarragon
or dill or 2.5 ml ($\frac{1}{2}$ tsp) dried**

**8 unshelled prawns and fresh
tarragon or dill sprigs, to garnish**

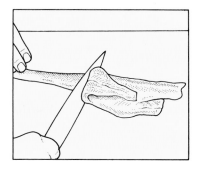

1 Skin the plaice fillets. Lay
them flat, skin side down, on a
board or work surface. Dip your
fingers in salt and grip the tail
end, then separate the flesh from
the skin at this point with a sharp
knife. Work the knife slowly
between the skin and flesh using a
sawing action until the opposite
end of the fillet is reached. Cut
each fillet into two lengthways.

2 Drain off any liquid from the
cottage cheese, then mash the
cheese with half of the Tabasco
sauce, the grated lemon rind and
seasoning to taste.

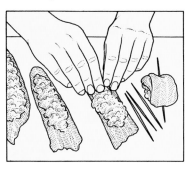

3 Lay the plaice fillets flat,
with their skinned side facing
upwards. Divide the cheese filling
equally between them, then roll
up and secure with wooden
cocktail sticks, if necessary.

4 Place the stuffed fish rolls close
together in a single layer in a
lightly oiled ovenproof dish.
Sprinkle the mushrooms around
the fish, then pour over the wine
mixed with the lemon juice and
remaining Tabasco. Sprinkle with
seasoning to taste.

5 Cover the dish with foil and
cook in the oven at 180°C
(350°F) mark 4 for 20 minutes or
until the fish is just tender.

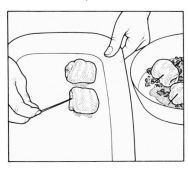

6 Remove the rolls from the
liquid and discard the cocktail
sticks. Arrange the fish on a
warmed serving dish, cover loosely
with foil and keep warm in the
oven turned to its lowest setting.

7 Put the cooked mushrooms in
a blender or food processor.
Add the tarragon or dill and blend
until smooth. Pour into a pan and
heat through. Taste and adjust
seasoning.

8 Pour a little sauce over each
plaice roll, then top with a
prawn and a tarragon or dill sprig.
Serve immediately, with any
remaining sauce handed separately
in a jug.

Menu Suggestion
Serve this low calorie dish with
jacket-baked potatoes or potatoes
boiled in their skins, and a
seasonal green vegetable or a
watercress and chicory salad.

STUFFED PLAICE FILLETS WITH MUSHROOM SAUCE

The cottage cheese with prawns
used in the stuffing for these
plaice fillets is available in
cartons from selected supermarkets. Look for a good-quality
brand which is thick and firm-
textured. Some brands of cottage
cheese are watery and will not be
suitable for this dish. If there is a
little water on the surface of the
cheese when you open the
carton, be sure to drain it off
before use.

FISH KEBABS

0.20* 187 cals

* plus 2 hours marinating

Serves 4

700 g (1½ lb) monkfish fillets, skinned

60 ml (4 tbsp) sunflower oil

juice of 2 limes or 1 lemon

1 small onion, skinned and roughly chopped

2 garlic cloves, skinned and crushed

2.5 ml (½ tsp) fennel seed

2.5 ml (½ tsp) dried thyme

freshly ground pepper

1 green pepper, halved, cored and seeded

16 whole cherry tomatoes or 4 small tomatoes, quartered

8 bay leaves

3 Thread the fish, green pepper, tomatoes and bay leaves on to 4 oiled skewers. Reserve the marinade for basting.

4 Cook the kebabs under a pre-heated moderate grill for about 10 minutes, basting with the marinade and turning once.

Menu Suggestion
Serve with steamed brown rice and a fennel salad to complement the flavour of the marinade.

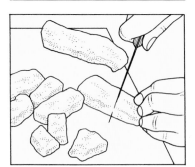

1 Cut the monkfish into 4 cm (1½ inch) chunks. Place the oil, lime or lemon juice, onion, garlic, fennel, thyme and pepper in a blender or food processor and blend until smooth. Toss the fish in this mixture, cover and marinate for at least 2 hours.

2 Meanwhile, place the green pepper in a saucepan of cold water and bring to the boil. Drain and cut into 12 pieces.

FISH KEBABS

In summertime, these kebabs would be excellent cooked on the barbecue—the additional flavour of the charcoal goes well with quick-cooking fish, and they would make an unusual alternative to steaks, chicken and chops. Follow the recipe exactly as above and make sure the barbecue coals are hot before cooking—they should look grey in daylight, glowing red at night. Food, especially delicately textured fish, should never be put over coals that are flaming, so wait for all flames to die down before starting to cook. Oil the barbecue grid well before placing the kebabs over the fire.

STUFFED COD CRÊPES

| 1.40 | ⌂ | £ | ✳ | 541 cals |

Serves 6

175 g (6 oz) plain flour, plus 45 ml (3 tbsp)

50 g (2 oz) salted peanuts, very finely chopped

2 eggs

15 ml (1 tbsp) vegetable oil

450 ml (¾ pint) milk and water mixed

700 g (1½ lb) cod fillets

568 ml (1 pint) milk

50 g (2 oz) butter

125 g (4 oz) celery, chopped

5 ml (1 tsp) curry powder

salt and freshly ground pepper

75 ml (5 tbsp) single cream

50 g (2 oz) Cheddar cheese, grated

chopped fresh parsley, to garnish

1 Make the batter for the crêpes. Whisk 175 g (6 oz) flour, the chopped peanuts, eggs, oil and half the milk and water mixture until quite smooth. Whisk in the remaining liquid.

2 Make twelve 18.5 cm (7½ inch) crêpes in the usual way (see page 349). Keep covered.

3 Wash and dry the fish and place in a large sauté or deep frying pan with the milk. Cover and poach gently for about 12 minutes until the fish is quite tender and begins to flake. Strain off and reserve the liquid. Flake the fish, discarding skin and bone.

4 Melt the butter in a heavy-based saucepan, add the celery and curry powder and fry gently for 1 minute, stirring. Remove from the heat and stir in the remaining flour, reserved liquid from cooking the fish and seasoning to taste. Bring to the boil, stirring; simmer for 1 minute. Remove from the heat and fold in the cream and flaked fish.

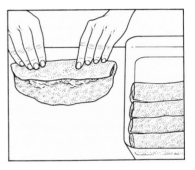

5 Divide the filling between the crêpes, roll up and place side by side in a single layer in a greased shallow ovenproof dish. Sprinkle the grated cheese over the top and cover loosely with foil. Chill in the refrigerator until required.

6 Bake in the oven at 180°C (350°F) mark 4 for about 40 minutes. Serve piping hot, sprinkled with chopped parsley.

187

SARSO WALI MACHCHLI
(MONKFISH WITH MUSTARD SEEDS)

| 0.35* | £ | 265 cals |

MILD

* plus several hours soaking

Serves 6

45 ml (3 tbsp) black mustard seeds

900 g (2 lb) monkfish fillet, skinned

30 ml (2 tbsp) plain flour

60 ml (4 tbsp) mustard oil or
    vegetable oil

1 medium onion, skinned and
    thinly sliced

300 ml ($\frac{1}{2}$ pint) natural yogurt

1 garlic clove, skinned and
    crushed

15 ml (1 tbsp) lemon juice

salt and freshly ground pepper

whole prawns and coriander,
    to garnish

1 Place 30 ml (2 tbsp) of the mustard seeds in a small bowl. Cover with 60 ml (4 tbsp) water and leave to soak for several hours. Finely grind the remaining seeds in a small electric mill or with a pestle and mortar.

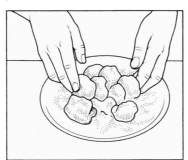

2 Cut the monkfish into 2.5 cm (1 inch) cubes and toss in the flour and ground mustard seeds.

3 Heat the oil in a large heavy-based frying pan, add the onion and fry for about 5 minutes until golden.

4 Drain the mustard seeds, then add to the pan with the monkfish. Fry over moderate heat for 3–4 minutes, turning *very gently* once or twice.

5 Gradually stir in the yogurt with the garlic, lemon juice and salt and pepper to taste. Bring to the boil, then lower the heat and simmer for 10–15 minutes or until the fish is almost tender.

6 Taste and adjust the seasoning. Turn into a warmed serving dish and garnish with the prawns and coriander. Serve immediately.

Menu Suggestion

Serve as a main course, with poppadoms and Khumbi Pullao (Mushroom Pilau) page 236.

SARSO WALI MACHCHLI

Mustard seeds, called sarson or rai, come in three different colours: black, brown and white. The black seeds are said to be the best, and are the ones most frequently used in Indian cooking. If you have difficulty finding them, go to an Indian or Pakistani grocer and he will be sure to stock them. To obtain their full flavour, it is a good idea to dry roast them before grinding.

TANDOORI FISH

| 0.45 | 95 cals |

Serves 2

225 g (8 oz) thick white fish fillet (monkfish, cod, haddock)

30 ml (2 tbsp) natural yogurt

15 ml (1 tbsp) lemon juice

1 small garlic clove, skinned and crushed

1.25 ml ($\frac{1}{4}$ tsp) ground coriander

1.25 ml ($\frac{1}{4}$ tsp) ground cumin

1.25 ml ($\frac{1}{4}$ tsp) ground turmeric

pinch of paprika

margarine or butter

fresh coriander and lime wedges, to garnish

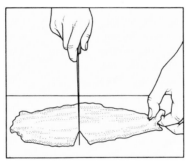

1 Skin the fish fillet, and then cut into 2 equal portions with a sharp knife.

2 Make the tandoori marinade. Put the yogurt and lemon juice in a bowl with the garlic and spices. Stir well to mix.

3 Place the fish on a sheet of foil and brush with the marinade. Leave in a cool place for 30 minutes.

4 Dot the fish with a few knobs of margarine or butter. Cook under a preheated moderate grill for about 8 minutes, turning frequently. Serve immediately, garnished with fresh coriander and lime wedges.

Menu Suggestion
Serve on a bed of saffron rice, accompanied by a green salad with plenty of chopped fresh coriander.

TANDOORI FISH

This recipe is given its name from the special clay *tandoor* oven which is used for cooking in India. Meat, poultry and fish are marinated in a yogurt and spice mixture to tenderise and add flavour, then cooked in the *tandoor*. It is the combination of the marinade and the searing temperatures of the charcoal-fired clay oven which gives such a spectacular colour and delicious taste. Small tandoori oven sets are available at specialist kitchen shops and departments, but these must be used outside for adequate ventilation and safety reasons. Obviously they cannot in any way compare with the real thing in size or intensity of heat, but if you like the flavour of tandoori food it is worth considering buying one as an alternative to cooking on a barbecue in summertime.

MACKEREL PARCELS

| 1.00 | £ | 319 cals |

Serves 4

4 fresh mackerel, weighing about 175 g (6 oz) each

about 25 g (1 oz) margarine or butter

½ large cucumber

60 ml (4 tbsp) white wine vinegar

30 ml (2 tbsp) chopped fresh mint

5 ml (1 tsp) sugar

salt and freshly ground pepper

natural yogurt and chopped fresh mint, to serve

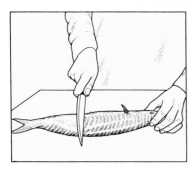

1 With the back of a knife and working from the tail towards the head, scrape off the scales from the skin of the mackerel.

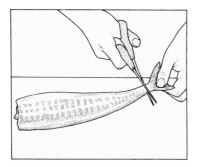

2 Cut off the heads just below the gills with a sharp knife. Cut off the fins and tails with kitchen scissors.

3 Slit the underside of the fish open from head to tail end with a sharp knife or scissors.

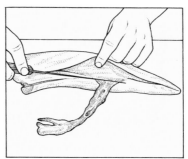

4 With the flat of the knife blade, scrape out the entrails of the fish, together with any membranes and blood. Wash the fish thoroughly inside and out under cold running water.

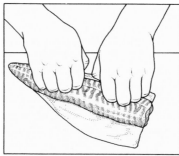

5 Lay the fish flat on a board or work surface with the skin uppermost. Press firmly along the backbone with your knuckles (this flattens the fish and loosens the backbone).

6 Turn the fish over and lift out the backbone with the help of a knife. Cut each fish lengthways into 2 fillets. Dry thoroughly with absorbent kitchen paper.

7 Brush 8 squares of kitchen foil with a little margarine. Put a mackerel fillet in the centre of each square, skin side down.

8 Arrange the cucumber slices on one half of the mackerel fillets, then sprinkle with the vinegar, mint, sugar and seasoning to taste. Dot with the remaining margarine in tiny pieces.

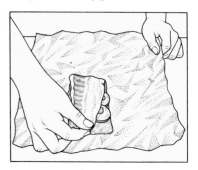

9 Fold the mackerel fillets over to enclose the cucumber filling, then wrap in the foil. Place the foil parcels in a single layer in an ovenproof dish. Cook in the oven at 200°C (400°F) mark 6 for 30 minutes until the fish is tender.

10 To serve, unwrap the foil parcels and carefully place the mackerel fillets in a circle on a warmed platter. Spoon yogurt in the centre and sprinkle with mint.

Menu Suggestion

Serve hot with potatoes boiled in their jackets, or serve cold with a potato salad.

MACKEREL PARCELS

Fresh mackerel, like herring, are an inexpensive yet much neglected fish. And yet they are a good source of first-class protein, plus the minerals calcium and phosphorus which are essential for healthy bones. Mackerel flesh is also rich in vitamins A and D, so it makes sense to include it regularly in a healthy diet. Always make sure to cook mackerel on the day of purchase as it quickly deteriorates after catching.

TALI MACHCHLI
(SPICED GRILLED MACKEREL)

| 0.40* | 🔲 | £ | 470 cals |

MEDIUM

* plus 2 hours marinating

Serves 4

4 fresh mackerel, each weighing about 275 g (10 oz), gutted and cleaned

juice of 1 lemon

60 ml (4 tbsp) chopped fresh coriander

10 ml (2 tsp) garam masala

5 ml (1 tsp) ground cumin

5 ml (1 tsp) chilli powder

salt and freshly ground pepper

50 ml (2 fl oz) ghee or melted butter

lemon wedges, to serve

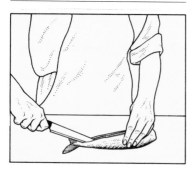

1 First bone the mackerel. With a sharp knife, cut off the heads just behind the gills. Extend the cut along the belly to both ends of the fish so that the fish can be opened out.

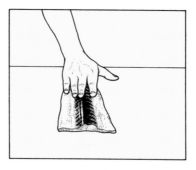

2 Place the fish flat on a board, skin side facing upwards. With the heel of your hand, press along the backbone to loosen it.

3 Turn the fish right way up and lift out the backbone, using the tip of the knife if necessary to help pull the bone away from the flesh cleanly. Discard the bone.

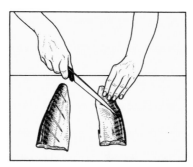

4 Remove the tail and cut each fish in half lengthways, then wash under cold running water and pat dry with absorbent kitchen paper. Score the skin side in several places with a knife.

5 In a jug, mix together the lemon juice, half of the coriander, the garam masala, cumin, chilli powder and salt and pepper to taste.

6 Put the mackerel in a grill pan and pour over the marinade. Cover and leave at cool room temperature for 2 hours, turning the fish once and brushing with the marinade.

7 When ready to cook, brush half of the ghee over the skin side of the mackerel. Cook under a preheated moderate grill for 5 minutes, then turn the fish over and brush with the remaining ghee. Grill for a further 5 minutes.

8 Transfer the fish to a warmed platter and sprinkle with the remaining coriander. Serve immediately, accompanied by lemon wedges.

Menu Suggestion

Spiced Grilled Mackerel is an economical dish for a midweek family meal. Serve with plain boiled rice and Hare Sem Aur Nariyal (Green Beans with Coconut) (see page 263).

TALI MACHCHLI

The spicy lemon marinade used in this recipe goes especially well with oily fish such as mackerel. In India there are numerous different varieties of both fresh- and sea-water fish, none of which are available here. The marinade can be used instead for familiar fish: fillets of plaice, haddock or cod, or even cubes of thick white monkfish, turbot or hake make excellent kebabs, especially when cooked outside on the barbecue.

RASEDAR JHINGA
(PRAWNS IN COCONUT MILK)

| 0.30 | £ £ | 200 cals |

MEDIUM

Serves 4

700 g (1½ lb) medium raw prawns in the shell or 900 g (2 lb) large frozen cooked prawns, thawed

10 ml (2 tsp) wine vinegar

5 ml (1 tsp) salt

2.5 cm (1 inch) piece of fresh root ginger, peeled and finely chopped

2 garlic cloves, skinned and crushed

2 medium onions, skinned and roughly chopped

45 ml (3 tbsp) ghee or vegetable oil

15 ml (1 tbsp) coriander seeds

10 ml (2 tsp) cumin seeds

5 ml (1 tsp) turmeric

2.5 ml (½ tsp) chilli powder

300 ml (½ pint) thick coconut milk (page 134)

chopped fresh coriander and sliced and seeded green chillies, to garnish

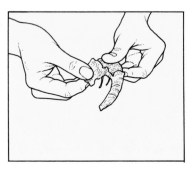

1 If using the raw prawns, remove the shells with your fingers leaving on the tail.

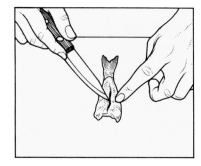

2 With the point of a sharp knife, cut down the back of each prawn and remove and discard the dark vein.

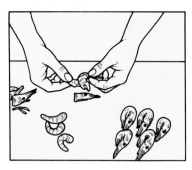

3 If using cooked prawns, remove the *whole* shell and de-vein in the same way as the raw prawns.

4 Wash the prawns and pat dry with absorbent kitchen paper. Place in a bowl with the vinegar and salt and leave to marinate for 30 minutes.

5 Place the ginger, garlic and onions in a blender or food processor and work to a smooth paste, adding a little water if the mixture sticks. Set aside.

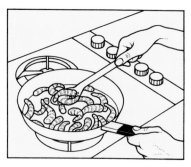

6 Heat half of the ghee in a heavy-based frying pan and add the prawns, reserving the marinade. Toss the raw prawns in the pan for 3–5 minutes until just turning pink. If using cooked prawns, toss for 1–2 minutes only. Remove the prawns with a slotted spoon, put back into the marinade and set aside.

7 Heat the remaining ghee in the same pan and add the onion paste. Fry gently for 5 minutes until just turning golden brown. Stir in the coriander, cumin, turmeric and chilli powder and fry, stirring constantly, for 1 minute.

8 Add the prawns and marinade and stir well to coat, then pour in the coconut milk and mix well. Bring to the boil, then lower the heat and simmer for 5 minutes.

9 Turn into a warmed serving dish and garnish with the chopped fresh coriander and rings of green chilli. Serve immediately.

Menu Suggestion
Serve for a quick supper or lunch dish, with plain boiled rice and Pudeene Ki Chutney (Mint Chutney) page 353.

SAAG JHINGA
(PRAWNS WITH SPINACH)

0.35	£ £ ✳*	373 cals

MEDIUM

Serves 4

60 ml (4 tbsp) ghee or vegetable oil
1 small onion, skinned and finely chopped
10 ml (2 tsp) ground ginger
10 ml (2 tsp) garam masala (page 140)
5 ml (1 tsp) mustard seeds
2.5 ml ($\frac{1}{2}$ tsp) chilli powder
2.5 ml ($\frac{1}{2}$ tsp) turmeric
450 g (1 lb) peeled prawns, thawed and thoroughly dried if frozen
450 g (1 lb) frozen leaf spinach
60 ml (4 tbsp) desiccated coconut
5 ml (1 tsp) salt

1 Heat half of the ghee in a heavy-based saucepan or flameproof casserole, add the onion and fry gently for about 5 minutes until soft.

2 Add the spices and fry, stirring, for a further 2 minutes. Add the prawns, increase the heat and toss to coat in the spiced onion mixture. Remove with a slotted spoon and set aside.

3 Heat the remaining ghee in the pan, add the spinach and heat gently until thawed. Stir frequently and cook for 8–10 minutes, or according to packet instructions.

4 Return the prawns to the pan, add half of the coconut and the salt and fold gently to mix. Cook for 5 minutes to allow the flavours to mingle, then turn into a warmed serving dish. Sprinkle with the remaining coconut and serve immediately.

Menu Suggestion
These prawns taste absolutely delicious served with plain boiled rice, poppadoms and Raita (Cucumber with Yogurt) page 353.

197

ITALIAN SQUID STEW

1.30* 🍴 🍴 320 cals

* plus 3 hours marinating

Serves 4

1 kg (2¼ lb) small squid

75 ml (5 tbsp) olive oil

salt and freshly ground pepper

75 ml (3 fl oz) dry white wine

2 garlic cloves, skinned and
    crushed

juice of ½ lemon

15 ml (1 tbsp) chopped fresh
    parsley

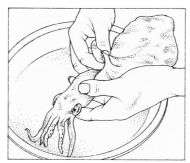

1 Wash the squid in plenty of
cold water. Grip the head and
tentacles firmly and pull them
away from the body. The entrails
will follow. Discard these and pull
out transparent quill.

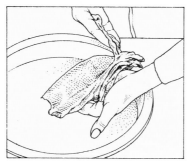

2 With your hands, carefully
peel the skin from the body
and the fins of the squid.

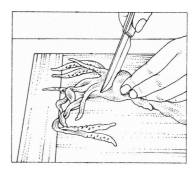

3 Cut the tentacles from head
and remove the skin. Reserve
two ink sacs being careful not to
pierce them. Discard rest of head.

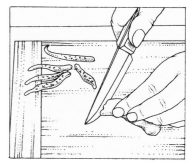

4 Cut the squid bodies into
0.5 cm (¼ inch) rings. Place in a
bowl with the tentacles and spoon
over 45 ml (3 tbsp) of the oil and
season well. Leave for 3 hours.

5 Pour the squid and marinade
into a large frying pan and
cook the squid for 5 minutes,
turning frequently. Add the wine
and garlic and cook for a further 5
minutes. Add the ink sacs, breaking them up with a spoon.

6 Cover and cook over a low
heat for about 40 minutes until
the squid is tender.

7 Add the remaining oil, the
lemon juice and parsley. Stir
for 3 minutes over a high heat,
adjust the seasoning and serve.

Menu Suggestion
In Italy, this rich stew of squid in
white wine would be served with
plain boiled rice or toasted bread.

MAIN COURSES
Vegetarian

Stuffed Baked Aubergines

| 1.00 | £ | 184 cals |

Serves 4

2 aubergines

25 g (1 oz) margarine or butter

4 small tomatoes, skinned and
chopped

10 ml (2 tsp) chopped fresh
marjoram or 5 ml (1 tsp) dried

1 shallot, skinned and chopped

1 onion, skinned and chopped

50 g (2 oz) brown breadcrumbs

salt and freshly ground pepper

50 g (2 oz) cheese, grated

parsley sprigs, to garnish

1 Steam or boil the whole
aubergines for about 30
minutes until tender.

2 Cut the aubergines in half
lengthways, scoop out the
flesh and chop finely. Reserve the
aubergine shells.

3 Melt the margarine in a pan,
add the tomatoes, marjoram,
shallot and onion and cook gently
for 10 minutes. Stir in the
aubergine flesh and a few breadcrumbs, then add salt and freshly
ground pepper to taste.

4 Stuff the aubergine shells with
this mixture, sprinkle with the
remaining breadcrumbs and then
with the grated cheese. Place in a
grill pan and grill until golden
brown on top. Serve hot, garnished
with parsley sprigs.

Menu Suggestion
Serve with brown rice and follow
with a cucumber and watercress
salad.

STUFFED BAKED AUBERGINES

This recipe can also be used for
courgettes. Allow 2–3 medium-
sized courgettes per person. Cut
them in half lengthways and
carefully scoop out the flesh with
a sharp-edged teaspoon. Blanch
in boiling salted water for 4
minutes only, then drain
thoroughly. Chop the scooped-
out raw courgette flesh and cook
for 10 minutes with the tomato
mixture. Stand the courgette
halves side by side (so that they
stand upright) in a well-buttered
baking tin before stuffing and
grilling. For a more substantial
main course dish, make a
separate cheese sauce and serve
with the stuffed courgettes so
that people can help themselves.
The flavour of Greek Feta
cheese goes well with courgettes
and aubergines and can also be
used with the breadcrumbs for
the topping.

VEGETABLE LASAGNE

| 1.10 | £ | 460 cals |

Serves 4

175 g (6 oz) lasagne verde

salt and freshly ground pepper

30 ml (2 tbsp) vegetable oil

2 medium onions, skinned and thinly sliced

350 g (12 oz) tomatoes, skinned and thinly sliced

350 g (12 oz) courgettes, trimmed and thinly sliced

15 ml (1 tbsp) tomato purée

5 ml (1 tsp) chopped fresh basil or 2.5 ml ($\frac{1}{2}$ tsp) dried

25 g (1 oz) walnut pieces, chopped

450 ml ($\frac{3}{4}$ pint) natural yogurt

2 eggs

75 g (3 oz) Cheddar cheese, grated

1.25 ml ($\frac{1}{4}$ tsp) ground cumin

a little vegetable oil, for brushing

1 Cook the lasagne in a large saucepan of boiling salted water with 15 ml (1 tbsp) oil for 15 minutes. Drain in single sheets on absorbent kitchen paper.

2 Heat the remaining oil in a pan, add the onion, tomatoes and 300 g (10 oz) of the courgettes and fry gently until the tomatoes begin to break down. Stir in the tomato purée, basil and plenty of seasoning.

3 Grease a deep-sided 2 litre ($3\frac{1}{2}$ pint) ovenproof dish. Layer the vegetables, lasagne and nuts in the dish, ending with a layer of lasagne.

4 Beat the yogurt and eggs together, then stir in the cheese, cumin and seasoning to taste. Pour over the lasagne.

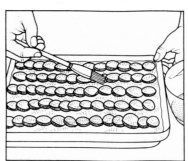

5 Arrange the remaining courgettes over the yogurt topping and brush them lightly with oil. Bake the lasagne in the oven at 200°C (400°F) mark 6 for about 40 minutes or until set. Serve hot, straight from the dish.

Menu Suggestion
Serve with crusty bread and a mixed green salad.

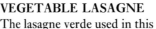

VEGETABLE LASAGNE
The lasagne verde used in this recipe is the green, spinach-flavoured lasagne. Most varieties must be pre-boiled before layering with the other ingredients in the dish, as indicated in the method here. To save time and trouble, look for the pre-cooked lasagne which can be placed straight in the dish from the packet without boiling. Most supermarkets and health food shops sell this type of lasagne, which comes in many different types, including wholewheat.

SPICY VEGETABLE PIE

| 1.00* | ⬠ | £ | ✳ | 690 cals |

* plus 2½ hours cooling and chilling

Serves 4

4 carrots, peeled and thinly sliced

4 leeks, washed, trimmed and thickly sliced

6 courgettes, washed, trimmed and thinly sliced

salt

175 g (6 oz) butter or margarine

1 onion, skinned and sliced

10 ml (2 tsp) ground cumin

175 g (6 oz) wholemeal flour

450 ml (¾ pint) milk plus 30 ml (2 tbsp)

100 g (4 oz) Cheddar cheese, grated

1.25 ml (¼ tsp) ground mace

freshly ground pepper

45 ml (3 tbsp) chopped fresh coriander or parsley

2.5 ml (½ tsp) baking powder

beaten egg, to glaze

10 ml (2 tsp) grated Parmesan

pinch of cayenne or paprika

1 Make the vegetable filling. Blanch the carrots, leeks and courgettes in boiling salted water for 1 minute only. Drain well.

2 Melt 40 g (1½ oz) butter in a heavy-based pan, add the onion and cumin and fry gently for 5 minutes until soft. Add the carrots, leeks and courgettes and fry for a further 5 minutes, stirring to coat in the onion mixture. Remove from the heat and set aside.

3 Melt 65 g (2½ oz) butter in a separate pan, sprinkle in 50 g (2 oz) of the flour and cook for 1–2 minutes, stirring, until lightly coloured. Remove from the heat and whisk in 450 ml (¾ pint) milk; return to the heat and simmer for 5 minutes until thick and smooth.

4 Stir in the Cheddar cheese, mace and salt and pepper to taste. Fold into the vegetables with the chopped coriander and 30 ml (2 tbsp) milk then turn into a 900-ml (1½-pint) ovenproof pie dish. Leave for 2 hours until cold.

5 Make the pastry. Sift 100 g (4 oz) flour, baking powder and a pinch of salt into a bowl. Rub in 50 g (2 oz) butter until the mixture resembles fine bread-crumbs, then add just enough water to mix to a firm dough.

6 Gather the dough into a ball, knead lightly and wrap in cling film; chill for 30 minutes.

7 Remove the dough from the refrigerator and roll out on a floured surface. Cut out a thin strip long enough to go around the rim of the pie dish. Moisten rim with water; place strip on rim.

8 Roll out the remaining dough for a lid, moisten the strip of dough, then place the lid on top and press to seal. Knock up and flute edge. Decorate the top.

9 Brush pastry with beaten egg; dust with Parmesan and cayenne. Bake in the oven at 190°C (375°F) mark 5 for 20–25 minutes.

VEGETABLE BIRYANI

| 0.55 | 519 cals |

Serves 4

350 g (12 oz) Basmati rice (see box)

1.4 litres (2½ pints) water

salt and freshly ground pepper

50 g (2 oz) ghee or clarified butter
(see box)

1 large onion, skinned and chopped

2.5 cm (1 inch) piece fresh root
ginger, skinned and grated

1–2 garlic cloves, skinned and
crushed

5 ml (1 tsp) ground coriander

10 ml (2 tsp) ground cumin

5 ml (1 tsp) ground turmeric

2.5 ml (½ tsp) chilli powder

3 medium carrots, peeled and
thinly sliced

225 g (8 oz) fresh or frozen green
beans, trimmed and cut in 2
lengthways

225 g (8 oz) cauliflower florets,
divided into small sprigs

5 ml (1 tsp) garam masala

juice of 1 lemon

hard-boiled egg slices and
coriander sprigs, to garnish

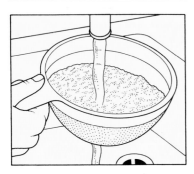

1 Put the rice in a sieve and hold under cold running water until the water runs clear.

2 Put the rice in a saucepan with 600 ml (1 pint) of the water and 5 ml (1 tsp) salt. Bring to the boil, then simmer for 10 minutes until only just tender.

3 Meanwhile, melt the ghee in a heavy-based large saucepan, add the onion, ginger and garlic and fry gently for 5 minutes until soft but not coloured. Add the coriander, cumin, turmeric and chilli powder and fry for 2 minutes more, stirring constantly to avoid catching and burning.

4 Remove the rice from the heat and drain. Add the remaining water to the onion and spice mixture with seasoning to taste. Stir well and bring to the boil. Add the carrots and beans and simmer for 15 minutes, then add the cauliflower and simmer for a further 10 minutes. Lastly, add the rice. Fold gently to mix and simmer until reheated.

5 Stir the garam masala and lemon juice into the biryani and simmer for a few minutes more to reheat and allow the flavours to develop. Taste and adjust the seasoning, then turn into a warmed serving dish. Garnish with egg slices and coriander and serve immediately.

Menu Suggestion
Serve this spicy dish with natural yogurt (raita) for a refreshing contrast, and a salad of sliced tomatoes, onions, cucumber and peppers dressed with oil, coriander, ginger and chilli powder to taste.

VEGETABLE BIRYANI

Indian basmati rice is expensive, but worth buying for its unique flavour and fluffy texture. Look for it in Indian shops and specialist supermarkets. Rinse or soak it before cooking, to remove excess starch.

Ghee is the Indian word for clarified butter. It is used in cooking because it can be heated to high temperatures without burning. Buy it at Indian shops, or clarify butter yourself.

BUCKWHEAT AND LENTIL CASSEROLE

1.45	453 cals

Serves 4

450 ml (¾ pint) water

salt and freshly ground pepper

150 g (5 oz) buckwheat

30 ml (2 tbsp) vegetable oil

1 red or green pepper, cored, seeded and cut into strips

1 onion, skinned and finely chopped

350 g (12 oz) courgettes, trimmed and sliced

175 g (6 oz) mushrooms, sliced

225 g (8 oz) red lentils

3 bay leaves

30 ml (2 tbsp) lemon juice

1 garlic clove, skinned and crushed

2 rosemary sprigs

5 ml (1 tsp) cumin seeds

600 ml (1 pint) vegetable stock

25 g (1 oz) butter

chopped fresh parsley, to garnish

1 Bring the water to the boil in a saucepan, add a pinch of salt, then sprinkle in the buckwheat and return to the boil. Boil rapidly for 1 minute. Reduce the heat, cover and cook gently for 12 minutes or until the water has been absorbed. Do not stir. Transfer to a buttered casserole.

2 Heat the oil in a flameproof casserole and fry the pepper and onion for 5 minutes. Add the courgettes and mushrooms and fry for 5 minutes. Stir in the lentils, bay leaves, lemon juice, garlic, rosemary, cumin and stock. Add to the casserole and stir well.

3 Simmer for about 45 minutes until the lentils are cooked, stirring occasionally. Add the butter, adjust the seasoning and sprinkle with parsley. Serve hot with a bowl of grated cheese, if liked.

Menu Suggestion
Packed with protein, this casserole makes a perfect main course dish for vegetarians, and is especially nutritious if served with boiled brown rice.

VEGETABLE HOT POT

| 1.30 | £ | ✳ | 533 cals |

Serves 4

450 g (1 lb) carrots, peeled and thinly sliced

2 large onions, skinned and thinly sliced

3 celery sticks, trimmed and thinly sliced

450 g (1 lb) potatoes, peeled and sliced

100 g (4 oz) swede, peeled and thinly sliced

450 ml ($\frac{3}{4}$ pint) vegetable stock (see page 350)

bouquet garni

salt and freshly ground pepper

425 g (15 oz) can butter beans, drained

100 g (4 oz) frozen peas

175 g (6 oz) fresh breadcrumbs

175 g (6 oz) hard cheese, grated

1 Layer the carrot, onion, celery, potato and swede in a 2.3 litre (4 pint) casserole.

2 Pour the vegetable stock into the casserole and add the bouquet garni and seasoning.

3 Cover and cook the stock and vegetables in the oven at 180°C (350°F) mark 4 for 1 hour.

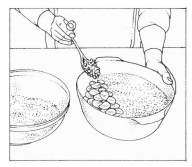

4 Remove the bouquet garni. Add the beans and peas to the casserole. Mix the breadcrumbs and cheese together. Spoon over the hot pot. Return to the oven, uncovered, for about 20 minutes.

Menu Suggestion
Vegetable Hotpot makes a delicious winter supper or lunch for the family. Serve with hot French bread and a glass or two of cider or beer.

VEGETABLE HOTPOT
Vegetable stock cubes are now becoming easier to obtain in supermarkets and delicatessens. Shops with kosher departments are likely to stock them, but if you still find them difficult to obtain, simply save the water from cooking vegetables. After straining, boil it until reduced, then store it in the refrigerator as you would meat stock.

STUFFED CABBAGE

| 2.00 | 🍴 | £ | 205 cals |

Serves 4

8–10 large cabbage leaves, trimmed

30 ml (2 tbsp) vegetable oil

2 onions, skinned and finely chopped

100 g (4 oz) mushrooms, chopped

50 g (2 oz) long grain rice

450 ml ($\frac{3}{4}$ pint) vegetable or chicken stock (see page 350)

397 g (14 oz) can tomatoes

5 ml (1 tsp) Worcestershire sauce

2.5 ml ($\frac{1}{2}$ tsp) dried basil

salt and freshly ground pepper

50 g (2 oz) hazelnuts, skinned and chopped

1 Blanch the cabbage leaves in boiling water for 3–4 minutes. Drain thoroughly.

2 Heat 15 ml (1 tbsp) of the oil in a frying pan and fry half the onions with the mushrooms for 5 minutes until browned. Add the rice and stir well.

3 Add 300 ml ($\frac{1}{2}$ pint) of the stock to the rice. Cover and cook for about 15 minutes until the rice is tender and the stock has been absorbed.

4 Meanwhile make a tomato sauce. Heat the remaining oil in a pan and fry the remaining onion for about 5 minutes until golden. Add the tomatoes, remaining stock, Worcestershire sauce, basil and seasoning. Bring to the boil, stirring, and simmer for 8 minutes. Blend until smooth.

5 Stir the hazelnuts into the rice with seasoning to taste, then remove from the heat.

6 Divide the rice mixture between the cabbage leaves and roll up to make neat parcels.

7 Arrange the cabbage parcels in an ovenproof dish. Pour over the tomato sauce.

8 Cover and cook in the oven at 180°C (350°F) mark 4 for about 1 hour until tender.

Menu Suggestion

These Stuffed Cabbage Rolls make a delicious vegetarian lunch or supper served with hot French bread. Follow with a tomato and onion salad for a well-balanced and colourful meal.

STUFFED PEPPERS

| 1.15 | 🍴 | 288 cals |

Serves 6

3 green peppers

3 red peppers

50 g (2 oz) butter

1 onion, skinned and finely chopped

100 g (4 oz) long grain rice

450 ml (¾ pint) vegetable or chicken stock (see page 350)

15 ml (1 tbsp) tomato purée

100 g (4 oz) mushrooms, sliced

salt and freshly ground pepper

75 g (3 oz) pine nuts or flaked almonds, roasted and chopped

10 ml (2 tsp) soy sauce

30 ml (2 tbsp) vegetable oil

4 Season well and stir in the nuts and soy sauce. Use this mixture to fill the peppers.

5 Replace lids, then place peppers in a deep ovenproof dish and pour over the oil. Cover and cook in the oven at 190°C (375°F) mark 5 for 30 minutes until tender.

Menu Suggestion
With their stuffing of rice, mushrooms and nuts, these stuffed peppers are substantial enough to serve on their own. Hot garlic or herb bread can be served with them, if extra carbohydrate is required.

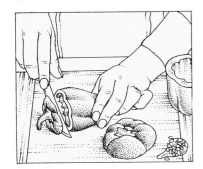

1 Cut a 2.5 cm (1 inch) lid from the stem end of the peppers. Scoop out the seeds and membrane. Blanch the shells and lids in boiling water for about 2 minutes. Drain and cool.

2 Melt the butter in a saucepan and gently fry the onion for 5 minutes until softened. Stir in the rice and cook for 1–2 minutes.

3 Add the stock, tomato purée and mushrooms. Bring to the boil and simmer for 13–15 minutes until the rice is tender and all the stock absorbed.

SOUTHERN BAKED BEANS

| 5.40* | £ | 323 cals |

* plus overnight soaking

Serves 4

275 g (10 oz) dried haricot beans, soaked overnight

15 ml (1 tbsp) vegetable oil

2 onions, skinned and chopped

225 g (8 oz) carrots, peeled and chopped

15 ml (1 tbsp) mustard powder

30 ml (2 tbsp) treacle

300 ml ($\frac{1}{2}$ pint) tomato juice

45 ml (3 tbsp) tomato purée

300 ml ($\frac{1}{2}$ pint) beer

salt and freshly ground pepper

1 Drain the beans and place in a saucepan of water. Bring to the boil and simmer for 25 minutes, then drain.

2 Meanwhile, heat the oil in a flameproof casserole and fry the onions and carrots for 5 minutes until lightly golden.

3 Remove from the heat, add the mustard, treacle, tomato juice and purée, beer and beans. Stir well.

4 Bring to the boil, cover and cook in the oven at 140°C (275°F) mark 1 for about 5 hours, stirring occasionally, until the beans are tender and the sauce is the consistency of syrup. Season well with salt and pepper.

Menu Suggestion

Serve these spiced, sweet beans as an accompaniment to roast or barbecued pork. Alternatively, serve them as a vegetarian dish with boiled rice or hot herb bread.

Pasta and Rice

SPAGHETTI ALLA CARBONARA
(SPAGHETTI WITH EGGS AND BACON)

0.20	683 cals

Serves 4

30 ml (2 tbsp) olive oil

1 onion, skinned and finely chopped

1 garlic clove, skinned and crushed

400 g (14 oz) spaghetti or other long thin pasta

6 rashers pancetta or unsmoked streaky bacon, rinded and cut into thin strips

60 ml (4 tbsp) dry white wine (optional)

3 eggs

60 ml (4 tbsp) freshly grated Parmesan cheese

30 ml (2 tbsp) single cream

30 ml (2 tbsp) chopped fresh parsley

salt and freshly ground pepper

1 Heat the oil in a pan, add the onion and fry gently for 5 minutes until soft but not coloured. Add the garlic and cook for a further minute.

2 Cook the spaghetti in a large pan of boiling salted water for 8–10 minutes or until just tender.

3 Meanwhile, add the bacon to the onion and fry for 2 minutes over high heat. Add the wine, if using, and boil until evaporated.

4 In a bowl, lightly beat the eggs with the Parmesan, cream, chopped parsley and salt and pepper to taste.

5 Drain the spaghetti, return to the pan with the bacon and onion mixture. Mix well over moderate heat for 1 minute.

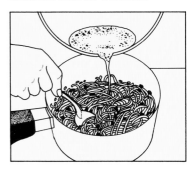

6 Remove from the heat and pour in egg mixture, mixing well. The heat from the spaghetti will cook the egg. Turn into a warmed serving dish and serve immediately.

Menu Suggestion
Serve for a family supper with fresh French bread and a green or mixed salad (see box below).

SPAGHETTI ALLA CARBONARA

This recipe originated in the region of Lazio—it is very popular in the capital city of Rome. The Romans happily eat Spaghetti alla Carbonara as a first course before their main meal of meat or fish and vegetables, but if you find this a little heavy going you can serve this quantity for a lunch or supper dish followed by a mixed or green salad and fresh bread. It's the perfect last-minute dish if you have eggs and bacon in the house, because it can be prepared in less than half an hour with hardly any effort and very few other ingredients.
Remember it next time everyone's hungry, and serve it as an unusual alternative to fried eggs and bacon.

FETTUCCINE ALLE VONGOLE
(FETTUCCINE WITH CLAM SAUCE)

0.45	£ £	565 cals

Serves 4

15 ml (1 tbsp) olive oil

1 onion, skinned and finely chopped

2–3 garlic cloves, skinned and crushed

700 g (1½ lb) tomatoes, skinned and roughly chopped, or one 397 g (14 oz) can tomatoes

two 200 g (7 oz) cans or jars baby clams in brine, drained (see box)

30 ml (2 tbsp) chopped fresh parsley

salt and freshly ground pepper

400 g (14 oz) fettuccine or other long thin pasta

1 Make the sauce. Heat 15 ml (1 tbsp) olive oil in a saucepan, add the onion and garlic and fry gently for 5 minutes until soft but not coloured.

2 Stir in the tomatoes and their juice, bring to the boil and cook for 15–20 minutes until slightly reduced.

3 Stir the drained clams into the sauce with 15 ml (1 tbsp) parsley and salt and pepper to taste. Remove from the heat.

4 Cook the fettuccine in a large pan of boiling salted water for 8–10 minutes until just tender.

5 Reheat the sauce just before the pasta is cooked, and taste and adjust seasoning. Drain the fettuccine well, tip into a warmed serving dish and pour over the clam sauce. Sprinkle with the remaining chopped parsley to garnish.

Menu Suggestion
Serve as a lunch or supper dish with fresh bread rolls.

FETTUCCINE ALLE VONGOLE

Fresh clams are easy to obtain in Italy, and are preferred for making this delicious sauce. If you are able to get fresh clams, so much the better. For this sauce, you will need about 2.3 litres (4 pints). Scrub them under cold running water with a stiff brush and scrape off any barnacles with a knife. Discard any clams which are not tightly closed, then put the remainder in a colander and leave them under running water for 20 minutes. Put the clams in a large saucepan with 300 ml (½ pint) water, cover and bring to the boil. Cook over high heat until all the shells are open (about 10 minutes), shaking the pan occasionally. If some remain closed after this time, discard them. Strain the clams, discarding the cooking liquid. Remove the meat from the shells (reserving a few whole ones to garnish, if liked), then use in step 3 of the recipe as drained canned clams.

TAGLIATELLE WITH CHEESE AND NUT SAUCE

| 0.15 | 770 cals |

Serves 4

400 g (14 oz) wholewheat or green (spinach) tagliatelle

salt and freshly ground pepper

100 g (4 oz) Gorgonzola cheese

100 g (4 oz) walnuts, chopped

5 ml (1 tsp) chopped fresh sage or 2.5 ml ($\frac{1}{2}$ tsp) dried sage

75 ml (5 tbsp) olive oil

15 ml (1 tbsp) chopped fresh parsley, to garnish

1 Plunge the tagliatelle into a large saucepan of boiling salted water. Simmer, uncovered, for 10 minutes or according to packet instructions, until *al dente* (tender but firm to the bite).

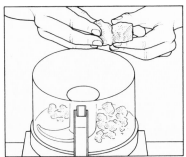

2 Meanwhile, crumble the cheese into a blender or food processor. Add two-thirds of the walnuts and the sage. Blend to combine the ingredients.

3 Add the oil gradually through the funnel (as when making mayonnaise) and blend until the sauce is evenly incorporated.

4 Drain the tagliatelle well and return to the pan. Add the nut sauce and fold in gently to mix. Add seasoning to taste.

5 Transfer the pasta and sauce to a warmed serving bowl and sprinkle with the remaining walnuts. Serve immediately garnished with chopped parsley.

Menu Suggestion
Quick to make at the last-minute, this nutritious dish makes an unusual lunch or supper. Serve with a crisp green salad tossed in a lemony vinaigrette dressing.

TAGLIATELLE WITH CHEESE AND NUT SAUCE

The Gorgonzola cheese used to make the sauce for this pasta dish must be one of the world's best-known blue cheeses. Real Gorgonzola cheese comes from the town of the same name in Lombardy, northern Italy. Originally it was made in the damp caves there, but nowadays it is mostly made in factories. The unique piquant flavour and creamy paste of Gorgonzola were produced naturally by the damp atmosphere in the caves, but in factories a similar result is achieved by using a bacteria known as *penicillium gorgonzola*. The process of making the cheese can now take as little as three months—as opposed to the twelve months taken by the traditional method.

SPAGHETTI WITH RATATOUILLE SAUCE

1.10 £ ✳* 458 cals

* freeze the ratatouille sauce separately at the end of step 6

Serves 4

1 aubergine
salt and freshly ground pepper
1 onion, skinned
1 garlic clove, skinned
1 green pepper
1 red pepper
3 medium courgettes
350 g (12 oz) tomatoes
10 ml (2 tsp) chopped fresh basil
400 g (14 oz) wholewheat spaghetti
freshly grated Parmesan cheese, to serve

1 Dice the aubergine, then spread out on a plate and sprinkle with salt. Dégorge for 30 minutes until the juices flow.

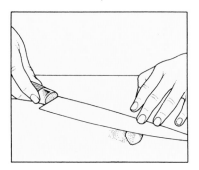

2 Meanwhile, prepare the remaining vegetables for the ratatouille sauce. Chop the onion finely. Crush the garlic on a board with a little salt and the flat of the blade of a large cook's knife.

3 Cut the peppers in half, remove the cores and seeds and wash well. Slice the flesh into thin strips.

4 Top and tail the courgettes, then slice them into very thin strips, leaving the skin on.

5 Skin the tomatoes. Put them in a heatproof bowl and pour in boiling water to cover. Leave to stand for 2 minutes, then drain and plunge into a bowl of cold water. Remove from the water one at a time, then peel off the skin with your fingers. Chop the flesh of the tomatoes finely.

6 Tip the diced aubergine into a sieve and rinse under cold running water. Put into a large, heavy-based pan with the prepared vegetables, basil and seasoning to taste. Cover and cook over moderate heat for 30 minutes. Shake the pan and stir the vegetables frequently during this time, to encourage the juices to flow.

7 Meanwhile, plunge the spaghetti into a separate large saucepan of boiling salted water. Simmer, uncovered, for 12 minutes or according to packet instructions, until *al dente* (tender but firm to the bite).

8 Drain the spaghetti thoroughly and turn into a warmed serving dish. Taste and adjust the seasoning of the ratatouille sauce, then pour over the spaghetti. Serve immediately, with the Parmesan cheese handed separately.

Menu Suggestion
The wholewheat spaghetti and rich, vegetable sauce together make this dish a complete meal.

Pasticcio di Maccheroni
(MACARONI PIE)

| 1.10 | f | 587 cals |

Serves 6

115 g (4½ oz) butter

30 ml (2 tbsp) olive oil

1 small onion, skinned and finely chopped

2 garlic cloves, skinned and crushed

397 g (14 oz) can tomatoes

5 ml (1 tsp) chopped fresh basil or 2.5 ml (½ tsp) dried, or mixed herbs

salt and freshly ground pepper

225 g (8 oz) large macaroni

75 g (3 oz) plain flour

568 ml (1 pint) milk

75 g (3 oz) Gruyère cheese, grated

1.25 ml (¼ tsp) freshly grated nutmeg

60 ml (4 tbsp) freshly grated Parmesan cheese

45 ml (3 tbsp) dried breadcrumbs

1 Make the tomato sauce. Melt 50 g (2 oz) of the butter in a heavy-based saucepan with the olive oil. Add the onion and garlic and fry gently for 5 minutes until soft but not coloured.

2 Add the tomatoes and their juices with the basil and seasoning to taste, then stir with a wooden spoon to break up the tomatoes. Bring to the boil, then lower the heat and simmer for 10 minutes, stirring occasionally.

3 Meanwhile, plunge the macaroni into a large pan of boiling salted water, bring back to the boil and cook for 10 minutes until just tender.

4 Make the cheese sauce. Melt the remaining butter in a separate saucepan, add the flour and cook over low heat, stirring with a wooden spoon, for about 2 minutes. Remove the pan from the heat and gradually blend in the milk, stirring after each addition to prevent lumps forming. Bring to the boil slowly, stirring all the time until the sauce thickens. Add the Gruyère cheese and seasoning to taste and stir until melted.

5 Drain the macaroni and mix with the tomato sauce. Arrange half of this mixture in a large buttered ovenproof dish.

6 Pour over half of the cheese sauce. Repeat the layers, then sprinkle evenly with the Parmesan and breadcrumbs.

7 Bake the pie in the oven at 190°C (375°F) mark 5 for 15 minutes, then brown under a pre-heated hot grill for 5 minutes. Serve hot.

LASAGNE AL FORNO
(PASTA LAYERED WITH MINCED BEEF AND BÉCHAMEL SAUCE)

2.10	£ ✳*	571–856 cals

* freeze after step 5

Serves 4–6

30 ml (2 tbsp) olive oil

1 onion, skinned and finely chopped

50 g (2 oz) carrot, peeled and finely chopped

100 g (4 oz) button mushrooms, wiped and sliced

50 g (2 oz) pancetta or unsmoked streaky bacon, rinded and finely diced

1 garlic clove, skinned and crushed

450 g (1 lb) lean minced beef or veal

350 g (12 oz) fresh tomatoes, skinned, seeded and sieved, or 226 g (8 oz) can tomatoes

15 ml (1 tbsp) tomato purée

150 ml ($\frac{1}{4}$ pint) dry white wine

150 ml ($\frac{1}{4}$ pint) beef stock (see page 350)

2 bay leaves

salt and freshly ground pepper

900 ml (1$\frac{1}{2}$ pints) milk

slices of onion, carrot and celery

6 peppercorns

100 g (4 oz) butter

75 g (3 oz) plain flour

12–15 sheets oven-ready lasagne (see box)

50 g (2 oz) freshly grated Parmesan cheese

1 Heat the oil in a large, heavy saucepan, add the onion, carrot, mushrooms, pancetta and crushed garlic. Fry, stirring, for 1–2 minutes. Add the beef or veal and cook over high heat for a further 2 minutes.

2 Stir in the tomatoes and juices, tomato purée, wine, beef stock, 1 bay leaf and seasoning to taste. Bring to the boil, reduce the heat to a simmer, cover and cook for about 35 minutes.

3 Meanwhile, pour the milk into a saucepan, add a few slices of onion, carrot and celery, the peppercorns and remaining bay leaf. Bring slowly to the boil, then remove from heat, cover and leave to infuse for about 15 minutes.

4 Make the béchamel sauce. Strain the infused milk into a jug. Melt the butter in a saucepan, add the flour and cook over low heat, stirring with a wooden spoon, for 2 minutes. Remove the pan from the heat and gradually blend in the milk, stirring after each addition to prevent lumps forming. Bring to the boil slowly and continue to cook for 2–3 minutes, stirring all the time until the sauce thickens. Add seasoning to taste.

5 Brush the inside of a baking dish with butter. Spoon one third of the meat sauce over the base of the dish. Cover this with 4–5 sheets of lasagne and spread over one third of the béchamel. Repeat these layers twice more, finishing with the béchamel sauce which should cover the lasagne completely. Sprinkle grated Parmesan over the top.

6 Stand the dish on a baking sheet. Bake in the oven at 180°C (350°F) mark 4 for about 45 minutes or until the top is well browned and bubbling.

Menu Suggestion
Serve as a main course dish followed by tomato and green salads, and a light dessert such as fresh fruit.

LASAGNE AL FORNO

There are numerous different recipes for lasagne al forno (lasagne baked in the oven): many like this one which combine layers of meat sauce, béchamel and pasta; some with three different cheeses (Parmesan, Mozzarella and Bel Paese) instead of the béchamel, and others with meatballs instead of meat sauce.

This recipe uses oven-ready lasagne, which is easy to use and saves preparation time. It is widely available both at supermarkets and delicatessens and

needs no pre-cooking—you simply take it straight from the box and layer it with the béchamel and meat sauces. The same thing can be done with homemade lasagne, which gives a beautiful light result and is well worth making for a dish such as this one which is heavy with other ingredients.

If only the ordinary dried lasagne is available this can of course be used, but you will find it time-consuming and messy, because it has to be boiled in

batches before it can be layered with the other ingredients. Always boil it in a very large pan, in *plenty* of boiling salted water (to prevent sticking). Adding 15 ml (1 tbsp) vegetable oil to the water before putting in the lasagne also helps with this problem. Only cook a few sheets at a time (4–6 at the most) to avoid overcrowding the pan, then drain and dry the sheets on a clean tea towel before layering them.

RAVIOLI
(PASTA FILLED WITH RICOTTA AND SPINACH)

 | 1.30 | | ✳* | 733 cals |

* freeze after step 7

Serves 4

350 g (12 oz) washed fresh spinach
  or 175 g (6 oz) frozen spinach

175 g (6 oz) Ricotta or curd cheese

115 g (4½ oz) freshly grated
  Parmesan

1 egg, beaten

pinch of freshly grated nutmeg or
  ground allspice

salt and freshly ground pepper

400 g (14 oz) freshly made pasta
  dough

75 g (3 oz) butter

a few fresh sage leaves, chopped,
  and a few extra, to garnish

1 Make the pasta stuffing. Place
the spinach in a saucepan
without any water and cook gently
for 5–10 minutes, or until thawed
if using frozen spinach. Drain very
well and chop the spinach finely.

2 Mix together the spinach,
Ricotta or curd cheese, 65 g
(2½ oz) Parmesan, the egg, nutmeg
and seasoning.

3 Cut the dough in two. Wrap
one half in cling film. Pat the
other half out to a rectangle, then
roll out firmly to an even sheet of
almost paper-thin pasta. If pasta
sticks, ease it carefully and flour
lightly underneath. Make sure
there are no holes or creases.
Cover with a clean damp cloth and
repeat with other half of dough.

4 Working quickly to prevent
the pasta drying out, place tea-
spoonfuls of the filling evenly
spaced at 4 cm (1½ inch) intervals
across and down the sheet of
dough that has just been rolled
out and is not covered.

5 With a pastry brush or your
index finger, glaze the spaces
between the filling with beaten
egg or water—this is of great
importance as it acts as a bond to
seal the ravioli.

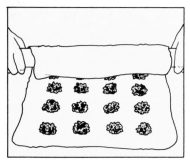

6 Uncover the other sheet of
pasta, carefully lift this on the
rolling-pin (to avoid stretching)
and unroll it over the first sheet,
easing gently. Press down firmly
around the pockets of filling and
along the dampened lines to push
out any trapped air and seal well.

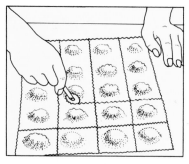

7 With a ravioli cutter, serrated-
edged wheel or even a sharp
knife, cut the ravioli into squares
between the pouches. Lift the
ravioli one by one on to a well-
floured baking sheet and leave to
dry for about 1 hour before cooking (or cover with cling film and
refrigerate overnight).

8 Pour at least 2.3 litres (4 pints)
water into a large saucepan
and bring to the boil. Add 10 ml
(2 tsp) salt.

9 Add the ravioli a few at a time,
stirring so that they do not
stick together. (A few drops of oil
added to the water will stop it
boiling over.) Cook the ravioli at a
gentle boil for about 5 minutes
until just tender. Remove with a
slotted spoon and place in a
warmed buttered serving dish.
Keep hot while cooking the remainder of the ravioli.

10 Melt the measured butter
in a saucepan and stir in the
rest of the grated Parmesan cheese
with the chopped sage. Pour over
the ravioli and toss to coat evenly.
Serve immediately, garnished with
fresh sage.

CANNELLONI
(PASTA FILLED WITH BEEF AND CHEESE)

0.45	🍴	✳*	998–1444 cals

* freeze after step 7

Serves 4–6

15 g (½ oz) butter

30 ml (2 tbsp) vegetable oil

1 onion, skinned and chopped

50 g (2 oz) pancetta or unsmoked
streaky bacon, rinded and
chopped

350 g (12 oz) lean minced beef

15 ml (1 tbsp) tomato purée

150 ml (¼ pint) red wine

2 egg yolks

pinch of freshly grated nutmeg

225 g (8 oz) Ricotta or curd cheese

50 g (2 oz) freshly grated
Parmesan cheese

salt and freshly ground pepper

1.1 litres (2 pints) béchamel sauce
(see page 352)

12–18 tubes oven-ready cannelloni

parsley sprigs, to garnish

1 Melt the butter and oil in a
medium, heavy saucepan, add
onion and fry for 5 minutes until
soft but not coloured. Add
pancetta and cook for 2 minutes.

2 Add the beef, increase the heat
and cook until well browned,
removing any lumps with a fork.

3 Stir in tomato purée and red
wine. Cook, stirring, until most
of liquid has evaporated. Set aside
to cool for 10 minutes.

4 Mix together the meat, egg
yolks, nutmeg, Ricotta, 25 g
(1 oz) Parmesan and seasoning.

5 Pour half of the béchamel
sauce into a shallow ovenproof dish which will take the
cannelloni in a single layer.

6 With a spoon, fill the cannelloni
with the meat. Lay them side
by side in the dish. Coat with
remaining béchamel, sprinkle over
remaining cheese and bake at
200°C (400°F) mark 6 for 20
minutes.

CHICKEN AND VEGETABLE RISOTTO

1.30	559 cals

Serves 4

175 g (6 oz) carrots, peeled

225 g (8 oz) turnips, peeled

175 g (6 oz) brown rice

350 ml (12 fl oz) chicken stock (see page 350)

50 g (2 oz) butter or margarine

4 chicken quarters, halved, about 900 g (2 lb) total weight

2 medium onions, skinned and chopped

1 stick of celery, chopped

50 g (2 oz) lean streaky bacon, rinded

salt and freshly ground pepper

90 ml (6 tbsp) dry white wine

chopped fresh parsley, to garnish

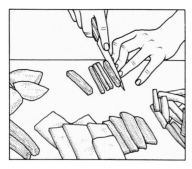

1 With a small sharp knife, cut the carrot and turnip into thick, even matchstick strips.

2 In a large saucepan, combine the rice and stock. Bring to the boil, then cover the pan and simmer for 15 minutes.

3 Melt 25 g (1 oz) fat in a flame-proof casserole. Add the chicken portions and fry for about 10 minutes until well browned. Remove from the pan.

4 Melt the remaining fat in the casserole, add all the vegetables and cook for 5 minutes until brown. Snip the bacon into the pan with kitchen scissors and fry gently for a further 2 minutes.

5 Stir in the rice mixture and season well. Arrange the chicken portions on top of the rice and vegetables. Spoon over the white wine.

6 Cover the casserole tightly with the lid or foil, then bake in the oven at 180°C (350°F) mark 4 for about 1 hour until the chicken is tender.

7 Just before serving, fork up the rice and vegetables round the chicken. Taste and adjust seasoning, then serve immediately, garnished with chopped parsley.

Menu Suggestion

Brown rice, chicken, bacon and vegetables make this risotto a substantial meal in itself. Serve for an informal family supper with hot garlic or herb bread, followed by a crisp mixed salad.

CHICKEN LIVER BOLOGNESE

0.40	835 cals

Serves 4

2 medium onions, skinned

125 g (4 oz) carrots, peeled

125 g (4 oz) celery

50 g (2 oz) lard

125 g (4 oz) streaky bacon, rinded

450 g (1 lb) chicken livers, chopped

45 ml (3 tbsp) tomato purée

150 ml ($\frac{1}{4}$ pint) red wine

150 ml ($\frac{1}{4}$ pint) chicken stock (see page 350)

2.5 ml ($\frac{1}{2}$ tsp) dried oregano

1 bay leaf

salt and freshly ground pepper

275 g (10 oz) spaghetti

25 g (1 oz) butter, melted

grated Parmesan cheese, to serve

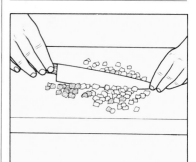

1 Chop the onions, carrots and celery finely. Melt the lard in a deep frying pan and fry the chopped vegetables until golden.

2 Snip the bacon into the pan, add the chicken livers and fry for about 5 minutes until the livers are browned on the outside and pink, but set, inside.

3 Stir in the tomato purée, red wine and stock. Add the oregano, bay leaf and seasoning, then bring to the boil. Lower heat, cover and simmer for 20 minutes.

4 Cook the spaghetti in boiling salted water for about 11 minutes until it is tender.

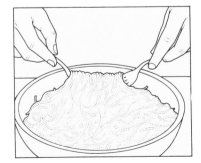

5 Drain the spaghetti and toss in the melted butter. Season with pepper. Serve with the chicken liver sauce, and grated Parmesan.

Menu Suggestion
Serve with a green salad, and chunks of French bread.

———————— VARIATIONS ————————

Instead of serving with pasta, use the chicken liver mixture as a filling for a herb-flavoured rice ring and serve with a tomato sauce handed separately. Or, spoon the mixture into puff pastry vol-au-vents or hot bread croustades, and serve as a starter or light main course.

To make bread croustades, choose a slightly stale unsliced white loaf. Cut into 5 cm (2 inch) thick rounds, 7.5 cm (3 inches) in diameter. Using a smaller cutter, cut through almost to the base, then carefully hollow out the centre. Place the rounds on a buttered baking sheet and brush with melted butter. Bake in the oven at 170°C (325°F) mark 3 for 40 minutes, turning occasionally, until crisp and brown all over.

Risotto alla Milanese
(SAFFRON RISOTTO)

| 0.35 | 🍴 | £ | 534 cals |

Serves 4

1.1 litres (2 pints) beef stock (see page 350)

75 g (3 oz) butter

1 small onion, skinned and finely chopped

350 g (12 oz) arborio rice

pinch of saffron strands

salt and freshly ground pepper

50 g (2 oz) freshly grated Parmesan cheese

1 Bring the stock to the boil in a large saucepan and keep at barely simmering point.

2 Meanwhile, in a large, heavy-based saucepan, melt 25 g (1 oz) butter, add the onion and fry gently for 5 minutes until soft but not coloured.

3 Add the arborio rice to the pan and stir well for 2–3 minutes until the rice is well coated with the butter.

4 Add a ladleful of stock to the pan, cook gently, stirring occasionally until the stock is absorbed. Add more stock as soon as each ladleful is absorbed, stirring frequently.

5 When the rice becomes creamy, sprinkle in the saffron with salt and pepper to taste. Continue adding stock and stirring until the risotto is thick and creamy, tender but not sticky. This process should take 20–25 minutes. It must not be hurried.

6 Just before serving, stir in the remaining butter and the Parmesan cheese.

RISOTTO ALLA VERONESE
(MUSHROOM AND HAM RISOTTO)

0.50	🝙 £	622 cals

Serves 4

90 g (3½ oz) butter

15 ml (1 tbsp) olive oil

2 small onions, skinned and finely chopped

1 garlic clove, skinned and crushed

225 g (8 oz) mushrooms, wiped and sliced

30 ml (2 tbsp) chopped fresh parsley

150 ml (¼ pint) white wine

900 ml (1½ pints) chicken stock (see page 350)

350 g (12 oz) arborio rice

50 g (2 oz) cooked ham, diced

25 g (1 oz) freshly grated Parmesan cheese

salt and freshly ground pepper

1 Melt 15 g (½ oz) butter and 15 ml (1 tbsp) olive oil in a saucepan. Add half the chopped onion and fry gently for 5 minutes until soft but not coloured.

2 Add the garlic, cook for 1 minute, then add the mushrooms and parsley. Cook gently for 10 minutes until the mushrooms are tender. Stir in 25 g (1 oz) butter and set aside while making the risotto.

3 Bring the stock to the boil in a large saucepan and keep at barely simmering point.

4 In a large, heavy-based saucepan, melt 25 g (1 oz) butter, add the rest of the onion and fry gently for 5 minutes until soft but not coloured.

5 Add the arborio rice and stir well for 2–3 minutes until the rice is well coated with the butter.

6 Add the wine, cook gently, stirring until absorbed. Add 150 ml (¼ pint) of stock as soon as this is absorbed. Continue to add stock in 150 ml (¼ pint) measures, stirring frequently until the risotto is thick and creamy, tender but not sticky. This should take 20–25 minutes. It must not be hurried.

7 Finally, stir in the remaining butter, ham, mushroom mixture and cheese. Taste and adjust seasoning. Serve immediately.

PRAWN RISOTTO

| 0.45 | £ £ | 293 cals |

Serves 4

75 g (3 oz) onion, skinned and
    thinly sliced

1 garlic clove, skinned and crushed

1 litre (1¾ pints) chicken stock (see
    page 350)

225 g (8 oz) long grain brown rice

50 g (2 oz) small button mushrooms

½ sachet saffron threads

salt and freshly ground pepper

225 g (8 oz) peeled prawns

50 g (2 oz) frozen petits pois

12 whole prawns, to garnish

1 Place the onion, garlic, stock,
rice, mushrooms and saffron
in a large saucepan or flameproof
casserole. Add seasoning to taste.
Bring to the boil and simmer,
uncovered, for 35 minutes, stirring
occasionally.

2 Stir in the prawns and petits
pois. Cook over high heat for
about 5 minutes, stirring occasionally until most of the liquid has
been absorbed.

3 Taste and adjust the seasoning, then turn into a warmed
serving dish. Garnish with the
whole prawns and serve
immediately.

Menu Suggestion

This succulent risotto made with
brown rice and prawns would be
perfectly offset by a tomato, onion
and basil salad.

CHINESE FRIED RICE

0.20* | £ | 475 cals

* plus 50 minutes soaking, and 2–3 hours or overnight chilling

Serves 4

350 g (12 oz) long grain rice

3 Chinese dried mushrooms, or 100 g (4 oz) button mushrooms, sliced

4 spring onions

30 ml (2 tbsp) vegetable oil

100 g (4 oz) beansprouts

100 g (4 oz) canned bamboo shoot, drained and cut into 2.5 cm (1 inch) matchsticks

100 g (4 oz) frozen peas

30 ml (2 tbsp) soy sauce

3 eggs, beaten

1 Put the rice in a sieve and wash thoroughly under cold running water until the water runs clear. Transfer the rice to a bowl, cover with cold water and leave to soak for 30 minutes.

2 Drain the rice and put in a medium saucepan. Cover with enough cold water to come 2.5 cm (1 inch) above the rice. Bring to the boil, cover tightly and simmer the rice very gently for 20 minutes. Do not stir.

3 Remove the pan from the heat, leave to cool for 20 minutes, then cover with cling film and chill in the refrigerator for 2–3 hours or overnight.

4 When ready to fry the rice, put the dried mushrooms in a bowl, cover with boiling water and leave to soak for about 20 minutes or until soft.

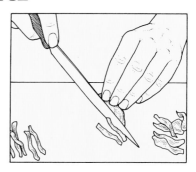

5 Squeeze out any excess moisture from the mushrooms, then cut into thin slivers. Cut the spring onions diagonally into 2.5 cm (1 inch) lengths.

6 Heat the oil in a wok or deep, heavy-based frying pan over high heat. Add all the vegetables and stir fry for 2–3 minutes. Add the soy sauce and cook, briefly, stirring.

7 Fork up the rice, add to the pan and stir fry for 2 minutes. Pour in the beaten eggs and continue to stir fry for 2–3 minutes, or until the egg has scrambled and the rice is heated through. Serve immediately.

Menu Suggestion
Fried Rice can be served in individual bowls with chopsticks, as an accompaniment to any Chinese main course.

KHUMBI PULLAO
(MUSHROOM PILAU)

0.30*	£	242–323 cals

* plus 30 minutes soaking

Serves 6–8

450 g (1 lb) basmati rice

225 g (8 oz) button mushrooms

30 ml (2 tbsp) ghee or vegetable oil

12 green cardamoms

6 whole cloves

5–6 pieces cassia bark

5 ml (1 tsp) salt

freshly ground pepper

1 Place the rice in a sieve and rinse under cold running water until the water runs clear. Transfer the rice to a bowl and cover with plenty of cold water. Leave to soak for 30 minutes.

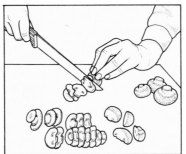

2 Wipe the mushrooms, then slice thinly. Heat the ghee in a large heavy-based saucepan or flameproof casserole, add the cardamoms, cloves and cassia bark with the mushrooms and fry over high heat for 1–2 minutes, stirring constantly.

3 Drain the rice well and leave to stand for 2 minutes. Remove the pan from the heat and stir in the rice. Add the salt and pepper to taste and mix well. Level the rice and pour in enough water to come approximately 2.5 cm (1 inch) above the rice.

4 Bring to the boil, cover tightly with a lid and cook very gently for 20 minutes. Do not uncover the pan during cooking.

5 Remove the lid and carefully fluff up the rice with a fork. All of the water should have been absorbed and the rice should be tender. Taste and adjust seasoning, then transfer the pilau to a warmed serving dish. Serve hot.

KHUMBI PULLAO

There are many different schools of thought on the preparation of rice for cooking. The method of rinsing and soaking used here has been tried and tested, and found to be especially good with basmati rice. Rinsing or washing under cold running water rids the rice of excess starch and any white polishing powder, and soaking helps ensure that the grains are separate and do not stick during cooking. Although both these processes may seem time-consuming, they are well worth it when you can be sure of perfect fluffy grains of rice, and the beautifully aromatic basmati, sometimes called the "king of rice", is too expensive to waste.

Pizzas

PIZZA NAPOLETANA
(PIZZA WITH TOMATOES, MOZZARELLA AND ANCHOVIES)

| 1.30* | £ | ✳* | 692 cals |

* plus 1½–2 hours rising; freeze after step 4

Serves 4

1 quantity of basic pizza dough (see page 349)

60 ml (4 tbsp) olive oil

450 g (1 lb) ripe tomatoes, skinned and chopped or 397 g (14 oz) can tomatoes, drained

pinch of sugar, or to taste

salt and freshly ground pepper

225 g (8 oz) Italian Mozzarella cheese, thinly sliced

50 g (2 oz) can anchovy fillets, drained and cut in half lengthways

20 ml (4 tsp) chopped fresh oregano or 10 ml (2 tsp) dried

1 Make the basic pizza dough according to the instructions on page 349 and leave to rise.

2 Put half of the olive oil in a pan with the tomatoes, sugar and salt and pepper to taste. Simmer for about 10 minutes, stirring from time to time.

3 Meanwhile, turn the risen dough out on to a floured surface. Roll out and cut into two 27.5-cm (11-inch) circles. (Use a large plate, flan dish or ring as a guide.) Make the edges slightly thicker than the centres.

4 Put the circles of dough on oiled baking sheets and spread the tomato mixture evenly over them, right to the edges. Arrange the slices of Mozzarella over the tomatoes.

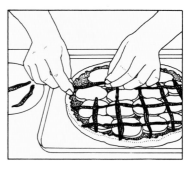

5 Arrange the anchovies in a lattice pattern over the top of the tomatoes.

6 Sprinkle over the remaining oil, with the oregano and salt and pepper to taste. Leave to prove in a warm place for about 30 minutes, then bake in a 220°C (425°F) mark 7 oven for 25 minutes or until the topping is melted and the dough well risen. Swap the baking sheets over half-way through the cooking time. Serve hot or cold.

Menu Suggestion
Serve as a lunch or supper dish with a crisp green salad tossed in an olive oil and lemon juice dressing.

PIZZA CASALINGA
(FARMHOUSE PIZZA)

| 1.30 | £ | ✳* | 566 cals |

* plus 1½–2 hours rising; freeze after step 5

Serves 6

1 quantity of basic pizza dough (see page 349)

60 ml (4 tbsp) olive oil

2 garlic cloves, skinned and crushed

225 g (8 oz) mushrooms, wiped

397 g (14 oz) can tomatoes

salt and freshly ground pepper

400 g (14 oz) Italian Mozzarella cheese, thinly sliced

100 g (4 oz) boiled ham, cut into strips

50 g (2 oz) bottled mussels or can anchovy fillets, drained

10 black olives, halved and stoned

20 ml (4 tsp) chopped fresh oregano or 10 ml (2 tsp) dried

1 Make the basic pizza dough according to the instructions on page 349 and leave to rise.

2 Heat 30 ml (2 tbsp) oil in a heavy-based frying pan. Add the garlic and mushrooms and fry for about 5 minutes until the oil is completely absorbed.

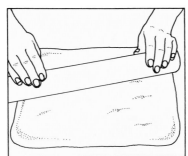

3 Turn the risen dough out on to a floured surface and roll out to a rectangle, approximately 30 × 25 cm (12 × 10 inches). Make the edges slightly thicker than the centre. Put the dough on an oiled baking sheet.

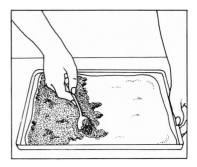

4 Mash the tomatoes with half of their juice so that there are no large lumps, then spread them evenly over the dough, right to the edges. Sprinkle with salt and pepper to taste.

5 Arrange the slices of Mozzarella over the tomatoes, then sprinkle over the strips of ham. Top with the mushrooms and mussels or anchovies, then dot with the olives.

6 Mix together the oregano and remaining oil, and add salt and pepper to taste. Drizzle over the top of the pizza.

7 Leave the pizza to prove in a warm place for about 30 minutes, then bake in the oven at 220°C (425°F) mark 7 for 25 minutes or until the topping is melted and the dough well risen. Cut into serving portions and serve hot or cold.

Menu Suggestion
Serve for a family supper with a crisp green salad of lettuce, chicory or endive and fennel.

PIZZA QUATTRO STAGIONI
(FOUR SEASONS PIZZA)

1.30*	£	✳*	782 cals

* plus 1½–2 hours rising; freeze after step 6

Makes 4

1 quantity of basic pizza dough (see page 349)

175 g (6 oz) button mushrooms, thinly sliced

45 ml (3 tbsp) olive oil

2 garlic cloves, skinned and crushed

10 ml (2 tsp) chopped fresh basil or 5 ml (1 tsp) dried

450 ml (¾ pint) simple tomato sauce (see page 352)

16 slices of Italian salami, rinded

50 g (2 oz) black olives, halved and stoned

8 bottled artichoke hearts, sliced

225 g (8 oz) Italian Mozzarella cheese, thinly sliced

4 tomatoes, skinned and sliced

10 ml (2 tsp) chopped fresh oregano or 5 ml (1 tsp) dried

salt and freshly ground pepper

1 Make the basic pizza dough according to the instructions on page 349 and leave to rise.

2 Fry the mushrooms lightly in 30 ml (2 tbsp) of the oil with the garlic and basil.

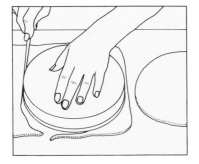

3 Turn the risen dough out on to a floured surface, roll out and cut into four 20-cm (8-inch) circles, using sandwich tins or flan rings as a guide. Make the edges slightly thicker than the centres.

4 Put the circles of dough into oiled sandwich tins. Spread the tomato sauce evenly over dough, right to edges.

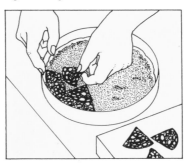

5 Cut each slice of salami into four quarters. Arrange these pieces in one quarter of each pizza, overlapping them to cover tomato sauce. Dot with olives.

6 Arrange the artichokes slices over another pizza quarter, the cheese and tomato over another and mushrooms over the last.

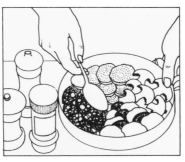

7 Sprinkle the remaining oil over the pizzas with the oregano and seasoning.

8 Leave the pizzas to prove in a warm place for about 30 minutes, then bake in the oven at 220°C (425°F) mark 7 for 25 minutes. Swap over quickly, half-way through the cooking time. Serve hot or cold.

PIZZA QUATTRO FORMAGGI
(PIZZA WITH FOUR CHEESES)

1.30*	£ ✳*	803 cals

* plus 1½–2 hours rising; freeze after step 5

Makes 4

1 quantity of basic pizza dough (see page 349)

226 g (8 oz) can tomatoes

salt and freshly ground pepper

100 g (4 oz) Italian Mozzarella cheese, diced

100 g (4 oz) Bel Paese or Provolone cheese, diced

100 g (4 oz) Fontina cheese, diced

100 g (4 oz) Taleggio cheese, diced

20 ml (4 tsp) olive oil

20 ml (4 tsp) chopped fresh mixed herbs or 10 ml (2 tsp) dried

1 Make the basic pizza dough according to the instructions on page 349 and leave to rise.

2 Turn the risen dough out on to a floured surface, roll out and cut into four 20-cm (8-inch) circles, using sandwich tins or flan rings as a guide. Make the edges slightly thicker than the centres.

3 Put dough into oiled sandwich tins or flan rings placed on oiled baking sheets.

4 Crush the tomatoes with their juice and spread evenly over the dough, right to the edges. Season to taste.

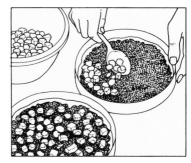

5 Mix the four cheeses together and sprinkle them evenly over the four pizzas.

6 Sprinkle over the oil and herbs, with salt and pepper to taste. Leave the pizzas to prove in a warm place for about 30 minutes, then bake in the oven at 220°C (425°F) mark 7 for 25 minutes or until the cheeses are melted and the dough is well risen. Swap the oven shelves over half-way through the cooking time. Serve hot or cold.

Menu Suggestion
Serve for lunch or supper followed by cold Peperonata (page 259).

CHILLI PIZZA FINGERS

| 1.00 | 🍴 | £ | ✳ | 461 cals |

Serves 6

225 g (8 oz) minced beef

2.5 ml (½ tsp) chilli powder

1 garlic clove, skinned and crushed

1 medium onion, skinned and chopped

1 small green pepper, cored, seeded and chopped

100 g (4 oz) mushrooms, wiped and sliced

225 g (8 oz) tomatoes, skinned and chopped

213 g (7.51 oz) can red kidney beans, drained

150 ml (¼ pint) beef stock (see page 350)

225 g (8 oz) plain wholewheat flour

50 g (2 oz) medium oatmeal

15 ml (1 tbsp) baking powder

salt and freshly ground pepper

50 g (2 oz) margarine or butter

1 egg, beaten

60 ml (4 tbsp) milk

15 ml (1 tbsp) tomato purée

175 g (6 oz) Mozzarella cheese, thinly sliced

basil sprigs, to garnish

1 First prepare the topping. Place the minced beef, chilli powder and garlic in a saucepan and fry for 3–4 minutes, stirring occasionally. Add the onion, green pepper and mushrooms and fry for a further 1–2 minutes. Stir in the tomatoes, red kidney beans and beef stock. Bring to the boil and simmer for about 15 minutes, stirring occasionally until most of the liquid has evaporated.

2 Meanwhile, combine the flour, oatmeal, baking powder and a pinch of salt in a bowl.

3 Rub in the margarine until the mixture resembles fine breadcrumbs. Bind to a soft dough with the egg and milk, then turn out on to a floured surface and knead lightly until smooth.

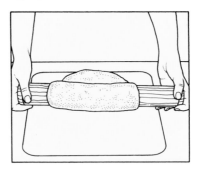

4 Roll out the dough to a 25 × 18 cm (10 × 7 inch) rectangle. Lift on to a baking sheet, then spread carefully with tomato purée. Pile the chilli mixture on top and cover with Mozzarella cheese.

5 Bake in the oven at 200°C (400°F) mark 6 for about 30 minutes until golden and bubbling. Cut into fingers for serving, garnished with basil sprigs.

Menu Suggestion

Serve as a substantial snack, or an easy supper dish accompanied by a salad of thinly sliced or grated courgettes dressed with a vinaigrette and snipped fresh chives.

PANZEROTTI
(DEEP-FRIED STUFFED PIZZAS)

1.00* £ ✳* 173 cals

* plus 1½–2 hours rising; freeze after step 7

Makes 16

1 quantity of basic pizza dough (see page 349)

300 ml (½ pint) Simple Tomato Sauce (see page 352)

100 g (4 oz) Italian Mozzarella cheese

25 g (1 oz) freshly grated Parmesan cheese

50 g (2 oz) boiled ham, finely diced

salt and freshly ground pepper

vegetable oil, for deep frying

1 Make the basic pizza dough according to the instructions on page 349 and leave to rise.

2 Cook the tomato sauce, over high heat, stirring constantly, until reduced to a thick pulp. Leave to cool for about 30 minutes.

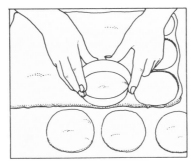

3 Meanwhile, turn the risen dough out on to a floured surface, roll out and cut into sixteen 10-cm (4-inch) circles. Use a plain pastry cutter or the rim of a wine glass or cup as a guide.

4 Spread the cold tomato sauce over the circles of dough, leaving a border at the edge.

5 Roughly chop the Mozzarella. Mix it with Parmesan, ham and seasoning. Sprinkle over one half of dough.

6 Brush the edge of the dough with water, then fold the plain half over the filled half.

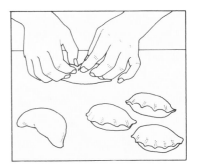

7 Press the edges of the panzerotti together well to seal in the filling, then crimp to make a decorative edge.

8 Heat the oil in a deep-fat frier to 180°C (350°F). Deep-fry the pizzas in batches for 2–3 minutes on both sides until golden. Drain and serve immediately.

Menu Suggestion
Serve hot as a snack on their own, or cold as part of a picnic or al fresco buffet.

PIZZETTE FRITTE
(PAN-FRIED MINI PIZZAS)

| 1.15* | 215 cals |

* plus 1½–2 hours rising
Makes 12

1 quantity of basic pizza dough
  (see page 349)

30 ml (2 tbsp) olive oil

1 small onion, skinned and finely
  chopped

1–2 garlic cloves, skinned and
  crushed

350 g (12 oz) ripe tomatoes,
  skinned and roughly chopped,
  or 397 g (14 oz) can tomatoes

20 ml (4 tsp) chopped fresh basil or
  10 ml (2 tsp) dried

pinch of sugar, or to taste

salt and freshly ground pepper

vegetable oil, for shallow frying

1 Make the basic pizza dough
according to the instructions
on page 349 and leave to rise.

2 Heat the olive oil in a pan, add
the onion and garlic and fry
gently for 5 minutes until soft and
lightly coloured. Add the tomatoes
and break them up with a spoon.
Bring to the boil, then lower the
heat, add the basil, sugar and salt
and pepper to taste. Simmer for
about 20 minutes, stirring
frequently.

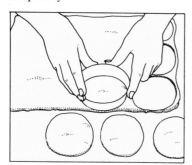

3 Meanwhile, turn the risen
dough out on to a floured surface, roll out and cut into twelve
10-cm (4-inch) circles.

4 Work the tomato mixture in a
blender or food processor.
Return to the rinsed-out pan, taste
and adjust seasoning, then reheat
gently while frying the pizzas.

5 Heat the vegetable oil in a
small frying pan and shallow
fry the pizzas in batches for about
2 minutes on each side until they
are golden.

6 Drain the pizzas quickly on
absorbent kitchen paper, then
spread with some of the sauce.
Serve immediately.

Menu Suggestion
Serve as a snack on their own, at
any time of day.

PIZZETTE FRITTE
This is just one of the many
versions of pizza, which
originated in Naples and is now
found all over the world. The
original pizza had a simple topping of tomatoes, anchovies and
cheese, but nowadays pizzerie
specialise in the most fanciful of
toppings. Pizzette Fritte make an
ideal snack, because they are
small enough to be eaten with
the fingers.

Vegetables

TRIO OF VEGETABLE PURÉES

0.40	249 cals

Serves 4

450 g (1 lb) carrots, scrubbed or peeled and roughly chopped

450 g (1 lb) parsnips or turnips, peeled and roughly chopped

salt and freshly ground pepper

350 g (12 oz) frozen peas

few fresh mint sprigs

5 ml (1 tsp) lemon juice

pinch of granulated sugar

40 g (1½ oz) butter or margarine

45 ml (3 tbsp) single or double cream

1.25 ml (¼ tsp) ground coriander

good pinch of freshly grated nutmeg

1 Cook the carrots and parsnips or turnips in separate pans of boiling salted water for about 20 minutes or until tender. At the same time, cook the frozen peas in boiling salted water according to packet instructions, with the mint sprigs, lemon juice and sugar.

2 Drain the vegetables, keeping them separate. Put the peas and mint in a blender or food processor with one-third of the butter and 15 ml (1 tbsp) of the cream. Work to a smooth purée, then add salt and pepper to taste.

3 Rinse out the machine, then add the carrots, another third of the butter, 15 ml (1 tbsp) cream and the coriander. Work to a smooth purée, then add salt and pepper to taste.

4 Repeat puréeing with the parsnips or turnips, the remaining butter and cream and the nutmeg. Add salt and pepper to taste.

5 Return all 3 purées to individual pans and reheat gently, stirring all the time. Spoon into 3 warmed serving bowls or in 3 or more sections in 1 large bowl. Serve immediately.

Menu Suggestion
Vegetable purées make an attractive alternative to plain boiled or mashed vegetables, especially for Sunday lunch or when entertaining.

TRIO OF VEGETABLE PURÉE

Garnish the top of the carrot purée with sprigs of fresh coriander, the pea purée with mint and the parsnips or turnips with a sprinkling of freshly grated nutmeg.

Ground coriander goes especially well with carrots, as do most Indian spices. For a spicier flavour, buy whole coriander seeds fresh from an Indian grocer and dry roast them for a few minutes in a non-stick, or heavy cast iron, frying pan. When the seeds begin to pop and burst, turn them into a mortar and grind to a fine powder with a pestle. Use fresh for maximum flavour, or store in an airtight container and use within a few weeks. If you are fond of coriander, splinkle the carrot purée liberally with the freshly chopped herb before serving.

RÖSTI
(SWISS POTATO CAKE)

| 0.45* | 🍴 | 292–585 cals |

* plus 10 minutes cooling

Serves 2–4

700 g (1½ lb) old potatoes, scrubbed

salt and freshly ground pepper

75 g (3 oz) butter, margarine or lard

1 small onion, skinned and finely chopped

1 Quarter any large potatoes and put in a saucepan of salted water. Bring to the boil and cook for 7 minutes. Drain well, leave to cool for about 10 minutes until cool enough to handle, then remove the skins.

2 Using a hand grater, grate the potatoes into a bowl. Melt 25 g (1 oz) of the butter in a frying pan, add the onion and fry gently for about 5 minutes until soft but not coloured.

3 Add the remaining butter to the onion and heat until melted. Add the grated potato and sprinkle with salt and pepper. Fry the potatoes, turning them constantly until they have absorbed all the fat.

4 Using a palette knife, form the potato into a neat, flat cake and flatten the top. Sprinkle with 15 ml (1 tbsp) water, cover the pan and cook gently for 15–20 minutes, until the underside is golden brown. Shake the pan occasionally to prevent the potato sticking to the bottom of the pan.

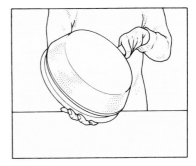

5 When cooked, place a large warmed serving plate on top of the frying pan. Invert the pan and turn the potatoes on to the plate so that the golden side is uppermost. Serve immediately, cut into wedges. Alternatively, serve straight from the pan, cut into wedges and inverted.

Menu Suggestion
Rösti is one of the most delicious of potato dishes. Serve with grilled or barbecued steak.

WATERCRESS AND OATMEAL CROQUETTES

| 1.05* | ⊟ | £ | ✳ | 425 cals |

* plus at least 30 minutes chilling

Serves 4

| 700 g (1½ lb) floury potatoes |
| 15 g (½ oz) butter, softened |
| 1 bunch watercress |
| 2 eggs |
| salt and freshly ground pepper |
| 15 ml (1 tbsp) plain flour |
| 50 g (2 oz) fresh breadcrumbs |
| 50 g (2 oz) medium oatmeal |
| vegetable oil, for deep frying |

1 Scrub the potatoes and boil in their skins until tender; about 20 minutes. Drain well.

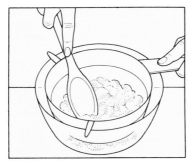

2 Peel the potatoes, then sieve them into a bowl or mash *well*. Beat in the butter.

3 Wash, drain and finely chop the watercress. Add to the bowl with 1 egg and seasoning to taste; mix well.

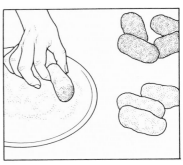

4 Mould the potato mixture into 12 cork-shaped pieces. Coat each croquette lightly in flour.

5 Break the remaining egg on to a plate; beat lightly. Combine the breadcrumbs and oatmeal on another plate.

6 Brush the croquettes with the beaten egg, then coat in the breadcrumb mixture, pressing it on firmly. Chill in the refrigerator for at least 30 minutes or until required.

7 Heat the oil in a deep fat frier to 190°C (375°F). Deep fry the croquettes for about 4 minutes or until golden brown on all sides. Drain on absorbent kitchen paper before serving.

Menu Suggestion
These croquettes make an unusual, colourful alternative to potatoes, and go especially well with lamb and fish dishes.

LENTIL AND CELERY PEPPERS

1.05	427 cals

Serves 2

125 g (4 oz) red lentils

salt and freshly ground pepper

2 green peppers, about 175 g (6 oz) each

25 g (1 oz) butter or margarine

1 medium onion, skinned and finely chopped

75 g (3 oz) celery, trimmed and finely chopped

75 g (3 oz) low fat soft cheese

1 egg

1 Cook the lentils in boiling salted water for 12–15 minutes until just tender.

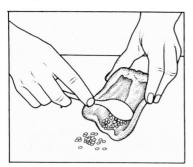

2 Meanwhile, halve the peppers and remove the cores and seeds. Place on a steamer and steam, covered, for about 15 minutes or until soft.

3 Melt the butter in a frying pan, add the onion and celery and fry gently for 2–3 minutes.

4 Drain the lentils and add to the onion and celery. Cook, stirring, for 1–2 minutes until heated through.

5 Remove the pan from the heat and beat in the cheese and egg with salt and pepper to taste.

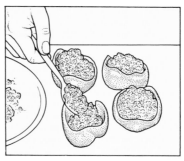

6 Remove the peppers from the steamer and fill with the mixture. Place under a hot grill for about 5 minutes or until golden brown. Serve hot.

Menu Suggestion
Serve these stuffed peppers for a tasty supper, accompanied by warm wholemeal bread and a tomato salad.

ROASTED OATMEAL VEGETABLES

1.30	260 cals

Serves 6

450 g (1 lb) medium onions

450 g (1 lb) carrots

450 g (1 lb) parsnips

120 ml (8 tbsp) vegetable oil

175 g (6 oz) coarse oatmeal

5 ml (1 tsp) paprika

salt and freshly ground pepper

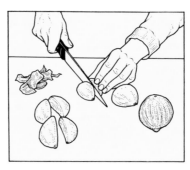

1 Skin and quarter the onions, keeping the root end intact. Peel the carrots and parsnips and cut into large chunks.

2 Put the carrots and parsnips in a saucepan of water, bring to the boil and cook for 2 minutes. Drain well.

3 Heat 30 ml (2 tbsp) of the oil in the saucepan and replace the carrots and parsnips. Add the onions, oatmeal, paprika and salt and pepper to taste. Stir gently to coat the vegetables.

4 Put the remaining oil in a large roasting tin and heat in the oven at 200°C (400°F) mark 6. When very hot, add the vegetable and oatmeal mixture and baste.

5 Roast in the oven for about 1 hour, or until the vegetables are just tender and golden brown. Baste occasionally during cooking. Spoon into a warmed serving dish and sprinkle over any oatmeal 'crumbs'. Serve hot.

Menu Suggestion
These crisp, oven-fried vegetables make a welcome alternative to plainly cooked vegetables. They can be served with any traditional meat or poultry.

SALSIFY AU GRATIN

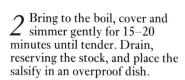

* plus 30 minutes cooling

Serves 4

450 g (1 lb) salsify, trimmed and peeled

300 ml (½ pint) chicken stock (see page 350)

25 g (1 oz) butter

45 ml (3 tbsp) plain flour

2.5 ml (½ tsp) mustard powder

175 g (6 oz) mature Cheddar cheese, grated

salt and freshly ground pepper

50 g (2 oz) fresh breadcrumbs

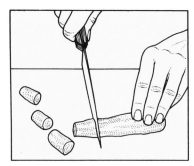

1 Cut the salsify into 2.5 cm (1 inch) lengths and place in a saucepan with the stock.

2 Bring to the boil, cover and simmer gently for 15–20 minutes until tender. Drain, reserving the stock, and place the salsify in an overproof dish.

3 Melt the butter in a saucepan, add the flour and mustard powder and cook over low heat, stirring with a wooden spoon, for 2 minutes. Remove the pan from the heat and gradually blend in the reserved stock, stirring after each addition to prevent lumps forming.

4 Bring to the boil slowly, then simmer for 2–3 minutes, stirring. Add half the cheese and seasoning to taste and pour over the salsify.

5 Mix the remaining cheese with the breadcrumbs and sprinkle over the dish. Cool for 30 minutes, cover and chill in the refrigerator until required.

6 Uncover and bake in the oven at 190°C (375°F) mark 5 for 20–25 minutes until the top is golden brown. Serve hot.

Menu Suggestion
Hot, cheesy and bubbling, this unusual vegetable dish taste delicious with plain roast meats, and can be cooked in the oven at the same time. Try it with the Sunday roast for a change.

SALSIFY AU GRATIN
Salsify is an inexpensive winter vegetable. It looks rather like a long, thin parsnip, and has a soft, white flesh. Years ago it used to be nicknamed the 'vegetable oyster', because its flavour was thought to be similar to that of oysters. Try coating chunks of salsify in batter after parboiling, then deep-frying them as a tasty alternative to chips.

PEPERONATA
(SWEET PEPPER AND TOMATO STEW)

| 0.45 | £ | ✳ | 156 cals |

Serves 6

75 ml (5 tbsp) olive oil

1 large onion, peeled and finely sliced

6 red peppers, cored, seeded and sliced into strips

2 garlic cloves, skinned and crushed

700 g (1½ lb) ripe tomatoes, skinned and roughly chopped

15 ml (1 tbsp) chopped fresh parsley

salt and freshly ground pepper

1 Heat the oil in a frying pan, add the onion and fry gently for 5 minutes until soft but not coloured.

2 Halve the peppers, remove the cores and seeds, then slice the flesh into strips.

3 Add the peppers and garlic, cook gently for 2–3 minutes, then add the tomatoes, parsley and salt and pepper to taste.

4 Cover and cook gently for 30 minutes until the mixture is quite dry: if necessary, remove the lid 10 minutes before the end of cooking and allow the liquid to evaporate. Taste and adjust seasoning before serving either hot or cold.

Menu Suggestion
Serve hot as a vegetable accompaniment to roast, grilled or barbecued meats. Serve cold with chunks of fresh bread for a starter.

CHINESE VEGETABLE STIR-FRY

| 0.30 | £ | 267 cals |

Serves 4

350 g (12 oz) mangetout

2 large red peppers

1 bunch of spring onions

225 g (8 oz) can water chestnuts

5 cm (2 inch) piece of fresh root ginger

1–2 garlic cloves

30 ml (2 tbsp) vegetable oil

15 ml (1 tbsp) sesame oil (optional)

30 ml (2 tbsp) dry sherry

30 ml (2 tbsp) soy sauce

10 ml (2 tsp) honey or soft brown sugar

10 ml (2 tsp) tomato purée

salt and freshly ground pepper

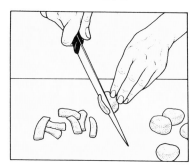

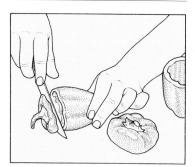

1 First prepare the vegetables. Top and tail the mangetout. Cut the tops off the peppers, remove the cores and seeds and wash thoroughly inside and out.

2 Pat the peppers dry with absorbent kitchen paper, then shred the flesh finely. Trim and shred the spring onions.

3 Drain the water chestnuts, rinse under cold running water, then shred finely.

4 Peel the root ginger, then cut the flesh into matchstick lengths. Skin and crush the garlic.

5 Heat the oils in a wok or deep, heavy-based frying pan. Add the spring onions, ginger and garlic and stir fry for 2–3 minutes. Add the remaining prepared vegetables and stir fry to mix them together.

6 In a bowl or jug, mix together the remaining ingredients, with salt and pepper to taste. Pour over the vegetables, moisten with about 60 ml (4 tbsp) water and mix well. Cook for about 5 minutes, stirring constantly, until the mangetout and red peppers are tender but still crunchy. Transfer to a warmed serving bowl and serve immediately.

Menu Suggestion
Serve this colourful stir-fried dish with pork, beef or duck, or with steamed or fried fish. Chinese egg noodles can be stir fried with the vegetables, or served separately.

CHINESE VEGETABLE STIR-FRY

Fresh water chestnuts are sometimes available in oriental specialist shops, but canned water chestnuts can be bought from most large supermarkets and delicatessens. Water chestnuts are not actually chestnuts, but the sweet root-bulb of an Asian marsh plant. The canned variety are ready peeled and have a good crunchy texture. They are bland tasting, so need to be combined with strong-tasting foods.

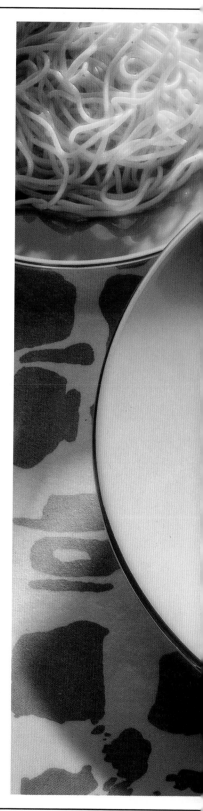

PIAZ AUR HARI MIRCH WALI BHINDI
(OKRA FRIED WITH ONION AND GREEN CHILLI)

0.30	£	130 cals

HOT

Serves 4

450 g (1 lb) fresh okra, or two 425 g (15 oz) cans okra in brine, drained

45 ml (3 tbsp) ghee or vegetable oil

1 medium onion, skinned and finely sliced

2 small green chillies

10 ml (2 tsp) ground cumin

2.5 ml ($\frac{1}{2}$ tsp) salt

freshly ground pepper

1 Wash the fresh okra and trim the ends. Dry well on absorbent kitchen paper. If using canned okra, rinse, drain and dry.

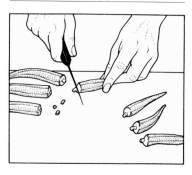

2 Heat the oil in a large, heavy-based frying pan or wok, add the onion and fry over moderate heat, stirring constantly, for about 5 minutes until turning golden.

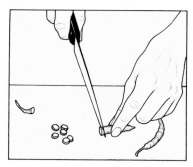

3 Meanwhile, trim the ends off the green chillies and cut the flesh into fine rings with a sharp knife. Remove as many seeds as you like, according to how hot the dish is to be.

4 Add the okra, chillies, cumin, salt and pepper to taste to the pan. Continue cooking over moderate heat, stirring constantly, for about 10–15 minutes. The fresh okra should be cooked but still quite crisp and the onions a deeper brown. The canned okra will become slightly sticky. Taste and adjust the seasoning, then turn into a warmed serving dish.

Menu Suggestion
Okra goes well with Khumbi Pullao (Mushroom Pilau) page 237 in a vegetarian menu. For meat eaters, the flavour of okra is especially good with lamb curries.

PIAZ AUR HARI MIRCH WALI BHINDI
Bhindi, translated as okra or ladies' fingers, are a long, thin tapering vegetable which are used extensively in Indian cooking. When trimming the ends in step 1, take care not to cut the flesh or a sticky substance will be released during cooking.

HARE SEM AUR NARIYAL
(GREEN BEANS WITH COCONUT)

0.30	£	200 cals

MILD

Serves 4

450 g (1 lb) French beans

salt and freshly ground pepper

450 g (1 lb) tomatoes

1 medium onion, skinned

115 g (4½ oz) desiccated coconut

45 ml (3 tbsp) ghee or vegetable oil

1 garlic clove, skinned and
   crushed

10 ml (2 tsp) garam masala

30 ml (2 tbsp) tomato purée

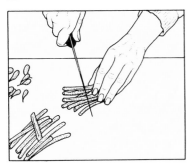

1 Top, tail and halve the French beans. Cook in a saucepan of boiling salted water for about 5 minutes or until just tender. Drain.

2 Roughly chop the tomatoes. Finely chop the onion. Place 100 g (4 oz) of the coconut in a measuring jug. Make up to 450 ml (¾ pint) with boiling water. Stir and leave to stand for 5 minutes. Strain through a sieve, pressing the coconut to squeeze out any liquid. Discard the contents of the sieve and reserve the coconut milk for later use.

3 Heat the ghee in a large, heavy-based frying pan, add the onion and fry gently for about 5 minutes until soft and lightly coloured.

4 Stir in the crushed garlic and garam masala and cook for 1–2 minutes, stirring. Add the coconut milk with the tomatoes, tomato purée and salt and pepper to taste. Bring to the boil, then boil the mixture rapidly, uncovered, for about 5 minutes.

5 Add the drained beans. Cook over gentle heat for 3–4 minutes, stirring occasionally, until heated through. Meanwhile, toast the remaining coconut under a preheated hot grill until golden. Taste and adjust seasoning, then turn into a warmed serving dish and sprinkle with the toasted coconut. Serve immediately.

Desserts

GINGER FRUIT SALAD

0.30*	86 cals

* plus 1 hour macerating

Serves 4

2 apricots

2 dessert apples

1 orange

241 ml (8½ fl oz) bottle low-calorie ginger ale

50 g (2 oz) white grapes, seeded

2 bananas

30 ml (2 tbsp) lemon juice

1 Prepare the fruits to be macerated. Plunge the apricots into a bowl of boiling water for 30 seconds. Drain and peel off the skin with your fingers.

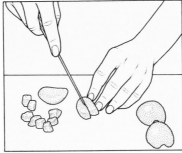

2 Halve the apricots, remove the stones and dice the flesh. Core and dice the apples, but do not peel them. Peel the orange and divide into segments, discarding all white pith.

3 Put the prepared fruits in a serving bowl with the ginger ale. Stir lightly, then cover and leave to macerate for 1 hour.

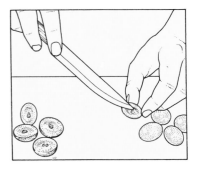

4 Cut the grapes in half, then remove the seeds by flicking them out with the point of a knife.

5 Peel and slice the bananas and mix them with the lemon juice to prevent discoloration.

6 Add the grapes and bananas to the macerated fruits. Serve in individual glasses.

Menu Suggestion
A refreshing end to any summer meal, Ginger Fruit Salad can also be topped with a spoonful of natural set yogurt.

GINGER FRUIT SALAD

If you wish to make this fruit salad in wintertime, then you can use dried apricots instead of the fresh ones suggested here. All the other fruits are available in winter.

Take a look at the wide choice of dried apricots at your local health food shop. The kind sold in packets in supermarkets are invariably bright orange in colour, which means that they are not necessarily naturally dried apricots—their good colour may come from an edible dye, so check the ingredients on the label before buying. Dried apricots sold loose in health food shops are a much better buy, especially the *hunza* variety, which are sun-dried and can be eaten just as they are, without soaking. Sun-dried apricots are often sold with their stones still in; these should be removed before using in fruit salads.

SUMMER FRUIT SALAD

| 1.20* | £ £ | 117–176 cals |

* plus 30 minutes cooling

Serves 4–6

100 g (4 oz) sugar
200 ml (7 fl oz) water
few fresh mint sprigs
1 strip of orange peel
225 g (8 oz) fresh strawberries
225 g (8 oz) fresh raspberries
1 small Ogen melon
30 ml (2 tbsp) orange-flavoured liqueur
30 ml (2 tbsp) finely chopped fresh mint
few whole fresh mint leaves, to decorate

1 Put the sugar in a heavy-based pan, add the water and heat gently for 5–10 minutes until the sugar has dissolved, stirring occasionally.

2 Add the mint sprigs and orange peel, then boil the syrup rapidly for 5 minutes, without stirring. Remove from the heat and leave for about 1 hour until completely cold.

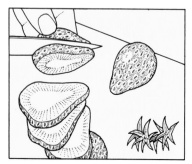

3 Meanwhile, prepare the fruit. Hull the strawberries, then slice them lengthways.

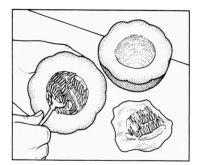

4 Leave the raspberries whole. Cut the melon in half, scoop out and discard the seeds.

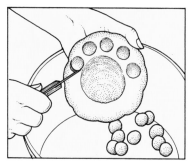

5 Cut the flesh into balls using a melon baller. Remove the mint sprigs and orange peel from the cold syrup, then stir in the liqueur and chopped mint.

6 Put the fruit in a serving bowl, pour over the syrup, then carefully fold together. Chill in the refrigerator for at least 30 minutes. Serve chilled, decorated with whole fresh mint leaves.

MELONS

The Ogen melon specified in this Summer Fruit Salad is available most of the year from specialist greengrocers and markets. The name 'Ogen' comes from the kibbutz in Israel where these melons were first grown.

Ogen melons are well worth looking for, because their flesh is very sweet—perfect for summer fruit salads, and also for winter desserts when other fresh fruits are scarce. Ogen melons are easily identified by their yellowy-green, stripy skins and their almost perfect round shape. Most Ogen melons are small enough for 1 serving, but large ones are also available which will serve 2–3 people. Both sizes are ideal for making into melon baskets—a pretty way to serve a fruit salad such as the one on this page. If you buy small Ogens, make individual baskets for each place setting; large Ogens, like honeydew melons, make spectacular table centrepieces.

To make a melon basket
1 Level the base of the melon so that it will stand upright.
2 With the tip of a sharp knife, score horizontally around the centre of the melon, keeping the line as straight as possible.
3 Cut down from the top of the melon to the scored line, working about 1 cm ($\frac{1}{2}$ inch) to one side of the centre.
4 Cut through the scored line on one side so that a wedge-shaped piece of melon is removed.
5 Repeat steps 3 and 4 so that both sides are removed.
6 Carefully scrape away the melon flesh inside the 'handle' left in the centre.
7 Scoop out and discard the seeds, then remove the flesh in the bottom half of the basket with a melon baller or sharp knife. Combine with the cut flesh from the reserved wedges.

LATE SUMMER PUDDING

| 0.20* | £ | ✳ | 271 cals |

* plus overnight chilling

Serves 6

450 g (1 lb) mixed fruits (e.g.
    blackcurrants, blackberries,
    redcurrants, raspberries)

30 ml (2 tbsp) water

150 g (5 oz) sugar

100–175 g (4–6 oz) white bread,
    thinly sliced

whipped cream, to serve

1 Strig the blackcurrants. Hull the blackberries. Place the fruits in a colander and wash under cold running water.

2 Stir the water and sugar together and bring slowly to the boil, add the fruits and stew gently for 5–10 minutes, until they are soft but retain their shape.

3 Cut the crusts from the bread and line the base and sides of a 900-ml (1½-pint) pudding basin with the slices so that there are no spaces between them.

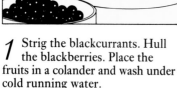

4 Pour in the fruit and completely cover with more slices of bread. Place a saucer with a weight on it on top of the pudding and refrigerate overnight. To serve, turn out on to a flat plate and serve with whipped cream.

SUMMER PUDDING

Summer pudding – made with freshly picked red and black fruits – is *the* traditional English pudding for hot summer days. Served outside at a summer lunch party, with lashings of fresh whipped cream, nothing could be more perfect.

The combination of fruits for summer pudding is a matter of personal choice and availability. Traditionally, two fruits should be used, and these are usually redcurrants and raspberries, although these days blackcurrants, blackberries, loganberries and strawberries are also often included.

If you have some juice left over when putting the fruit into the bread-lined basin, save it until serving time. When you turn the pudding out onto its serving plate, you may find that some of the bread slices show white, in which case spoon over reserved fruit juice to cover any gaps.

EARLY SUMMER PUDDING WITH CHANTILLY CREAM

0.30*	£ ✳*	451 cals*

* plus overnight chilling; freeze
pudding only; calories include Cream

Serves 4

450 g (1 lb) mixed redcurrants, cherries and raspberries
30 ml (2 tbsp) water
150 g (5 oz) sugar
100–175 g (4–6 oz) white bread, thinly sliced
15 ml (1 tbsp) Kirsch
150 ml (5 fl oz) double cream
½ an egg white
15 g (½ oz) icing sugar
vanilla flavouring

1 Strig the redcurrants. Stone the cherries. Hull the raspberries. Place the fruits in a colander and wash under cold water.

2 Cook the fruits as indicated in step 2, opposite. Line the pudding basin with bread as indicated in step 3.

3 Add the fruit and liqueur and cover with more slices of bread. Place a saucer with a weight on it on top of the pudding; refrigerate overnight.

4 Lightly whip the cream. In a separated bowl, whisk the egg white until stiff. Fold in the whipped cream. Sift the icing sugar into the bowl and then fold in with a few drops of vanilla. Chill.

5 To serve, turn the pudding out on to a flat plate and serve with the chantilly cream.

Menu Suggestion
Serve with Spicy Crab Dip
(page 27) and Vitello Tonnato
(page 60).

STRAWBERRY CREAM

| 0.15* | 79 cals |

* plus 1 hour chilling

Serves 6

100 g (4 oz) cottage cheese
150 ml ($\frac{1}{4}$ pint) natural yogurt
clear honey, to taste
700 g ($1\frac{1}{2}$ lb) fresh strawberries

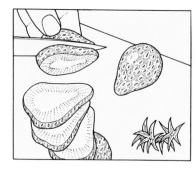

1 Work the cottage cheese in a blender or food processor until smooth. Alternatively, work through a fine wire sieve by pushing with the back of a metal spoon.

2 In a bowl, beat the cheese and yogurt together with honey to taste. Set aside.

3 Hull the strawberries and slice finely, reserving 6 whole ones to decorate.

4 Divide the sliced strawberries equally between 6 individual glasses or glass serving dishes.

5 Pour the cheese mixture over the strawberries and chill in the refrigerator for about 1 hour. Serve chilled, decorated with the reserved whole strawberries.

Menu Suggestion
Strawberry Cream is rich and creamy in flavour yet surprisingly low in calories. Serve as a special summertime dessert, with langues de chat or wholemeal shortbread biscuits.

BANANA WHIPS

| 0.20 | 208 cals |

Serves 4

2 egg whites

300 ml (½ pint) natural set yogurt

finely grated rind and juice of ½ orange

60 ml (4 tbsp) soft brown sugar

2 medium bananas

50 g (2 oz) crunchy breakfast cereal

1 Whisk the egg whites until standing in stiff peaks. Put the yogurt in a bowl and stir until smooth. Fold in the egg whites until evenly incorporated.

2 In a separate bowl, mix together the orange rind and juice and the sugar. Peel the bananas and slice thinly into the juice mixture. Fold gently to mix.

3 Put a layer of the yogurt mixture in the bottom of 4 individual glasses. Cover with a layer of cereal, then with a layer of the banana mixture. Repeat these 3 layers once more. Serve immediately.

Menu Suggestion
A quickly made dessert that appeals particularly to children of all ages.

SHERRIED APRICOT TRIFLE

1.00* | 573 cals

* plus cooling, setting and overnight chilling
Serves 8–10

410 g (14½ oz) can apricot halves in natural juice
127 g (4½ oz) packet orange- or tangerine-flavoured jelly
350 g (12 oz) Madeira cake
300 ml (½ pint) sherry
1 egg
2 egg yolks
25 g (1 oz) caster sugar
15 ml (1 tbsp) cornflour
450 ml (¾ pint) milk
300 ml (½ pint) double or whipping cream
few strips of angelica and some glacé cherries, to decorate

1 Drain the apricots and measure the juice. Make up the jelly according to packet instructions, using the apricot juice as part of the measured liquid. Leave in a cool place until cold and just beginning to set.

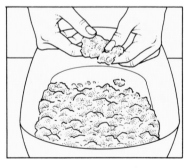

2 Meanwhile break up the cake with your fingers and place in the bottom of a glass serving dish. Pour over the sherry, place the apricots on top, reserving one for decoration, cover and leave to stand while making the custard.

3 Make the custard. Put the egg and egg yolks in a bowl with the sugar and whisk lightly together. Add the cornflour and a few tablespoons of the milk and whisk again until combined.

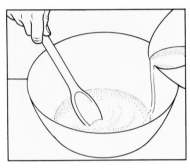

4 Scald the milk in a heavy-based saucepan. Pour on to the egg mixture, stirring constantly, then return the custard to the rinsed-out pan. Cook over low to moderate heat, stirring all the time until the custard thickens and coats the back of the spoon. Pour immediately into a bowl, cover the surface of the custard closely with cling film and leave until cold.

5 Pour the cold, setting jelly over the apricots in the serving dish, spreading it evenly, then chill in the refrigerator until set.

6 Pour the cold custard over the jelly, cover closely with cling film and chill overnight.

7 Whip the cream until stiff, then swirl or pipe over the trifle leaving the centre uncovered. Decorate with the remaining apricot, angelica 'stalks', and glacé cherry 'flowers'. Serve chilled.

SHERRIED APRICOT TRIFLE

Trifle is an old-fashioned English dish, traditionally served at Sunday tea time. Every English family has its own version, but the authentic English trifle which was so popular in Victorian days was a simple layered concoction of Madeira cake soaked in sherry, almond-flavoured macaroons or ratafias, a rich egg custard and a topping of thickly whipped cream. Today's modern trifle with fruit and jelly would have been frowned upon by the Victorians.

The essence of making a good trifle lies in using a large quantity of sherry for soaking the Madeira cake base. It may seem extravagant when you are making it, but unless you use the amount specified in the recipe, you will not get the proper 'boozy' flavour, which is vital to a really good special-occasion trifle like this.

BLACK FOREST TRIFLES

0.20	266 cals

Serves 4

350 g (12 oz) fresh cherries or 425 g (15 oz) can cherries

½ packet (4) trifle sponges or 75 g (3 oz) sponge cake

150 ml (¼ pint) soured cream

15 ml (1 tbsp) kirsch or orange-flavoured liqueur (optional)

1 egg white

15 ml (1 tbsp) caster sugar

chocolate curls, to decorate

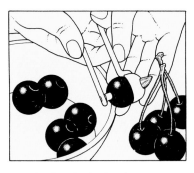

1 If using fresh cherries, stone them, then simmer them gently in a little water for 2–3 minutes. Leave to cool. If using canned cherries, drain and stone them, reserving the juice.

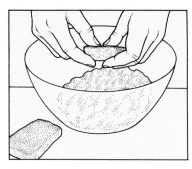

2 With your fingers, break the trifle sponges or cake roughly into a bowl. Stir in 30 ml (2 tbsp) of the soured cream and the liqueur, if using.

3 Divide the sponge mixture between 4 stemmed glasses. Spoon the cherries on top, with 120 ml (8 tbsp) of the cooking liquid or reserved juices from the canned cherries.

4 Whisk the egg white until stiff, add the sugar and continue whisking until very stiff. Fold into the remaining soured cream.

5 Top each glass with the soured cream mixture and chill in the refrigerator until ready to serve. Decorate with chocolate curls just before serving.

Menu Suggestion
Exceptionally quick to prepare, these trifles make a delicious dessert for Sunday lunch, or even Sunday tea when there's no time to bake something special.

BLACK FOREST TRIFLES
Kirsch is a cherry brandy which comes from the border area of France, Germany and Switzerland. The Germans call their version *kirschwasser*, and it is traditional to use it in the famous Black Forest chocolate and cherry gâteau, Schwarzwalder Kirschtorte. These Black Forest Trifles are a variation on the theme, so the addition of kirsch gives them authenticity.

YOGURT AND ORANGE WHIP

0.15	£	225 cals

Serves 4

2 eggs, separated

50 g (2 oz) caster sugar

finely grated rind of 1 orange

15 ml (1 tbsp) orange-flavoured liqueur

150 ml (¼ pint) natural yogurt

orange shreds, to decorate

1 In a deep bowl, whisk the egg yolks with half of the sugar until pale and creamy. Whisk in the orange rind and liqueur.

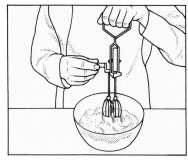

2 In a separate bowl, whisk the egg whites until stiff but not dry, add the rest of the sugar and whisk again until stiff.

3 Fold the yogurt into the egg yolk mixture, then fold in the whisked egg whites until evenly incorporated.

4 Spoon the mixture into 4 individual glasses and decorate with orange shreds. Serve immediately, or the mixture will begin to separate.

Menu Suggestion
Yogurt and Orange Whip makes the perfect last-minute cold dessert. Serve with sponge fingers or brandy snaps.

CRUNCHY PEARS IN CINNAMON AND HONEY WINE

| 1.00 | 230–344 cals |

Serves 4–6

60 ml (4 tbsp) white wine, vermouth or sherry

60 ml (4 tbsp) clear honey

5 ml (1 tsp) ground cinnamon

50 g (2 oz) margarine or butter

100 g (4 oz) wholewheat breadcrumbs (made from a day-old loaf)

50 g (2 oz) demerara sugar

4 ripe dessert pears

1 In a jug, mix together the wine, honey and half of the cinnamon. Set aside.

2 Melt the margarine in a small pan, add the breadcrumbs, sugar and remaining cinnamon and stir together until evenly mixed. Set aside.

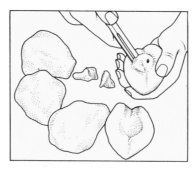

3 Peel and halve the pears. Remove the cores. Arrange the pear halves, cut side down, in a greased ovenproof dish and pour over the white wine mixture.

4 Sprinkle the pears evenly with the breadcrumb mixture and bake in the oven at 190°C (375°F) mark 5 for 40 minutes. Serve hot.

Menu Suggestion
Accompany with yogurt flavoured with grated orange rind.

CRUNCHY PEARS IN CINNAMON AND HONEY WINE

For this recipe you can use Comice dessert pears, but be careful that they are not too ripe—Comice pears very quickly become over-ripe and bruised, and cannot be stored for any length of time. Buy them on the day you intend to cook them and check they are perfect and *just* only ripe before purchase. Conference pears are a dual-purpose pear; they are ideal for cooking and eating, so these too can be used for this recipe.

RHUBARB BROWN BETTY

| 0.55 | ✳ | 228 cals |

450 g (1 lb) rhubarb

225 g (8 oz) fresh wholewheat
 breadcrumbs

50 g (2 oz) Barbados sugar

2.5 ml ($\frac{1}{2}$ tsp) ground ginger

50 ml (2 fl oz) fresh orange juice

300 ml ($\frac{1}{2}$ pint) natural yogurt,
 to serve

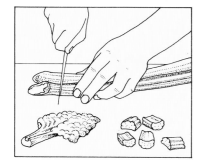

1 Trim the rhubarb and cut the
 stalks into short lengths. Put in
a greased 900 ml (1$\frac{1}{2}$ pint) ovenproof dish.

2 Mix the breadcrumbs, sugar
 and ground ginger together
and sprinkle over the fruit. Spoon
the orange juice over the crumbs.

3 Bake in the oven at 170°C
 (325°F) mark 3 for 40 minutes
or until the fruit is soft and the
topping browned. Serve hot or
cold, with natural yogurt.

Menu Suggestion
Rhubarb Brown Betty is equally
good served hot or cold, with
natural yogurt. Any leftover will
also reheat well.

AMERICAN CHOCOLATE PIE

1.00* £ 609 cals

* plus 30 minutes chilling and 4 hours setting

Serves 8

225 g (8 oz) shortcrust pastry (see page 348)

100 g (4 oz) sugar

50 g (2 oz) plain flour

pinch of salt

450 ml ($\frac{3}{4}$ pint) milk

50 g (2 oz) plain chocolate

3 egg yolks

40 g (1$\frac{1}{2}$ oz) butter or margarine

5 ml (1 tsp) vanilla flavouring

225 ml (8 fl oz) double or whipping cream

chocolate curls (see page 345) or grated chocolate, to decorate

1 Roll out the pastry on a lightly floured surface and use to line a 23-cm (9-inch) loose-bottomed fluted flan tin or ring placed on a baking sheet. Crimp edges of pastry and refrigerate for 30 minutes.

2 Prick the base of the pastry case then bake blind in the oven at 200°C (400°F) mark 6 for 10–15 minutes until set. Remove paper and beans and bake for a further 5–10 minutes until lightly coloured. Leave to cool.

3 While the pastry case is cooling, mix the sugar with the flour and salt in a large saucepan and stir in the milk.

4 Break the chocolate into small pieces and add to the pan. Heat gently until the chocolate has melted, stirring continuously.

5 Whisk until the chocolate and milk are blended, then increase the heat and cook for about 10 minutes, stirring constantly. Remove saucepan from heat.

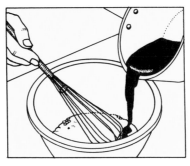

6 Beat the egg yolks and whisk in a small amount of the hot chocolate sauce.

7 Slowly pour the egg mixture into the saucepan, stirring rapidly. Cook over low heat stirring, for 10–15 minutes, until the mixture is very thick and creamy. Do not allow to boil.

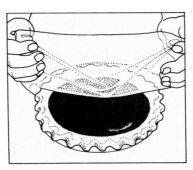

8 Remove from the heat. Stir in the fat and vanilla flavouring and pour into the cold pastry case. Cover to prevent a skin forming and refrigerate for about 4 hours until set.

9 Just before serving, whip the cream lightly and spread it evenly over the chocolate filling. Decorate the top with chocolate curls or grated chocolate. Serve the pie chilled.

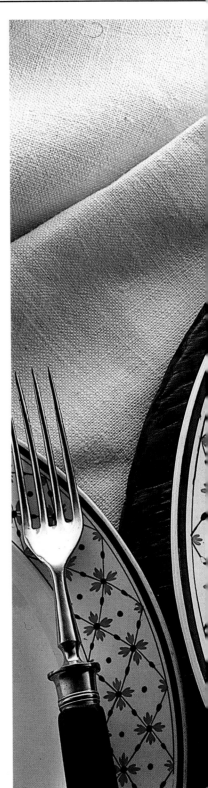

LIME MERINGUE PIE

1.35* ☐ £ 520 cals

* plus 30 minutes chilling

Serves 6

200 g (7 oz) shortcrust pastry (see page 348)

2 limes

75 g (3 oz) granulated sugar

45 ml (3 tbsp) cornflour

2 eggs, separated

knob of butter

125 g (4 oz) caster sugar

lime slices, to decorate (optional)

pouring cream, to serve

1 Roll out the pastry on a floured work surface and use to line a 20.5-cm (8-inch) flan ring. Refrigerate for 30 minutes. Bake blind in the oven at 200°C (400°F) mark 6 for 10–15 minutes.

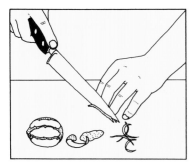

2 Pare a few strips of lime peel, shred finely, blanch in boiling water for 1 minute, drain, cool.

3 Finely grate the remaining rind from the limes into a small saucepan. Strain the juice, make up to 300 ml (½ pint) with water and add to the pan with the granulated sugar. Heat gently to dissolve the sugar.

4 Blend the cornflour with 30 ml (2 tbsp) water to a smooth paste. Add some of the heated liquid and stir. Return to the pan and boil for 2 minutes, stirring all the time. Cool slightly, then beat in the egg yolks and butter. Pour into the warm pastry case.

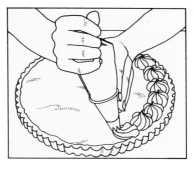

5 Whisk the egg whites until stiff, then fold in the caster sugar. Spread a thin layer of meringue over the pie, then pipe the rest around the edge.

6 Bake in the oven at 150°C (300°F) mark 2 for about 45 minutes until the meringue is crisp and lightly browned.

7 Decorate with the shredded lime rind and slices (if using). Serve the pie warm, with cream.

BAKEWELL PUDDING

| 0.45 | £ | 659–933 cals |

Serves 4–6

225 g (8 oz) frozen puff pastry, thawed, or shortcrust pastry (see page 348)

45 ml (3 tbsp) red jam

175 g (6 oz) ground almonds

100 g (4 oz) caster sugar

50 g (2 oz) unsalted butter

3 eggs, beaten

1.25 ml ($\frac{1}{4}$ tsp) almond flavouring

pouring cream or custard, to serve

1 Roll out the pastry on a floured surface and use to line a 900-ml (1½-pint) oval pie dish.

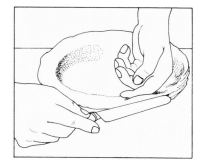

2 Knock up the edge of the pastry in the pie dish with the back of a knife.

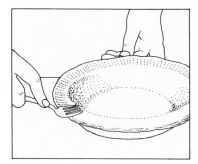

3 Mark the rim with the prongs of a fork. Brush the jam over the base. Chill in the refrigerator while making the filling.

4 Make the filling. Beat the almonds with the sugar, butter, eggs and almond flavouring.

5 Pour the filling over the jam and spread it evenly. Bake in the oven at 200°C (400°F) mark 6 for 30 minutes or until the filling is set. Serve warm or cold, with pouring cream or custard.

BAKEWELL PUDDING

This rich pudding was first created by the cook at an inn in Bakewell, Derbyshire in 1859. It is still made in the town today, according to a secret recipe. Our version is like the original, and not to be confused with the similar but drier Bakewell tart, which is made with bread or cake crumbs.

OLD-FASHIONED TREACLE TART

| 1.00 | £ | 528–721 cals |

Serves 4–6

150 g (6 oz) plain flour

pinch of salt

40 g (1½ oz) caster sugar

50 g (2 oz) butter or block margarine

25 g (1 oz) lard

15–30 ml (1–2 tbsp) iced water

225 g (8 oz) golden syrup

finely grated rind and juice of 1 lemon

75 g (3 oz) fresh white breadcrumbs

a little beaten egg or milk, to glaze

whipped cream, to serve

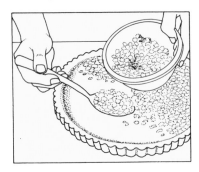

1 Place the flour and salt into a bowl, then stir in the sugar. Rub in half the butter or margarine with the lard until the mixture resembles fine breadcrumbs. Add enough iced water to mix to a firm dough.

2 Gather the dough together with your fingers and form into a ball, then roll out on a floured surface and use to line a 20.5-cm (8-inch) loose-bottomed flan tin. Reserve the pastry trimmings. Chill in the refrigerator while making the filling.

3 Make the filling. Warm the golden syrup in a heavy-based pan with the remaining butter and the lemon rind and juice.

4 Sprinkle the breadcrumbs evenly over the base of the pastry case, then slowly pour in the melted syrup.

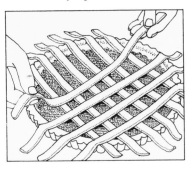

5 Make strips from the reserved pastry trimmings and place these over the tart in a lattice pattern, brushing the ends with water to stick them to the pastry case. Glaze with a little beaten egg or milk.

6 Bake in the oven at 190°C (375°F) mark 5 for about 25 minutes until the filling is just set. Serve warm, with whipped cream.

TREACLE

You may wonder why recipes for treacle tart always contain golden syrup rather than treacle. The explanation is quite simple. Treacle is the syrup which is left in the sugar refining process when the sugar has been crystallised; in the seventeenth century, when West Indian sugar cane was first refined to make sugar, treacle was unrefined and recipes for treacle tart such as this one would have used black treacle rather than syrup. It was not until the late nineteenth century that treacle itself was refined to make the golden syrup which is so popular today. As tastes changed, recipes which had originally used treacle began to specify syrup instead.

COLLEGE PUDDINGS

| 0.50 | £ | 473 cals |

Serves 4

100 g (4 oz) shredded suet

100 g (4 oz) fresh white breadcrumbs

50 g (2 oz) sultanas

50 g (2 oz) raisins

pinch of ground cinnamon

pinch of ground cloves

pinch of grated nutmeg

50 g (2 oz) sugar

2.5 ml ($\frac{1}{2}$ tsp) baking powder

pinch of salt

2 eggs, beaten

custard sauce, to serve (see page 352)

1 Mix the suet with the bread-crumbs and add the fruit, spices, sugar, baking powder and salt. Mix very well together, then stir in the eggs.

2 Pour into four greased dariole moulds or small individual foil dishes placed on a baking tray and bake in the oven at 180°C (350°F) mark 4 for about 30 minutes. Turn out and serve hot with custard.

FUDGY NUT PIE

| 1.35 | £ £ ✳ | 607 cals* |

* excluding ice cream; 702 cals with
50 g (2 oz) ice cream

Serves 8

225 g (8 oz) shortcrust pastry (see
page 348)

50 g (2 oz) plain chocolate, broken
into small pieces

50 g (2 oz) butter or margarine

175 g (6 oz) caster sugar

75 g (3 oz) light soft brown sugar

100 ml (4 fl oz) milk

75 g (3 oz) corn syrup or golden
syrup

5 ml (1 tsp) vanilla flavouring

1.25 ml ($\frac{1}{4}$ tsp) salt

3 eggs

100 g (4 oz) chopped mixed nuts

icing sugar, to decorate

vanilla ice cream, to serve

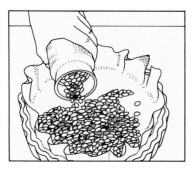

1 Roll out the pastry on a
floured work surface and use to
line a 23-cm (9-inch) flan dish or
fluted flan ring placed on a baking
sheet. Bake blind in the oven at
200°C (400°F) mark 6 for 10–15
minutes until set. Set aside to cool.

2 While the pastry case is cooling, put the chocolate and fat
in a large heatproof bowl standing
over a pan of simmering water.
Heat gently until melted.

3 Remove bowl from the pan
and add the remaining ingredients, except for the chopped nuts.
Beat with a wooden spoon until
well mixed, then stir in the nuts.

4 Pour the filling into the pastry
case and bake in the oven at
180°C (350°F) mark 4 for 45–60
minutes or until puffy and golden.
Dredge with icing sugar. Serve
hot or cold with ice cream.

FUDGY NUT PIE

Rich and nutty, this pie has a
definite 'American' flavour.
Corn syrup is a popular ingredient in American pies and
desserts. A by-product of sweetcorn, it is similar to golden syrup
but has a thinner consistency and
lighter flavour. Look for it in
delicatessens and large supermarkets if you want to give your
pie an authentic flavour.
Americans use unsweetened
'baker's' chocolate for dessert
making and baking, but this is
very difficult to obtain outside
the U.S. Instead, use a good-
quality plain chocolate: French
and Belgian varieties are the
least sweet and have good
melting qualities.

Magic Chocolate Pudding

0.45	£	241–362 cals

Serves 4–6

50 g (2 oz) butter or margarine

75 g (3 oz) caster sugar

2 eggs, separated

40 g (1½ oz) self raising flour

25 ml (5 tsp) cocoa powder

350 ml (12 fl oz) milk

1 Cream the fat and sugar together until light and fluffy, then beat in the egg yolks.

2 Sift the flour and cocoa powder together over the creamed mixture, then beat in until evenly mixed. Stir in the milk. Whisk the egg whites until stiff and fold into the mixture.

3 Pour into a greased 1-litre (1¾-pint) ovenproof dish. Bake in the oven at 180°C (350°F) mark 4 for 35–45 minutes until the top is set and spongy to the touch. This pudding will separate into a custard layer with a sponge topping. Serve hot.

MAGIC CHOCOLATE PUDDING

This delicious chocolate pudding, which is a great hit with children, is called 'magic' because it separates magically during baking into a rich chocolate sauce at the bottom and a sponge cake on top.

BAKED RUM AND RAISIN CHEESECAKE

| 1.40* | 🎩 £ £ ✳ | 452 cals |

* plus 1 hour cooling

Serves 8

75 g (3 oz) raisins

75 ml (5 tbsp) dark rum

225 g (8 oz) self-raising flour

5 ml (1 tsp) bicarbonate of soda

5 ml (1 tsp) cream of tartar

75 g (3 oz) butter

rind of 1 lemon

150 ml ($\frac{1}{4}$ pint) soured cream

125 g (4 oz) cottage cheese

125 g (4 oz) full-fat soft cheese

2 eggs, separated

50 g (2 oz) caster sugar

150 ml ($\frac{1}{4}$ pint) double cream

15 ml (1 tbsp) icing sugar,
   to decorate

1 Put the raisins and rum in a saucepan and bring to the boil. Turn off the heat and leave to cool for 15 minutes.

2 Meanwhile, sift the flour into a bowl with the bicarbonate of soda and cream of tartar. Rub in the butter.

3 Grate in the lemon rind, using the finest side of the grater. Bind to a smooth dough with the soured cream, then use to line a greased 25 cm (10 inch) flan dish.

4 In a bowl, beat together the cottage and cream cheeses. Stir in the rum and raisins.

5 In a separate bowl, whisk the egg yolks and caster sugar until pale and fluffy. Whisk in the double cream, and continue whisking until the mixture is the consistency of lightly whipped cream. Fold into the cheese, rum and raisin mixture.

6 Whisk the egg whites until stiff and fold into the mixture. Pour it into the prepared pastry case and bake in the oven at 180°C (350°F) mark 4 for about 1 hour. Turn off the heat and leave to cool in the oven for 15 minutes. Remove from the oven and cool for a further 45 minutes.

7 Cut into slices and dust with icing sugar.

Menu Suggestion
Serve this traditional, rich cheesecake after a light main course such as grilled steak, chops or Minted Lamb Grill (page 102).

FRUIT AND NUT CRUMBLE

| 1.05 | £ ✳* | 410 cals |

* freeze at the end of step 4

Serves 4

100 g (4 oz) plain wholewheat flour

pinch of salt

50 g (2 oz) butter or margarine

100 g (4 oz) demerara sugar

25 g (1 oz) walnuts, finely chopped

3 cooking pears

1 large cooking apple

30 ml (2 tbsp) redcurrant jelly

finely grated rind and juice of
1 lemon

1 Mix the flour and salt in a bowl. Add the butter or margarine and rub in until the mixture resembles fine breadcrumbs. Stir in half the sugar and the walnuts. Set aside.

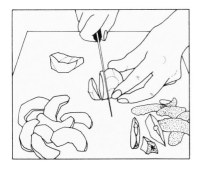

2 Peel and quarter the pears and apple. Remove the cores, then slice the flesh thinly.

3 In a bowl, mix the redcurrant jelly and the lemon rind and juice with the remaining sugar. Add the sliced fruit and fold gently to mix.

4 Turn the fruit into an oven-proof dish and sprinkle the crumble mixture over the top. Leave in a cool place or the refrigerator until ready to cook (overnight if convenient).

5 Bake in the oven at 180°C (350°F) mark 4 for 40 minutes or until the fruit feels soft when pierced with a skewer and the crumble topping is crisp and golden. Serve hot.

Menu Suggestion
This nutty pear and apple crumble is a filling family pudding. Serve with pouring cream, custard or ice cream.

COFFEE CHEESECAKE

1.00*	✳	380 cals

* plus 2–3 hours chilling

Serves 8

50 g (2 oz) butter, melted

175 g (6 oz) gingernut biscuits, finely crushed

15 ml (1 tbsp) gelatine

45 ml (3 tbsp) cold water

15 ml (1 tbsp) instant coffee powder

30 ml (2 tbsp) coffee-flavoured liqueur

300 ml (½ pint) boiling water

150 g (5 oz) soft brown sugar

450 g (1 lb) curd cheese

300 ml (10 fl oz) whipping cream

coffee beans, to decorate

1 Lightly oil a 20-cm (8-inch) loose-bottomed deep cake tin or spring-release cake tin.

2 Stir the butter into the crushed biscuits. Press firmly into the base of the tin. Refrigerate for 30 minutes until set.

3 Sprinkle the gelatine on to the cold water. Leave to soak for 10 minutes.

4 Stir the coffee and coffee liqueur into the boiling water. Add the soaked gelatine, stirring until dissolved. Stir in the sugar.

5 Put the coffee mixture and curd cheese into a blender and work until just smooth. Leave until beginning to set then lightly whip the cream and fold half into the cheese mixture.

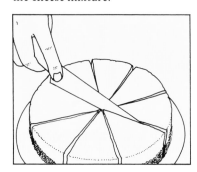

6 Turn the mixture into the prepared tin and refrigerate for 2–3 hours or until set. When set, remove from the tin. To serve, cut into eight, pipe a cream whirl on top of each slice and decorate with coffee beans.

ALTERNATIVE DECORATIONS

For even better effect, buy sugar coffee beans, available from high-class confectioners. Alternatively, thin chocolate leaves or squares would look attractive and taste good.

QUICK CHERRY CHEESECAKE

| 1.00* | ✳ | 699–1049 cals |

* plus 2–3 hours chilling

Serves 4–6

65 g (2½ oz) unsalted butter, melted

150 g (5 oz) digestive biscuits, crushed

225 g (8 oz) full fat soft cheese

2.5 ml (½ tsp) vanilla flavouring

60 ml (4 tbsp) icing sugar, sifted

300 ml (10 fl oz) double cream

400-g (14-oz) can cherry pie filling

1 Stir the melted butter into the crushed biscuits and mix well, then press into the base and sides of a 22-cm (8½-inch) fluted flan dish. Refrigerate for 30 minutes.

2 Put the cheese into a bowl and beat until soft and creamy, then beat in the vanilla flavouring and icing sugar.

3 Whip the cream until it holds its shape, then fold into the cheese until evenly blended.

4 Spoon the mixture into the biscuit base and level the surface. Refrigerate for 30 minutes.

5 Spoon the pie filling over the top of the cheesecake. Refrigerate for 2–3 hours to set.

BLACKCURRANT SORBET ▶

| 0.30* | £ | ✳ | 120 cals |

* plus 6 hours freezing, 1 hour cooling and 30 minutes standing

Serves 6

450 g (1 lb) fresh blackcurrants, washed and stringed

100 g (4 oz) caster sugar

finely grated rind and juice of $\frac{1}{2}$ a lemon

60 ml (4 tbsp) blackcurrant-flavoured liqueur (optional)

2 egg whites, stiffly whisked

fresh mint sprigs, to decorate

1 Cook the blackcurrants with 60 ml (4 tbsp) water until soft. Push through sieve to form purée.

2 Dissolve sugar in 300 ml ($\frac{1}{2}$ pint) water over low heat, add lemon rind; boil for 10 minutes. Cool for 1 hour. Add lemon juice; strain into bowl. Stir blackcurrant purée and liqueur, if using, into cooled syrup. Pour into a shallow freezer container and leave for 3 hours.

3 Transfer mixture to a chilled basin and break up with a fork. Fold in egg whites. Return to freezer for 3 hours. 30 minutes before serving, refrigerate to soften. Decorate with mint.

MIXED BERRY SORBET

| 0.30* | £ | ✳ | 117 cals |

*plus 6 hours freezing, 1 hour cooling and 30 minutes standing time

Serves 6

225 g (8 oz) strawberries

225 g (8 oz) redcurrants

150 ml ($\frac{1}{4}$ pint) and 30 ml (2 tbsp) water

100 g (4 oz) caster sugar

150 ml ($\frac{1}{4}$ pint) sparkling white wine

2 egg whites

3 Stir the wine and fruit purée into the cooled syrup. Pour into a shallow freezer container and leave for 3 hours.

4 Transfer frozen mixture to a chilled basin and break up with a fork. Whisk the egg whites until stiff and fold into the mixture. Return to the freezer for 3 hours. 30 minutes before serving, re-frigerate to soften.

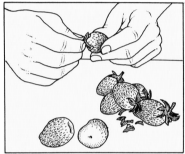

1 Hull the strawberries. Then remove the stalks from the red-currants and place the fruit in a saucepan with 30 ml (2 tbsp) water. Cook for about 10 minutes until soft. Push the blackcurrants and strawberries through a sieve to form a purée.

2 Dissolve the sugar in 150 ml ($\frac{1}{4}$ pint) water over low heat and boil gently for 10 minutes. Leave to cool for 1 hour.

FRUIT SORBETS

Fresh strawberries and black-currants are specified here, although it is not absolutely essential to use these two fruits if they are not readily available. Frozen redcurrants can be used instead of fresh—and they need not be defrosted before using. Blackcurrants or even white-currants can be used as a sub-stitute for the redcurrants, and raspberries, loganberries or blackberries as a substitute for the strawberries. As long as the fruit is unblemished and fully ripe, the sorbet is bound to look and taste good.

PRALINE ICE CREAM

0.50* 🄳 £ £ ✳ 393 cals

* plus 45 minutes cooling, 9 hours freezing and 30 minutes softening

Serves 6

50 g (2 oz) whole unblanched almonds

50 g (2 oz) granulated sugar

300 ml (½ pint) milk

1 vanilla pod

1 egg

2 egg yolks

75 g (3 oz) caster sugar

200 ml (7 fl oz) double cream

coarsely grated plain chocolate, to decorate (optional)

1 Place the almonds and granulated sugar in a heavy-based pan. Heat slowly until the sugar caramelises, turning occasionally.

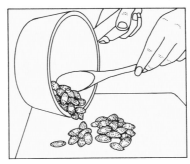

2 Pour the mixture on to an oiled baking sheet to cool and harden for about 15 minutes.

3 Use a mouli grater, blender or food processor to grind the cooled praline to a powder.

4 Bring the milk and vanilla pod to the boil, take off the heat and leave to infuse for 15 minutes.

5 Beat the egg, egg yolks and caster sugar until pale in colour, strain in the milk, stir, and return to the saucepan. Cook slowly for about 10 minutes until the custard coats the back of a wooden spoon—do not boil. Cool completely for 30–40 minutes. Lightly whip the cream and fold into the custard.

6 Freeze the mixture for about 3 hours until mushy. Beat well, then fold in the praline powder. Spoon into a freezer container and freeze for about 6 hours until firm.

7 Transfer to the refrigerator to soften for 30 minutes before serving. Serve scooped into glasses and decorated with coarsely grated chocolate, if liked.

PRALINE

Praline is a French confection made by cooking almonds and sugar together until the sugar caramelises, then crushing the set mixture to a powder. This recipe for Praline Ice Cream uses white praline, although brown praline can also be used. Brown praline has a stronger flavour than white; they are both made in exactly the same way, the only difference is that for brown praline almonds in their skins are used, whereas white praline uses blanched almonds.

TUTTI FRUTTI ICE CREAM

| 0.45* | 🫕 | £ £ | ✳ | 475–593 cals |

* plus 2–3 hours soaking, 30 minutes cooling and 5 hours freezing

Serves 8–10

| 90 ml (6 tbsp) dark rum |
| 50 g (2 oz) sultanas |
| 50 g (2 oz) stoned dates |
| 50 g (2 oz) glacé cherries |
| 50 g (2 oz) dried plump apricots |
| 568 ml (1 pint) milk |
| 1 vanilla pod or a few drops of vanilla flavouring |
| 6 egg yolks |
| 175 g (6 oz) caster sugar |
| 600 ml (20 fl oz) double cream |

1 Pour the rum into a screw-top jar or a bowl. Add the sultanas, then roughly snip the dates, cherries and apricots into the jar or bowl. Make sure all the fruit is coated with rum. Cover and leave to macerate for 2–3 hours shaking or tossing occasionally until the rum is absorbed.

2 Meanwhile, make the ice cream. Put the milk and vanilla pod or flavouring into a heavy-based saucepan and bring almost to the boil. Remove from the heat, cover and leave to infuse for 15 minutes.

3 Beat the egg yolks and sugar together in a bowl until thick and pale, stir in the milk and strain back into the saucepan.

4 Cook the custard gently over a low heat, stirring all the time, until it coats the back of a wooden spoon. Do not boil or it will curdle. Cover and leave the custard for about 30 minutes until completely cold.

5 Pour into a chilled, shallow freezer container and freeze for about 2 hours until mushy.

6 Turn the frozen mixture into a large, chilled basin and mash with a whisk or fork.

7 Lightly whip the cream and fold into the mixture with the macerated fruit. Return to the freezer and freeze for 3 hours, or until required, until firm.

8 Allow to soften for about 30 minutes in the refrigerator before serving.

——————— VARIATION ———————

For a short-cut version of this ice cream, you can use a 425 g (15 oz) can of custard instead of making the egg custard as here. With vanilla flavouring added and the heady flavour of fruit macerated in rum, no-one will guess the custard came out of a can! If you are making the ice cream with children in mind, add 25 g (1 oz) chocolate polka dots to the mixture in stage 7 when adding the macerated fruit.

Teatime Treats/ Baking

LEMON CREAM GÂTEAU

0.50*	✳*	304–405 cals

* plus 30–40 minutes cooling; freeze without lemon decoration

Serves 6–8

100 g (4 oz) plain flour

pinch of salt

4 eggs

175 g (6 oz) caster sugar

finely grated rind and juice of 1 lemon

90 ml (6 tbsp) lemon curd

100 g (4 oz) low-fat soft cheese

45 ml (3 tbsp) single cream

15 ml (1 tbsp) icing sugar

crystallised lemon slices, to decorate

1 Sift the flour and salt into a bowl and set aside.

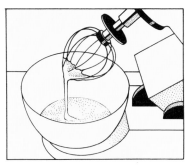

2 Beat the eggs and sugar in a tabletop electric mixer until thick enough for the beaters to leave a trail behind when lifted.

3 Fold in the sifted flour, lemon rind and juice; then immediately turn into a buttered 20.5 cm (8 inch) cake tin. Bake in the oven at 190°C (375°F) mark 5 for 20–25 minutes. Turn the cake out onto a wire rack. Leave the cake until completely cold, about 30–40 minutes.

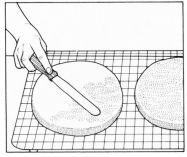

4 Split the cake in half and spread the cut side of each half with 45 ml (3 tbsp) lemon curd. Whip the cheese and cream together with the icing sugar, then sandwich the cakes together with about one-third of the mixture, between the lemon curd.

5 Place the cake on a serving plate and swirl the remaining cheese and cream mixture over the top and sides. Decorate with lemon slices and chill in the refrigerator until serving time.

Menu Suggestion
Whisked sponges are so quick to make once you know how, and make perfect last-minute desserts or coffee morning treats when sandwiched together with yummy fillings like this one.

LEMON CREAM GÂTEAU
Making a whisked sponge in a tabletop electric mixer is by far the quickest and easiest method. Whisked sponges are fatless; they rely on lots of air to make them light and fluffy in texture, and beating in air is hard work and time-consuming. Tabletop electric mixers have heavy-duty motors which can beat in large amounts of air in a relatively short time; with a hand-held electric whisk or a balloon whisk, you will find the only way to incorporate so much air is to whisk the mixture over hot water. This is a successful method, but it can take anything up to 20 minutes before the whisk leaves a ribbon trail behind it when lifted, and then you must continue whisking off the heat until the mixture is cold before folding in the flour.

ALMOND AND CHERRY CAKE

| 1.25* | 🍴 | £ £ | ✳* | 497 cals |

* plus 1–2 hours chilling; freeze after stage 5

Serves 10

275 g (10 oz) glacé cherries

65 g (2½ oz) self-raising flour

225 g (8 oz) unsalted butter, softened

225 g (8 oz) caster sugar

6 eggs, beaten

pinch of salt

175 g (6 oz) ground almonds

2.5 ml (½ tsp) almond flavouring

icing sugar, to decorate

1 Grease a deep 23-cm (9-inch) cake tin. Line with greaseproof paper and grease the paper.

2 Dust the cherries lightly with a little of the flour. Arrange in the bottom of the tin.

3 Put the butter and sugar into a bowl and beat together until pale and fluffy. Beat in the eggs a little at a time, adding a little of the flour if the mixture shows signs of curdling.

4 Sift in remaining flour with salt and add the almonds and almond flavouring.

5 Turn the mixture into the pre-pared tin. Bake in the oven at 180°C (350°F) mark 4 for 1 hour. Cover with greaseproof paper if browning too quickly. Leave in the tin for 1–2 hours to cool. Sift icing sugar on top to decorate.

ALMONDS

The moist fragrance of this delicious Almond and Cherry Cake comes from the ground almonds blended into the mixture. Rich in fat and protein, almonds boost the calorie content of each slice, but they also give an inimitably moist texture.

Ready ground almonds are the easiest to use for this recipe; you can buy them in small 50 g (2 oz) packets or in larger quantities. Beware of buying too many at once as they tend to loose their flavour once the pack is opened. The best flavour comes from nuts that you have ground freshly yourself. Buy them either in the shell or shelled but unblanched. Remove the shells with nut crackers, then soak the kernels in boiling water until the skins will slip off easily. Grind the almonds in a blender or food processor (beware of over-grinding the almonds and turning them to a paste if you use a food processor), or use a nut mill.

FROSTED COCONUT CAKE

| 2.00* | £ | ✱ | 580 cals |

* plus 1 hour cooling

Serves 8

50 g (2 oz) shelled hazel nuts

225 g (8 oz) butter or block margarine

225 g (8 oz) caster sugar

5 eggs

2.5 ml ($\frac{1}{2}$ tsp) vanilla flavouring

125 g (4 oz) plain flour

125 g (4 oz) self-raising flour

40 g ($1\frac{1}{2}$ oz) desiccated coconut

75 g (3 oz) icing sugar

shredded coconut

1 Grease a 20-cm (8-inch) base measurement spring-release cake tin. Base-line with grease-proof paper and grease the paper.

2 Spread the nuts out on a baking sheet and brown in the oven at 200°C (400°F) mark 6 for 5–10 minutes. Put into a soft tea towel and rub off the skins. Chop the nuts finely.

3 Put the butter and sugar into a bowl and beat until pale and fluffy. Whisk 4 whole eggs and 1 yolk together and gradually beat into the creamed mixture with the vanilla flavouring.

4 Fold the flours into the mixture with 25 g (1 oz) desiccated coconut, and half the nuts.

5 Turn the mixture into the prepared tin and bake in the oven at 180°C (350°F) mark 4 for 45 minutes.

6 Meanwhile prepare a meringue topping: whisk the egg white until stiff and gradually sift and whisk in the icing sugar, keeping the mixture stiff. Fold in the remaining desiccated coconut and chopped hazel nuts.

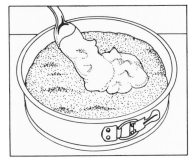

7 Spoon the meringue topping on to the cake, after it has cooked for 45 minutes, and scatter with shredded coconut.

8 Return to the oven for 20–30 minutes or until a skewer comes out of the cake clean. Check after 15 minutes and cover with a layer of greaseproof paper if it is over-browning. Leave to cool completely for 1 hour.

SQUIDGY CHOCOLATE MOUSSE CAKE

| 1.30* | 🍶 £ £ ✳* | 586 cals |

* plus 1 hour cooling and overnight chilling; freeze after stage 6

Serves 8

| 450 g (1 lb) plain chocolate |
| 45 ml (3 tbsp) orange-flavoured liqueur |
| 9 eggs, 5 of them separated |
| 150 g (5 oz) caster sugar |
| 100 g (4 oz) unsalted butter, softened |
| blanched julienne strips of orange rind and grated chocolate, to decorate |

1 Grease a 20-cm (8-inch) spring-release tin, line with greaseproof paper and grease the paper.

2 Break half the chocolate into a heatproof bowl and place over a pan of simmering water and stir gently until the chocolate has melted. Stir in 15 ml (1 tbsp) liqueur, then remove from the heat.

3 Using an electric whisk, whisk five egg yolks and the sugar together until thick and creamy, then beat in the butter a little at a time until smooth. Beat in the melted chocolate until smooth.

4 Whisk the five egg whites until stiff, then fold into the chocolate mixture. Turn into the prepared tin and bake in the oven at 180°C (350°F) mark 4 for 40 minutes until risen and firm. Leave the cake to cool in the tin for 1 hour.

5 Make the top layer: melt the remaining chocolate as before, then stir in the remaining liqueur. Remove from the heat, cool for 1–2 minutes. Separate the remaining eggs and beat the egg yolks into the chocolate mixture. Whisk the egg whites until stiff, then fold into the chocolate mixture.

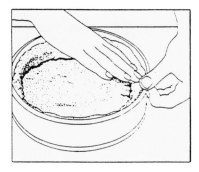

6 Press the crust down on the baked cake with your fingers and pour the top layer over it. Refrigerate overnight.

7 The next day, remove the cake carefully from the tin and put on to a serving plate.

8 Arrange blanched strips of orange rind around the outside edge and decorate with grated chocolate.

SAFFRON CAKE

2.30* ☐ £ £ ✳ 393 cals

* plus 2 hours infusing and 1–2 hours cooling

Serves 8

25 g (1 oz) fresh yeast or 7.5 ml (1½ tsp) dried yeast plus a pinch of sugar

150 ml (¼ pint) tepid milk

450 g (1 lb) strong plain flour

5 ml (1 tsp) salt

50 g (2 oz) butter, cut into pieces

50 g (2 oz) lard, cut into pieces

175 g (6 oz) currants

finely grated rind of ½ a lemon

25 g (1 oz) caster sugar

2.5 ml (½ tsp) saffron strands, infused for 2 hours in 150 ml (¼ pint) boiling water

1 Grease a 20-cm (8-inch) round cake tin. Crumble the fresh yeast into a bowl and cream with the milk, until smooth. If using the dried yeast and sugar, sprinkle the mixture into the milk and leave in a warm place for 15 minutes until frothy.

2 Sift the flour and salt into a bowl. Rub in the butter and lard until the mixture resembles fine breadcrumbs. Stir in the currants, lemon rind and sugar.

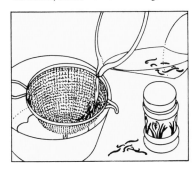

3 Strain the saffron infusion into a pan and warm slightly. Add to the dry ingredients with the yeast liquid and beat well.

4 Turn the dough into the prepared tin, cover with a clean cloth and leave to rise in a warm place for about 1 hour until the dough comes to the top of the tin.

5 Bake in the oven at 200°C (400°F) mark 6 for 30 minutes. Lower the oven temperature to 180°C (350°F) mark 4 and bake for a further 30 minutes. Turn out on to a wire rack to cool for 1–2 hours.

APPLE PARKIN

| 2.05* | £ | ✳ | 632–766 cals |

* plus 2 hours cooling and 2 days storing

Serves 6–8

450 g (1 lb) eating apples
25 g (1 oz) butter or margarine
225 g (8 oz) plain flour
10 ml (2 tsp) baking powder
15 ml (3 tsp) ground ginger
50 g (2 oz) lard
125 g (4 oz) medium oatmeal
75 g (3 oz) caster sugar
125 g (4 oz) golden syrup
125 g (4 oz) black treacle
1 egg, beaten
30 ml (2 tbsp) milk
Cheddar cheese wedges, to serve

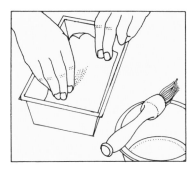

1 Grease and base line a 1.7 litre (3 pint) loaf tin.

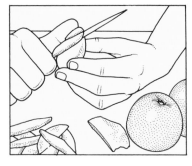

2 Peel, quarter, core and chop the apples. Melt the butter in a small saucepan, add the apples, cover and cook gently until soft. Beat the apples to a purée, then cool for about 1 hour.

3 Sift the flour, baking powder and ginger into a large bowl. Rub in the lard; stir in the oatmeal and sugar.

4 Warm the syrup and treacle together until evenly mixed, then stir into the dry ingredients with the apple purée, egg and milk. Stir until evenly blended.

5 Turn into the prepared tin and bake in the oven at 180°C (350°F) mark 4 for about 1½ hours, covering loosely with foil after 45 minutes.

6 Turn out of the tin and cool on a wire rack for 1 hour. Wrap and store for 2 days before eating.

7 Slice and accompany with wedges of Cheddar cheese.

Menu Suggestion

Yorkshire parkin is traditionally eaten with cheese, and the apples in this version go particularly well with it. Try it with a sharp Cheddar or Wensleydale for an unusual packed lunch.

FRUITY GINGERBREAD

| 1.05* | £ | ✳ | 164 cals |

* plus cooling and 3 days maturing

Makes about 20 squares

75 g (3 oz) butter or margarine
100 g (4 oz) dark soft brown sugar
100 g (4 oz) golden syrup
100 g (4 oz) black treacle
225 g (8 oz) medium oatmeal
100 g (4 oz) self-raising flour
50 g (2 oz) mixed dried fruit
10 ml (2 tsp) ground ginger
pinch of salt
175 ml (6 fl oz) milk
butter for spreading (optional)

1 Melt the butter or margarine in a saucepan with the sugar, syrup and treacle.

2 Meanwhile, in a bowl, mix together the oatmeal, flour, fruit, ginger and salt.

3 Pour the melted mixture into the bowl, then the milk. Beat vigorously with a wooden spoon until all the ingredients are evenly combined.

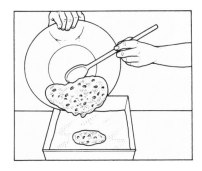

4 Pour the mixture into a greased and base-lined 25 cm (10 inch) square baking tin. Bake in the oven at 180°C (350°F) mark 4 for 45 minutes or until firm to the touch.

5 Allow to cool in the tin for 10 minutes, then turn out on to a wire rack and leave until cold. Wrap in cling film or foil and store in an airtight tin for 3 days until the gingerbread is really moist.

6 Unwrap and cut into about 20 squares. Spread with butter if liked.

Menu Suggestion
This moist gingerbread, with its added fruit, is bound to be popular with children. Pop a slice or two in the school packed lunch box.

HONEY HAZEL NUT TWIST

| 3.00* | ⬚ | ✳ | 139–166 cals |

*plus 1 hour cooling
Serves 10–12

| 60 ml (4 tbsp) tepid milk |
| 15 ml (1 tbsp) caster sugar |
| 5 ml (1 tsp) dried yeast |
| 175 g (6 oz) strong plain flour |
| 2.5 ml (½ tsp) salt |
| 75 g (3 oz) butter or block margarine, cut into pieces |
| 1 egg, size 6 |
| 50 g (2 oz) shelled hazel nuts |
| 75 ml (5 tbsp) thick honey |

1 Lightly oil a bowl and set aside. Grease an 18-cm (7-inch) straight-sided sandwich tin. Base-line with greaseproof paper and grease the paper.

2 Put the milk into a small bowl and sprinkle over 5 ml (1 tsp) sugar and the yeast. Leave in a warm place for about 15 minutes until frothy.

3 Sift the flour with the salt into a bowl and rub in 50 g (2 oz) of the butter until the mixture re-sembles fine breadcrumbs. Stir in the remaining sugar and beat in the egg and the yeast liquid to form a soft dough.

4 Turn out on to a lightly floured surface and knead until smooth, about 5 minutes. Put into the oiled bowl, cover with oiled cling film and leave to double in size, about 45 minutes.

5 Meanwhile, spread the nuts out on a baking sheet and brown in the oven at 200°C (400°F) mark 6 for 5–10 minutes. Put into a soft tea towel and rub off the skins. Grind the nuts in an electric blender or food processor.

6 Beat the remaining butter with the nuts and 45 ml (3 tbsp) honey to a smooth paste.

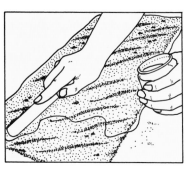

7 Turn the dough out on to a floured surface, knead again lightly and roll out to an oblong 61 × 20 cm (24 × 8 inch). Spread the honey over the surface.

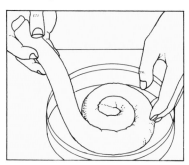

8 Roll up from a long edge. Coil into the prepared sandwich tin. Press down firmly. Cover as in stage 4 and leave to double in size, about 45 minutes.

9 Bake at 200°C (400°F) mark 6 for 20–25 minutes until golden brown. Turn out on to a plate and brush at once with the remaining honey, warmed. Cool for 1 hour before serving.

DROP SCONES

| 0.20 | £ | 55–62 cals |

Makes 16–18

150 g (5 oz) self-raising flour

pinch of salt

15 ml (1 tbsp) caster sugar

15 ml (1 tbsp) vegetable oil

1 egg, beaten

150 ml ($\frac{1}{4}$ pint) milk

lard or oil, for greasing

1 Sift the flour, salt and sugar into a bowl, then add the oil, egg and milk. Stir with a wooden spoon to combine to a thick batter the consistency of double cream.

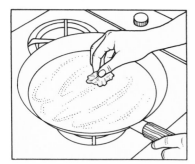

2 Grease a girdle or heavy frying pan with a little lard or oil and place over moderate heat until hot.

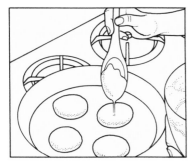

3 Drop spoonfuls of the mixture from the point of the spoon on to the pan, keeping them well apart to allow for spreading.

4 Cook over moderate heat for 2–3 minutes until bubbles rise and burst all over the surface of the scones and the undersides are golden brown. Turn them over with a palette knife and cook for 2–3 minutes on the other side.

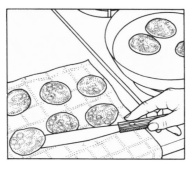

5 Transfer the cooked scones to a clean tea-towel and fold the cloth over to enclose them while making the remaining scones. Serve hot, as soon as all the scones are made.

Menu Suggestion

Made from storecupboard ingredients, Drop Scones are ideal for an impromptu tea party. Serve them with butter and jam or honey. You can also serve them for a dessert with golden or maple syrup and lashings of whipped cream!

DROP SCONES

Drop scones take their name from the fact that the mixture is 'dropped' from the mixing spoon onto the hot girdle. In the old days, they were made on the kitchen range and every cook had a girdle or griddle which was made of thick iron (an excellent conductor of heat) and had a half-hoop handle for easy lifting. Girdles can still be found in antique shops, and some kitchen specialist shops sell modern equivalents, but a heavy-based frying pan can be used with equal success.

APRICOT OAT CRUNCHIES

0.45*	✳	166 cals

* plus overnight soaking and 1 hour cooling

Makes 12

75 g (3 oz) self-raising wholewheat flour

75 g (3 oz) rolled (porridge) oats

75 g (3 oz) demerara sugar

100 g (4 oz) margarine or butter

100 g (4 oz) dried apricots, soaked in cold water overnight

1 Lightly grease a shallow oblong tin measuring 28 × 18 × 3.5 cm (11 × 7 × 1½ inches).

2 Mix together the flour, oats and sugar in a bowl. Rub in the margarine until the mixture resembles breadcrumbs.

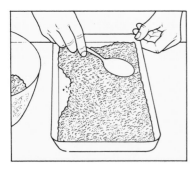

3 Spread half the mixture over the base of the prepared tin, pressing it down evenly.

4 Drain and chop the apricots. Spread them over the oat mixture in the tin.

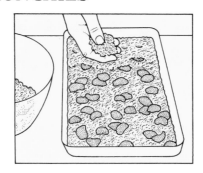

5 Sprinkle over the remaining crumb mixture and press down well. Bake in the oven at 180°C (350°F) mark 4 for 25 minutes until golden brown. Leave in the tin for about 1 hour until cold. Cut into bars to serve.

Menu Suggestion
These delicious chewy teatime bars will keep well for several days if tightly wrapped in kitchen foil and kept in an airtight tin.

WHOLEWHEAT DATE AND BANANA BREAD WITH HAZELNUTS

| 2.00* | ✳* | 266–319 cals |

* plus cooling; freeze without honey and nut decoration

Serves 10–12

225 g (8 oz) stoned dates, roughly chopped

5 ml (1 tsp) bicarbonate of soda

300 ml (½ pint) milk

275 g (10 oz) self-raising wholewheat flour

100 g (4 oz) margarine or butter

75 g (3 oz) shelled hazelnuts, chopped

2 medium ripe bananas

1 egg, beaten

30 ml (2 tbsp) clear honey

1 Put the dates in a pan with the soda and milk. Bring slowly to boiling point, stirring, then remove from the heat and leave until cold.

2 Put the flour in a large bowl and rub in the margarine with your fingertips. Stir in the hazelnuts, reserving 30 ml (2 tbsp) for decorating.

3 Peel and mash the bananas, then add to the flour mixture with the dates and the egg. Beat well to mix.

4 Spoon the mixture into a greased and base-lined 1 kg (2 lb) loaf tin. Bake in the oven at 180°C (350°F) mark 4 for 1–1¼ hours until a skewer inserted in the centre comes out clean.

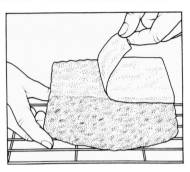

5 Leave the loaf to cool in the tin for about 5 minutes. Turn out, peel off the lining paper and place the right way up on a rack.

6 Heat the honey gently, then brush over the top of the loaf. Sprinkle the reserved hazelnuts on to the honey and leave until cold. Store in an airtight tin if not eating immediately.

Menu Suggestion
This lovely moist bread, more like a dense cake in texture, can be served unbuttered at tea time.

> **WHOLEWHEAT DATE AND BANANA BREAD WITH HAZELNUTS**
>
> It may seem unusual to have a cake made entirely without sugar, but this is because of the high proportion of dates used in this recipe. Dates have the highest natural sugar content of all dried fruit and if used in cakes such as this one there is no need to add extra sugar.

REFRIGERATOR COOKIES

0.35*	37–49 cals

* plus overnight chilling and about 30 minutes cooling; freeze dough at the end of step 3

Makes 30–32

225 g (8 oz) plain flour
5 ml (1 tsp) baking powder
100 g (4 oz) butter or margarine
175 g (6 oz) caster sugar
5 ml (1 tsp) vanilla flavouring
1 egg, beaten

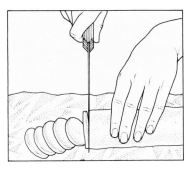

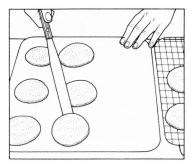

4 To shape and bake: slice the roll very thinly into as many cookies as required. (The remainder of the roll can be wrapped again in the foil and returned to the refrigerator for up to 1 week.)

5 Place the cookies well apart on a buttered baking sheet. Bake in the oven at 190°C (375°F) mark 5 for 10–12 minutes until golden.

6 Leave the cookies to settle on the baking sheet for a few minutes, then transfer to a wire rack and leave to cool completely. Store in an airtight tin if not eating immediately.

Menu Suggestion

Serve for children's teas or when unexpected visitors call. Keep a roll of dough in the refrigerator ready to make a batch of cookies at a moment's notice.

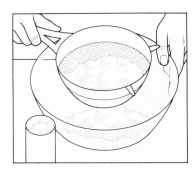

1 Sift the flour and baking powder into a bowl. Rub in the fat until the mixture resembles breadcrumbs, then add the sugar and stir until evenly combined.

2 Add the vanilla flavouring and egg and mix to a smooth dough with a wooden spoon.

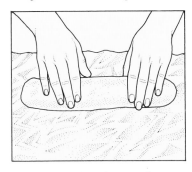

3 Turn the dough onto a large sheet of foil and shape into a long roll about 5 cm (2 inches) in diameter. Wrap in the foil and chill in the refrigerator overnight.

VARIATIONS

Walnut: add **50 g (2 oz) very finely chopped walnuts** with the sugar in step 1.
Coconut: add **50 g (2 oz) desiccated coconut** with the sugar in step 1.
Sultana: add **50 g (2 oz) very finely chopped sultanas** with the sugar in step 1.
Chocolate: add **50 g (2 oz) very finely grated plain chocolate** with the sugar in step 1.
Spicy: omit the vanilla and sift in **10 ml (2 tsp) ground mixed**

spice with the flour in step 1.
Lemon: omit the vanilla and add the **finely grated rind of 1 lemon** with the sugar in step 1.
Ginger: omit the vanilla and sift in **7.5 ml (1½ tsp) ground ginger** with the flour in step 1.
Cherry: add **50 g (2 oz) very finely chopped glacé cherries** with the sugar in step 1.
Orange: omit the vanilla and add the **finely grated rind of 1 orange** with the sugar in step 1.

ICED MARZIPAN ROUNDS

1.10* 🥄 £ £ ✳* 235 cals

* plus 1 hour chilling, 30 minutes cooling and 30 minutes drying; freeze at the end of step 7

Makes 8

100 g (3½ oz) plain flour	
40 g (1½ oz) caster sugar	
40 g (1½ oz) butter or margarine	
1 egg yolk	
75 g (3 oz) yellow-coloured marzipan	
25 ml (5 tsp) dark rum	
30 ml (2 tbsp) apricot jam	
100 g (4 oz) icing sugar	
yellow food colouring	

1 Mix the flour and caster sugar together in a bowl. Add the butter or margarine and rub in with the fingertips. Mix to a smooth dough with the egg yolk and 5 ml (1 tsp) water.

2 Turn the dough out on to a floured surface and knead lightly until smooth. Wrap and chill in the refrigerator for 30 minutes.

3 On a floured surface, roll the dough out to a 3 mm (⅛ inch) thickness. With a 5 cm (2 inch) round fluted cutter, stamp out 16 rounds. Prick with a fork.

4 Place the rounds on lightly greased baking sheets, then chill again in the refrigerator for 30 minutes.

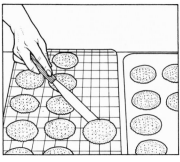

5 Bake in the oven at 180°C (350°F) mark 4 for about 20 minutes. Transfer to a wire rack and leave to cool for 30 minutes.

6 Knead the marzipan with a few drops of the rum. Lightly dust the work surface with a little icing sugar, then roll the marzipan out to a 3 mm (⅛ inch) thickness. With the same 5 cm (2 inch) cutter, stamp out 8 rounds.

7 Brush each cooled biscuit with a little melted apricot jam. Sandwich together with a marzipan round in the centre.

8 Beat the icing sugar and remaining rum together. Divide in half. Add a few drops of colouring to one half.

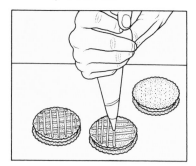

9 Using small piping bags and plain nozzles, lattice the rounds with icing. Leave to dry for at least 30 minutes.

10 Serve immediately, or store in a single layer in airtight containers for up to 5 days.

Menu Suggestion
Make these unusual sandwich biscuits for a special teatime treat. The children will love the marzipan and apricot jam filling, and the different coloured icings make the biscuits really eye-catching.

ICED MARZIPAN ROUNDS
Marzipan is another name for almond paste, made from sugar, almonds and egg white. The origins of marzipan are uncertain. Some say it was introduced to Europe by the Arabs, others that it was created by a French order of nuns. Literally translated, the word marzipan means 'St Mark's bread', and European cuisines have a fair number of marzipan specialities connected with religious festivals. Sicily and Germany, for example, have marzipan fruits and vegetables at Christmas, whereas England has simnel cake at Easter and iced cakes with marzipan are served for Christmas and other celebrations. Marzipan can be either yellow or white.

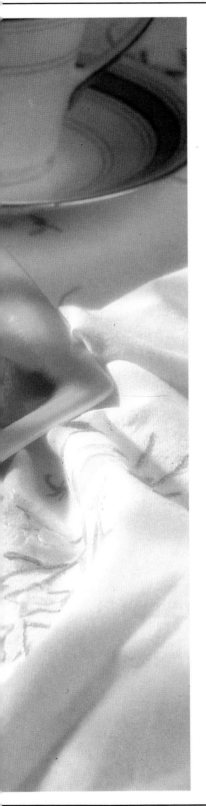

LEMON AND LIME COOKIES

0.55* £ ✳* 91 cals

* plus 30 minutes cooling; freeze after cooling in step 4

Makes 24

100 g (4 oz) butter or margarine

100 g (4 oz) caster sugar

1 egg yolk

50 g (2 oz) full-fat soft cheese

175 g (6 oz) plain flour

finely grated rind of 1 small lemon

15 ml (1 tbsp) lemon juice

20 ml (4 tsp) lime marmalade

1 Put the butter or margarine and caster sugar in a bowl and beat together until light and fluffy.

2 Beat in the egg yolk, cheese, flour, lemon rind and juice, until a soft mixture is formed.

3 Place small spoonfuls of the mixture on to greased baking sheets, allowing room for spreading.

4 Bake in the oven at 190°C (375°F) mark 5 for about 17 minutes or until light brown. Transfer to a wire rack to cool for at least 30 minutes. Store in an airtight container for up to 3 days.

5 Melt the marmalade in a small saucepan and brush over the cookies, to glaze. Leave to set for 5 minutes before serving.

Menu Suggestion

With their tangy marmalade glaze, these cookies taste good at any time of day, but they go particularly well with morning coffee.

LEMON AND LIME COOKIES

These cookies are simplicity itself to make, almost like craggy, flat rock cakes. If you have a food processor, steps 1 and 2 can be made in moments, by working all the ingredients together in one go.

You will find the flavours of lemon and lime together are just perfect with a morning cup of coffee, but children may find the lime a little too tangy. You can of course use ordinary orange marmalade for the glaze if you wish, together with the finely grated rind of 1 small orange and 15 ml (1 tbsp) orange juice, instead of the lemon in the recipe. This makes the cookies quite a bit sweeter.

CHOCOLATE VIENNESE FINGERS

| 1.00* | £ | ✳* | 89 cals |

* plus 1 hour cooling and setting;
freeze after stage 5

Makes about 18

125 g (4 oz) butter or block
  margarine

25 g (1 oz) icing sugar

75 g (3 oz) plain chocolate

125 g (4 oz) plain flour

1.25 ml ($\frac{1}{4}$ tsp) baking powder

15 ml (1 tbsp) drinking chocolate
  powder

few drops of vanilla flavouring

1 Grease two baking sheets. Put the butter into a bowl and beat until pale and soft, then beat in the icing sugar.

2 Break 25 g (1 oz) chocolate into a heatproof bowl and place over simmering water. Stir until the chocolate is melted, then remove from heat and leave to cool for 10 minutes.

3 When the chocolate is cool, but not thick, beat it into the creamed mixture.

4 Sift in the flour, baking powder and drinking chocolate. Beat well, adding a few drops of vanilla flavouring.

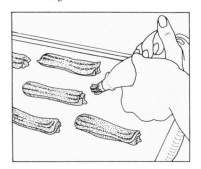

5 Spoon into a piping bag fitted with a medium star vegetable nozzle and pipe finger shapes about 7.5 cm (3 inches) long on to the prepared baking sheets, allowing room between each for the mixture to spread. Bake at 190°C (375°F) mark 5 for 15–20 minutes until crisp and pale golden. Cool on a wire rack for 30 minutes.

6 When the fingers are cold, break the remaining 50 g (2 oz) chocolate into a heatproof bowl. Stand the bowl over a pan of simmering water and stir until the chocolate has melted. Remove from the heat and dip both ends of the fingers into the melted chocolate. Leave on a wire rack for 30 minutes to set.

USEFUL INFORMATION
AND
BASIC RECIPES

Kitchencraft and Cooking Techniques

Busy cooks deserve good tools to work with, and pleasant surroundings in which to work. Often having to conjure up meals in minutes, today's cook can turn to many gadgets and appliances which will make life in the kitchen a lot easier. There is no magic about cooking. There is a simple explanation for everything that happens when a food is cooked. The section on cooking techniques will help you understand why you should cook foods in a certain way in order to prepare them with speed and ease.

KITCHENCRAFT AND COOKING TECHNIQUES

A good cook, like a good craftsman, needs good tools. This does not mean necessarily buying the most expensive equipment and the latest gadgets. It means working out which utensils will be most useful to your style of cooking and eating and making the most of them to save you both time and effort.

The most sophisticated kitchen equipment is of little use if you do not have a well planned kitchen. Kitchens need to have method in the way in which they are laid out; they should save you time and effort in your daily domestic routine; and they should be pleasing places in which to work.

Ingredients for an easy-to-work-in kitchen
Here are some guidelines for use when planning your kitchen. They are aimed at making your time in the kitchen as pleasant and as efficiently spent as possible.
- Make your kitchen physically comfortable, as well as practical to work in.
- Plan activity centres in your kitchen so that they are well positioned in relation to one another.
- These activity centres need, ideally, to be arranged in the logical order for preparing a meal ie store cupboard, preparation area/work surface, and serving/eating area.
- Wherever possible avoid narrow gaps between work surfaces and appliances.
- Store cupboards/larders should allow for the storage of all types of food: dry cupboards for canned and packaged goods; ventilated racks for vegetables and firm fruits. You will also need a refrigerator and a freezer.

- For the work surface choose a durable material, that will withstand fairly hard wear. There should be a good chopping surface, either separate or inset into the work top—wood or some other non-slip surface. Marble and slate are also good as they can serve the dual purpose of chopping surface and a perfect pastry-making surface.
- If possible, keep all large pieces of equipment on the work surface so that they are to hand when you need them. Keep all small preparation equipment and gadgets close to the work surface.
- Storage of saucepans, baking tins etc, depends very much on how your cooking facilities are arranged. If you have a split level cooker, with a hob set into the work surface, then it is advisable to have a cupboard close to the hob; most wall-mounted ovens are set into a housing unit, with drawer space underneath for storing pans and tins.

With a free-standing cooker, keep all cooking pots and pans, colanders and sieves as close as possible in adjacent cupboards, or hang them on the wall or suspend them from hooks on the ceiling or units.
- Serving and eating areas should, ideally, be close to one another.
- You will also need good lighting, effective ventilation, and a comfortable floor. You need a good source of light directed on all principle work areas. An extractor hood or fan is essential, both to remove excess cooking smells and steam, and to keep the kitchen as cool as possible. The kitchen floor should obviously look nice, but it should also be comfortable to stand on and easy to keep clean. Choose a non-slip surface, which is easy on the feet.

COOKING EQUIPMENT

Choosing the right piece of equipment for a particular job will, in the end, save you time. It pays to invest in good quality equipment as it lasts longer and does the job consistently better than inferior equipment. Here is a guide to the types of equipment you will need to produce delicious food efficiently.

SAUCEPANS

Good pans are usually expensive, but they last; cheap saucepans do not last and often give off toxic metal substances into the food, which is not desirable.

The best pans to use are those made of metals that conduct heat well: copper, cast iron, or good-quality enamelled steel or stainless steel are good choices. Saucepans with a non-stick finish are excellent for boiling milk and making sauces, but they are not such a good choice for some of the 'tougher' cooking jobs. Long term they are a bad buy for the non-stick coating starts to wear off. The heavier the pan the safer it is to use; solid based pans are also less prone to sticking. Handles are another important aspect to be considered when buying pans. If they are riveted they are much more secure than handles which have been screwed on.

Four saucepans of varying sizes, and one good-sized frying pan, is the minimum that you can probably get away with. In addition, most kitchens can make good use of one very large pan, with a handle fixed on either side; it is useful for cooking whole chickens and large pieces of gammon and can double as a preserving pan.

FRYING PANS

Deep frying pans are better than shallow ones; they will hold more food and there is less likelihood of liquids spitting and bubbling over. A lid is essential.

Omelette and pancake pans are by no means musts, but they do make the cooking of both these foods a great deal easier. The sides

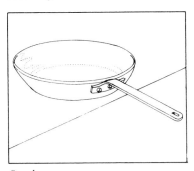

Omelette pan

of an omelette pan are curved and not too high, so that the omelette will roll up readily and fall onto the plate without breaking.

WOKS

A wok is a Chinese cooking utensil which is now very popular in the West as well. It looks like a curve-based large frying pan with two rounded handles and is traditionally made of cast iron though nowadays you can also buy stainless steel and non-stick ones.

Balance it on a metal collar directly over the heat, so that the wok can be moved backwards and forwards to ensure even cooking when stir frying. The wok is a very versatile cooking utensil. Food can be deep fried in it, and then drained on a semi-circular rack which clips on to the rim of the wok; this is very useful when you are frying food in batches. A small circular rack can be positioned in the centre of the wok and used as a steamer with a domed lid fitted neatly over the top.

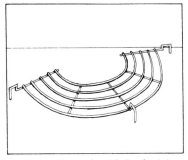

Semi-circular wok rack for draining

FISH KETTLE

A fish kettle is best for poaching whole, large fish. The long oval-shaped pan has handles at either end, and the draining rack that the fish lies on fits neatly inside. The shape of the kettle allows the fish to lie completely flat, without curling; once cooked, the fish can be lifted out easily on the rack, without any danger of it breaking or splitting. If the fish is to be eaten cold it is usually left in the fish kettle in its cooking liquid to cool, and then lifted out.

Choose good quality pans

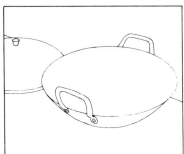

Cast iron wok

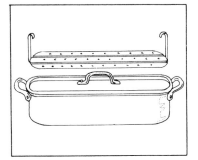

Fish kettle and rack

EGG POACHERS

If you like regular shaped poached eggs, then an egg poacher is the answer. A poacher consists of a base pan (rather like a deep frying pan) which you half fill with water

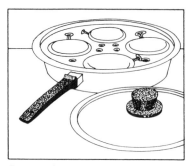

Egg poacher

and a tray containing small poaching cups that sits on top (these are often non-stick). A lid goes over the top of the pan while the eggs are poaching gently in the buttered cups.

BAKING TINS

Baking is a skill; it relies on the precision of the cook, good quality ingredients, and the right shape and size of tin. Even a straight-forward packet cake mix can turn out to be a flop if the wrong tin is used. Most recipes specify a particular size of tin, and this should always be used. Rich mixtures should be baked in strong tins; if the tin is too thin then the mixture will burn.

The greatest worry with baking tins is that of sticking; mixtures that are relatively high in fat are usually fairly safe, but those that contain little fat or are high in sugar, can be very difficult to turn out of a tin.

To line a tin really neatly takes time and patience. The perfect solution is to use baking tins with a non-stick surface; all the familiar shaped tins that are used in every-day baking are available with a non-stick lining. Here is a list of tins you will need for quick, easy baking:

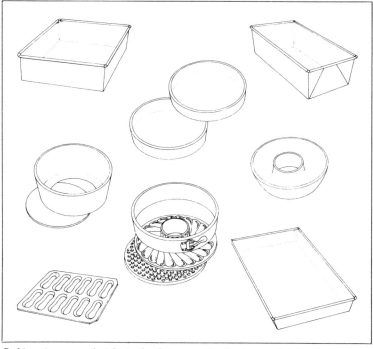

Baking tins: a sandwich tin, loaf tin, round cake tins, madeleine tins and a Swiss roll tin

BASIC TINS

Loaf tins—these come in 450 g (1 lb) and 900 g (2 lb) sizes. Use them for cakes and breadmaking.

Flan rings and tins—use a round tin with plain or fluted sides and a removable base for pastry flans.

Sandwich tins—these come in sizes 18–25.5 cm (7–10 inches) and are shallow, round tins with straight sides for making sandwich and layer cakes. (You can also use spring release tins.)

Swiss roll tins

Lining a deep tin for fruit cake

Standard cake tins—you will need 15-cm (6-inch), 16-cm (7-inch) and 17-cm (8-inch) tins.

KNIVES

Good sharp knives are the cook's most important tools. Knives vary enormously in quality, the best ones have taper ground blades—the blade, bolster and tang is forged from one piece of steel, and the handle is fixed securely in place with rivets.

Cook's knives are the classic knives used by all top chefs and professional cooks. They have strong, broad and very sharp blades, and the handles are firmly riveted to give added strength while chopping. Classic cook's knives have heavy handles, there-fore if they fall they land handle first, avoiding damage to the blade. The larger size cook's knives, those with blades between 15–20 cm (6–8 inches) long, are extremely versatile—they can be used for chopping, cubing, slicing, 'mincing', and crushing. Small

Two useful sizes of cook's knife

Boning knife

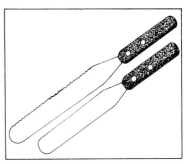

Two types of palette knife

Filleting knife

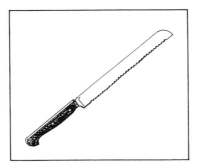

Bread knife with serrated edge

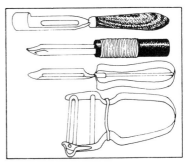

Varieties of potato peeler

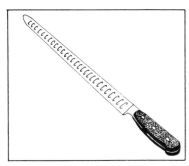

Fishmonger's knife

cook's knives, with blades about 10 cm (4 inches) long are very good for paring vegetables and shaping vegetable garnishes.

Filleting knives have a long, slim, pliable blade. Sharpness and flexibility are essential, as the blade has to follow the bones of the fish very closely. These knives are also useful for skinning.

Fishmonger's knives have a strong, rigid, scalloped blade. These are very heavy knives which make them ideal for cutting through the backbones of fish.

Boning knives have rigid, narrow, broad-backed blades, with very sharp points. They come in different lengths, depending on what they are going to be used to bone. The handles are indented and shaped to prevent your hand from slipping.

Carving knives come in many different styles and sizes. Knives suitable for carving large joints of meat are shaped like an elongated filleting knife; sturdy, but flexible towards the tip of the blade. Serrated knives tend to tear the texture of hot meat, and are best reserved for cutting cold joints.

A bread knife should have a fairly rigid blade, but it should be long enough to slice through the largest of loaves—many bread knives have serrated blades, and they tend to cause less crumbs than a plain-edged knife. Serrated knives can also cope with crisp crusts much better.

The palette knife gets its name from its artistic associations; it is the same shape as the knife that painters use to mix paint colour with oil. It has a long evenly-wide blade, which is extremely pliable. A palette knife is used primarily for spreading soft mixtures, such as icings, and for flipping foods such as pancakes.

Serrated palette knives are very useful for slicing sponges and other cakes into layers.

Potato peelers are not strictly speaking knives, but they do have a cutting blade and are a must for every kitchen.

CHOPPERS

Choppers have very heavy, deep rectangular blades; they are extremely strong and need to be used with care. They are blade-heavy and tend to drop forward when held. Choppers will cut through most bones, and they are particularly useful for cutting up oxtail. The cleaver is the Chinese equivalent of the chopper, but it is much more versatile; the blade is finer and sharper and can be used for chopping, slicing, 'mincing' and scraping, and for making vegetable garnishes.

SCISSORS

All-purpose kitchen scissors can be used for removing bacon rinds; splitting bread dough decoratively; roughly cutting parsley, chives and other herbs; removing the cores from kidneys.
Fish scissors have serrated blades, with one slightly longer than the other. Use for trimming fins and tails, and cutting through bones.
Poultry shears have a strong spring between the two blades, which makes them extremely robust. They are excellent for cutting through the bones and carcass of all poultry.

KITCHEN SCALES

There are basically two different types of kitchen scales: balance (the traditional variety) and spring balance. Long term, balance scales are a better buy as there is less that can go wrong; unlike spring balance scales they are not dependent on a spring.

Spring balance scales are extremely easy to use and fairly accurate. However, the needle on the dial occasionally gets knocked out of position, so it should be reset each time the scales are used. Some spring balance scales are designed to sit on the work surface, while others can be mounted on the kitchen wall. Unless you have very smooth and level kitchen walls, it is better to buy free-standing scales for accuracy.

Manual juice extractors

SQUEEZERS

Juice squeezers
Juice squeezers or citrus presses come in different shapes and sizes; some are manual and others are operated electrically. The basic principle behind all of them is exactly the same. A ridged dome of glass or plastic presses into the centre of the halved fruit, thus squeezing out the juice. Some of the juicers are hand held, which means that you hold them over a bowl; others have a container beneath the squeezer which collects the juice. Apart from those squeezers which will take halved grapefruits and oranges, there are also smaller ones.

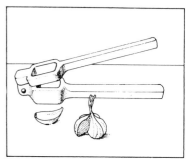

Garlic press

Garlic presses
These are the smallest squeezers of all. They look like small potato ricers, and work in a similar manner. Put the peeled clove of garlic into the press and squeeze down gently—if you squeeze very gently you just get the juice of the garlic—harder, you get the flesh.

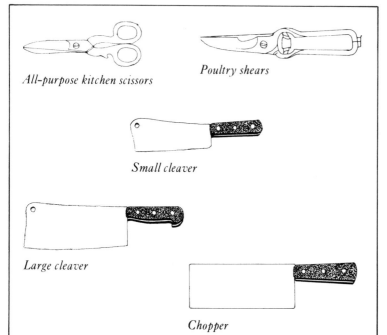

All-purpose kitchen scissors

Poultry shears

Small cleaver

Large cleaver

Chopper

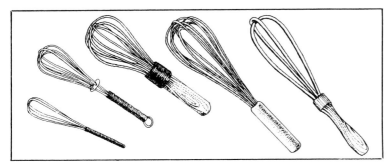

Balloon whisks are available in varying sizes for different tasks

WHISKS

Whisks and beaters cope with a variety of culinary tasks. There are three different kinds of hand whisks: balloon, coiled and rotary. **Balloon whisks** come in different sizes and weights and they are extremely effective. The large, lightweight, very round whisks are the best for egg whites—they are easy to handle and can be used at quite a speed. Slimmer, thicker ridged, and heavier balloon whisks are better for coping with thick sauces, choux pastry or semi-set ice cream mixtures. They will incorporate more air into a mixture than any other type of whisk, and they are extremely easy to clean. **Coiled whisks**, which look just as their name suggests, are cheaper than balloon whisks, but nowhere near as effective. You need to use a lot of effort for not much result. **Rotary whisks** have two four-bladed beaters, which are operated by a small handle. Although you need one hand to steady the whisk and one to turn the handle, it is a speedy and efficient way of whisking slack mixtures such as egg whites and thin sauces.

Electric whisks and whisk attachments

Hand-operated electric whisks, with two beaters like a rotary whisk, are very efficient. The

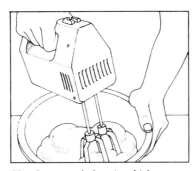

Hand operated electric whisk

beaters can be moved around the inside of a bowl or saucepan (non-stick) with relative ease. This is an advantage when making sauces.

The whisk attachment which goes with several food processors is not that effective; the size of the

beaters is relatively small and they cannot move freely through a mixture to incorporate a noticeable amount of air. It is reasonably effective with whisked cake mixtures, but one must not forget that the bowl of most food processors is relatively small. The whisk attachment on large electric mixers is particularly powerful; it is shaped like a squashed balloon whisk and reaches almost every part of the mixing bowl.

BLENDERS

Electric blenders, also called liquidisers, have become very much an integral part of the kitchen gadget scene. They are extremely labour saving. Some

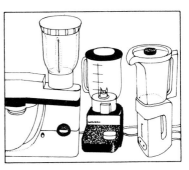

Different types of blender

blenders operate freely as a separate gadget, while others fit onto an electric food mixer. The only way in which they differ tends to be as far as capacity and speed are concerned; some are larger and faster than others. The blades in the base of the plastic or glass goblet rotate at a high speed, pulverising the ingredients inside. It is an invaluable gadget for liquidising soups, sauces, and fruit and vegetable purées, but it can also chop and grind ingredients to varying degrees. There is a hole in the lid of the blender, so ingredients can be dropped through the top while the blades are whirring.

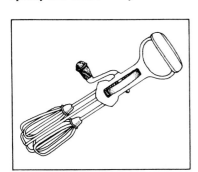

Rotary egg whisk

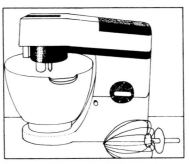

Electric mixer and whisk attachment

ELECTRIC MIXERS AND FOOD PROCESSORS

Electric mixers and food processors can tackle most of the day-to-day culinary tasks, and they are great labour-saving devices for those who are pushed for time and/or have a large family to feed.

The electric mixer

The large size electric mixers, or table mixers as they are often called, have very powerful motors, which can drive a variety of attachments such as: potato peelers, bean shredders and cream makers. The main disadvantage with the table mixer is that it is so bulky, and consequently takes up a lot of space, either on the work surface or in a cupboard. The bowl of the standard table mixer is very capacious, and will hold twice as much as most food processors.

The food processor

The food processor is a compact machine, which is primarily used for chopping, mincing, grinding and blending. It is simple to use, strong, and comparatively quiet. The plastic processor bowl fits over a spindle; the cutting, shredding and whisking attachments in turn fit over the spindle.

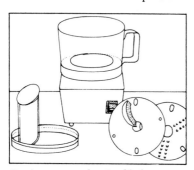

Food processor showing blades

The lid that fits over the bowl has a funnel through which food or liquid can be fed. When the machine is turned on, the cutting blade or other attachments move very fast — vegetables are chopped in 10 seconds, minced in

15 seconds, and puréed in 20 seconds. Food processors have revolutionsed some of our methods of preparation, for example, they are a great help when making pastry and bread doughs, soups, pâtés and terrines.

A word of warning: even though you can buy whisking attachments for food processors, they are not as effective as the beaters on a traditional electric table mixer.

MINCERS

This useful gadget quickly turns cooked or raw meat, fish and vegetables into tiny particles. It is an asset when using up leftover cooked food and is also excellent for preparing your own freshly minced meat at home.

Hand mincers are usually made from cast iron or a strong plastic. They fit firmly onto the work surface, either by means of small rubber suction pads or a screw clamp; the latter is the most secure, and the larger mincers are always fitted with a clamp. The handle on the mincer turns a 'screw' which pushes the food to be minced towards small cutting blades or extruding discs. The size of the perforations in the metal discs dictates the final texture of the minced food, which will either be fine, medium or coarse.

Mincer attachments can also be bought to fit into many table electric mixers.

PRESSURE COOKERS

Pressure cookers can save you a great deal of time. There are many different models available, but basically a pressure cooker looks like a heavy duty saucepan, with a domed lid. It has a weight on it which helps determine the level of pressure at which the food will cook and it also has a safety valve for steam to escape. It works on the principle of increasing the boiling temperature of water and then trapping the resultant steam. (This is achieved by means of added pressure.) Some models of

pressure cooker only operate under one pressure; however, the more recent models operate under three; so you can choose which pressure to use according to the type of food you are cooking.

The food is put into the base of the cooker with the appropriate amount of liquid; the lid is then firmly closed and the pan placed over the heat until steam comes through the vents. The necessary pressure weight is then added until a hissing noise is emitted; at this point the heat is turned down for the remainder of the cooking time. (This is always indicated in individual recipes.) After cooking, the pressure has to be released, either slowly or quickly, depending on the food inside. Most recent pressure cookers have an automatic setting on the lid, complete with a timer; this enables you to set both the cooking time and the speed at which pressure should be released.

The pressure cooker is particularly good for cooking the following types of foods:

STOCKS AND SOUPS

Meat—the less expensive, tougher cuts
Poultry and game (especially boiling fowl and casserole game)
Firm textured fish (pressure cooking eliminates the fishy smell)
Root vegetables, such as swedes
Pulses
Grain—brown rice
Steamed puddings—both sweet and savoury

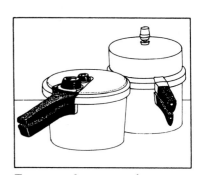

Two types of pressure cooker

Preserves — jams, marmalade, bottled fruits and chutney

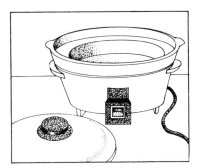

Crockpot or slow cooker

CROCKPOTS

Cooking in a crockpot (or slow-cooker) is an up-dated version of a traditional method of cooking: our great-grandmothers would leave casseroles cooking gently all day in the very coolest part of the kitchen range.

The crockpot consists of an earthenware bowl which sits neatly inside an outer casing. An electric element is fixed between the base of the bowl and the casing, and it operates on two settings — low (75 watts) and high (130 watts). When plugged in it only uses about the same amount of power as a light bulb.

As the name suggests, a crockpot or slow-cooker cooks foods very slowly; so slowly that it can cook food while you are out of the house. It saves time, money and fuel. With most recipes, all the ingredients can be put into the crockpot at once and then left to cook for several hours. The steam which condenses on the crockpot lid returns to the pot, thus keeping the food moist. Subtle, rich flavours develop during long, slow cooking, and it is ideal for the tougher and cheaper cuts of meat. The crockpot heats very gently so there is no risk of burning, sticking or boiling over; consequently it is very easy to clean. Food does not need to be stirred during cooking and it is important to resist the temptation to remove the lid while cooking. If it is removed,

heat is lost from the crockpot and it takes a long time for the original temperature to be regained.

General guidelines

- The crockpot needs pre-heating before food is added.
- Meat has a better appearance and flavour if it is lightly fried before it goes into the crockpot.
- Always bring stock and other liquids to the boil before adding them to the crockpot.
- Most foods should be started off on the High setting, and then reduced to Slow for the remainder of the time; chicken and pork to be 'roasted' should be cooked on High for the whole cooking time.
- Always follow the given quantities of liquid in a recipe accurately; too much liquid can result in overcooking.
- Meats with a high fat content should be trimmed very well before being put into the crockpot; fats do not bake-off as they do in a conventional oven.
- A crockpot should not be used for re-heating any cooked frozen food.
- Leftovers from food that has been cooked in a crockpot must be brought to boiling point in a saucepan before being eaten.

A crockpot is suitable for cooking most foods, as long as recipes are adapted accordingly. It is, however, particularly successful when preparing the following:

Soups
Cooked pâtés
Root vegetables
Meat and poultry — casseroles and 'roasts'
Fish casseroles
Cheese fondue
Steamed puddings
Rice pudding (and other grain puddings)
Lemon curd

COOKING BRICKS

Cooking bricks are simplicity itself to use and always produce delicious-tasting, moist and tender

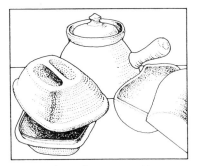

Unglazed, earthenware cooking bricks

food. They come in a variety of shapes and sizes and can be used for cooking most meats, fish and even potatoes, although they always tend to be referred to as 'chicken bricks'. Made of porous, unglazed earthenware, with close-fitting lids, these bricks are very similar in concept to the clay pots used in Greek and Roman times. Before using a brick, always give it a preliminary soaking in cold water each time that you use it in order for it to impart moisture to the food being cooked.

After draining, place the seasoned food into the cooking brick with herbs, chopped vegetables, and any other flavourings or seasonings that you like, and put the lid on top. Put the brick into a cold oven, and then turn it on. As the oven heats up, condensation forms on the lid of the brick, and trickles back onto the food; this acts as a baste and keeps the food moist. All the flavour, juices and aroma of the food are conserved naturally, and the food is far less fatty than it is when cooked by many other more conventional methods, such as roasting or frying.

Cooking bricks should never be washed with detergent as this will taint the food. Just wipe out well with a clean damp cloth or wash in water to which a little vinegar has been added. The bricks do darken with use, but this does not mean that they are dirty, just discoloured.

ELECTRIC DEEP FRYERS

Many people avoid deep frying if they can, because they hate the smell and mess that are associated with it. However careful you are when deep frying food in an open fryer, you cannot prevent the lingering odour. Frying in hot deep fat can also be extremely dangerous. If the temperature of the fat is not regulated very carefully, it can burn; and if moisture gets into the hot fat, it can bubble up and boil over. Electrically operated deep fryers are not only safer, but they also guarantee successful results every time and there is little or no smell. Most electric deep fryers are thermostatically controlled, so that the temperature of the fat or oil is controlled automatically. When the fryer is plugged in and switched on, an indicator light comes on; once the desired temperature of the oil or fat has been reached, the light goes out. The

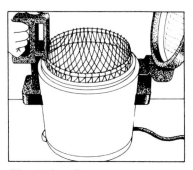

Electric deep fryer

frying basket clips onto the inside of the fryer and can be fixed at various heights. This enables you to put the food that is to be fried into the basket, before the oil or fat is heated — there is no need to lift the lid of the fryer off, as the basket can be lowered into the hot fat from the outside of the fryer. A special filter is fitted into the lid of the fryer which neutralises all the fat and cooking smells. The controlled temperature of the fat ensures that foods are fried to just the right degree.

COOKING TECHNIQUES

When cooking you can use a variety of different techniques from grilling to frying and roasting to poaching. As well as understanding all the techniques you must also bear in mind the type of food that you are going to cook and the time you have to cook it in. Under each technique are given guidelines as to which foods are best suited to this particular method of preparation.

Here are some quick and easy techniques — including grilling and frying — as well as a number of longer cooking methods, like casseroling. Once you have grasped the basics of these you will find them extraordinarily straightforward.

GRILLING

Grilling is one of the simplest and quickest methods of cooking. It simply involves placing the food under the heat source, turning it and then removing it when cooked. Generally, small pieces of food are grilled like chicken portions, sausages or fish fillets, all of which cook relatively quickly.

To perfect the technique always preheat the grill before using it. The high temperature sears the surface of the food, sealing in all the juices, before cooking continues. With thick pieces of food, such as steaks or chops, sear both sides, but you do not need to do this with finer foods such as thin cutlets or fillets of fish, ideal foods when you are in a hurry. To speed up cooking time place foods to be seared near the source of heat, then lower the grill pan for the remainder of the cooking time.

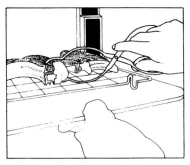

Turning meat under the grill

To make the food taste its best keep it moist throughout grilling; brush it from time to time with oil, melted butter or a marinade. However, do not be tempted to season meat with salt until after it has been cooked as this can toughen it. Test the food while it is cooking to see if it is done.

When grilling chicken and pork, always grill them very thoroughly to ensure that they are cooked through. Steak and lamb, however, can be cooked according to personal preference and to the amount of time available.

Use tongs for turning the food during grilling, and never pierce it with a fork or skewer or you may get hot fat sprayed at you. Always serve grilled foods immediately as they dry out quickly and toughen if kept warm.

Brushing meat with marinade

IDEAL GRILLING FOODS

Beef—steaks (fillet, rump, sirloin, entrecôte and T-bone), sausages and beefburgers
Lamb—chump chops, loin chops, cutlets, leg steaks (cut from fillet end), liver and kidneys
Pork—fillet, spare-rib chops, loin chops, sausages, liver and kidney
Bacon and Gammon—rashers and chops
Veal—fillet (as kebabs), cutlets, loin chops, liver (calf's)
Chicken—breasts, drumsticks, leg and wing joints, split and flattened poussins
Fish—thick fillets, steaks, small whole fish
Mushrooms
Tomatoes

FRYING

Foods can be deep fried, shallow fried or stir fried. It is useful to have all these ways of cooking at your fingertips since they all give quick results and are easy to do once you have mastered the technique. Basically they all depend on two simple principles which are that you use relatively small pieces of food and that you use hot fat to cook them in.

DEEP FRYING

A variety of foods can be successfully deep fried from potatoes to cheese, chicken and fish. Indeed, entire meals can be deep fried.

The technique involves heating a large amount of oil, usually vegetable oil, in a solid-based pan or deep-fat fryer, lowering food into it, letting it cook for a few minutes and then taking it out. Here are some steps on deep frying.

Steps to deep frying

Fill a heavy-based pan no more than two-thirds full of oil. Start heating the oil very gently at first, and then raise the heat. Check the temperature of the oil carefully, either by using a frying thermometer, or test with a cube of stale bread (see below).
● Coat the foods for deep frying

with breadcrumbs or batter, this protects them while being cooked and also prevents

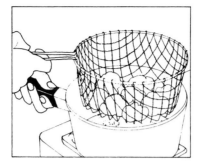

Deep frying small portions

moisture from the food leaking into the oil.
● When cooking small portions or pieces of food, lower them into the fat in a wire frying basket; this makes it easier to remove them from the hot fat.
● Always lower the food into the hot oil slowly.
● Once the food is cooked, remove it carefully using a wire basket or a perforated spoon, and drain on absorbent kitchen paper.
● Remove all crumbs and remnants of fried food with a perforated spoon, otherwise they will burn and taint the flavour of the oil. Do not allow water or other liquids to get into the fat or it will 'spit'.
● Turn the heat off as soon as

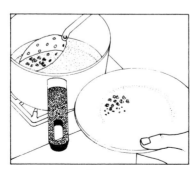

Removing crumbs after frying

you have finished deep frying, and leave the pan to cool without moving it.

Straining cooled oil for storage

● Once the oil is quite cool, strain it thoroughly, and store in a clean bottle for future use.

Deep frying temperatures

The temperature of hot oil for deep frying varies considerably according to the type of food and on whether it is raw or has already been cooked. Raw food is cooked at a lower temperature than cooked. A frying thermometer is the most accurate method of gauging the heat of the oil; alternatively, use a cube of day-old bread.

The bread cube method

● If the bread cube sinks to the bottom of the pan of oil, and does not frizzle at all, then the oil is not yet hot enough.
● If the bread cube frizzles gently, then the oil has reached about 180°C (350°F) and you can fry beignets and do the 'first frying' of chipped potatoes.
● If a light blue haze rises from the oil and the bread cube browns in 1 minute then the oil has reached about 190°C (375°F) and is at the right temperature for frying coated fish fillets, croquettes and fruit fritters.
● If a noticeable blue haze rises from the oil and the bread cube browns in 30 seconds, then the oil has reached about 200°C (400°F) and it is ready for frying small fritters, croûtons, coated cooked foods (such as fish cakes), and the second frying of chipped potatoes.

SHALLOW FRYING

Shallow frying is another quick and easy method of cooking, although not quite as quick as deep frying. It is ideal for cooking chops, steaks, escalopes, liver, sausages, bacon, eggs and fish. All you need to do is fry the food in a shallow amount of hot fat (about 1–2.5 cm/$\frac{1}{2}$–1 inch) over a moderate heat. Turn the food once during cooking. You can use a variety of fats from cooking oil, vegetable oil, olive oil, white cooking fat, lard, margarine, butter, or a mixture. If you want to use butter don't use it on its own as it burns at a relatively low temperature. It is advisable to mix it with oil or margarine.

It is best to coat the food before shallow frying it; this helps to protect it from the temperature of the fat, and also prevents fragile items, such as fish fillets, from collapsing.

The guidelines for safe and successful shallow frying are very similar to those for deep fat frying, although there are distinct differences. The fat must be heated gently at all times, even during the actual cooking; there is no need to use a fat thermometer to test the heat of the fat, just drop a small piece of stale bread into the hot fat and it should sizzle steadily without spitting. Lower the coated food into the hot fat gently, and turn it during frying with a per-

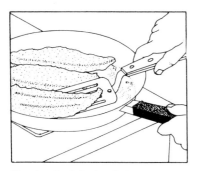

Turning food during frying

forated spoon or fish slice. (Scoop off any crumbs or remnants of food from the surface of the cooking fat so they don't burn.)

Remove the cooked food with a perforated spoon or slice and drain thoroughly.

STIR FRYING

Stir frying is a traditional Chinese method of cooking, which has gained tremendous popularity throughout Europe in recent years. It is a quick and versatile technique that can be used for vegetables, meat, fish, rice and noodles. The secret of the technique lies in cutting up the food into uniformly-sized small pieces and then cooking them very quickly in oil. The beauty of this method of cooking is that the food retains its shape, texture and taste.

A wok, the traditional Chinese cooking utensil, is the best receptacle to use for stir frying. It is a large, deep metal pan, with a completely spherical base and two looped handles.

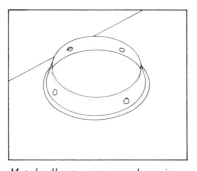

Metal collar to support wok on ring

Place the wok directly on the gas or electric ring. (It works better on gas.) You can buy a metal collar which you fit around your cooking ring, which acts as a support for the wok. This makes it easier to move the wok around as the food is cooking, ensuring that each surface of the wok comes in contact with an even temperature; an all essential fact in stir frying.

When you stir fry foods you'll find that they cook very quickly, so it's important to have everything well prepared in advance. Chop your food up into evenly-sized small pieces and, if using meat or fish, coat it in flour. Place

the wok over the heat, preferably standing on a metal collar, and add a few spoonfuls of oil to it. Once the oil is hot, add the finely cut ingredients, either all in one go or in stages, depending on the recipe. Garlic, root ginger and other highly flavoured ingredients are often used. These should be fried first and then the other ingredients should be added. Tilt the wok backwards and forwards

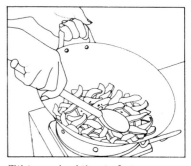

Tilting wok while stir-frying

over the heat, while you stir and turn the ingredients with a long-handled spatula until cooked.

POACHING

This is a subtle cooking technique used for preparing delicate foods which cook quickly. Poaching describes the gentle agitation of a hot liquid by natural movement of the liquid. Odd bubbles occur, but not the steady bubbling that one associates with simmering. The choice of cooking liquid depends

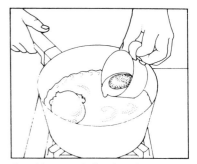

Poaching eggs in hot liquid

to a large extent on what you are poaching; for fish, a court bouillon or wine would be most appropriate; for meat, a vegetable or meat stock or wine; for eggs, water.

When poaching eggs and quenelles, add them to the liquid, once it is hot and 'quivering'. Fish fillets, on the other hand, should be put into the pan with cold liquid and then brought to the correct temperature for poaching. Fish is usually poached covered, but many other foods are poached without a lid.

Suitable poaching foods
Boned and skinned chicken breasts
Meat and fish quenelles
Fish fillets and thin fish cutlets
Shellfish, such as scallops
Eggs
Gnocchi
Soft fruits, such as peaches

STEAMING
This is a quick and nutritious way of cooking food and is generally applied to vegetables. All you need is a simple metal steamer which you place in a saucepan. Pour in

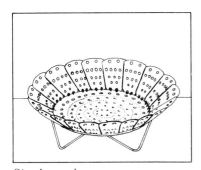

Simple metal steamer

boiling water to just beneath the steamer, add the vegetables and cover with a lid. The vegetables will cook in the steam and, unlike when they are cooked in water, very little nutritious value will be lost. Steaming is also an excellent way of reheating food.

ROASTING
Roasting is certainly a very effort-less way of cooking. Once the food is in the oven, you can virtually forget about it, apart from giving it the occasional baste. However, roasting is only suitable for prime, tender cuts of meat, and for poultry and most game.

Roasting is a direct heat method of cooking, and the food needs to be kept moist throughout cooking. Before putting the joint or bird into the oven spread it with fat (duck is the only exception to this rule—it is naturally fatty and should be pricked with a skewer before roasting). With meat, poultry or game that dries out quickly, like chicken, veal, venison, pheasant and grouse, it is advisable to cover it with strips of

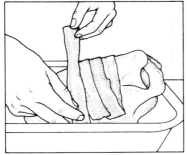

Adding moisture with strips of bacon

streaky bacon. This gives added moisture.

Veal, lamb and pork can be boned, stuffed and rolled before roasting as can poultry and game. Use a well-flavoured stuffing which will moisten and enhance the flavour of the meat during cooking. Stuffing makes the meat go further, but it takes longer to cook.

Another way of keeping the food moist during roasting, is to cover it with cooking foil, dull side uppermost; the foil can be re-moved either for the first or last part of the cooking time, to allow the food to brown. When using foil, add on an extra few minutes cooking time.

Place your meat, poultry or feathered game on a grid or rack in a roasting tin. This is important since it makes it easy to baste the food during cooking and to roast vegetables under it.

Roast in a preheated oven for the given time, basting with the

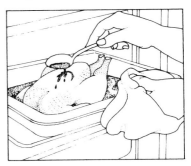

Basting poultry during cooking

juices and fat in the roasting tin from time to time. Test to see whether the meat is done. Push a skewer right into the meat, take it out and feeling it, when it is hot to the touch the meat is done. Beef, lamb and game are often served underdone, but chicken, turkey and pork should always be cooked right through. If you are using a meat thermometer, insert the thermometer in the thickest part of the meat before it goes into the oven, making sure that it does not touch the bone. All roast meats are

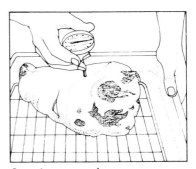

Inserting a meat thermometer

much easier to carve or cut if they are first allowed to 'settle' after cooking. Remove from the oven and keep warm for about 15 minutes until ready to serve.

What to roast
Beef—whole fillet, rump, fore rib, sirloin on the bone, boned sirloin, wing rib, topside, silverside
Lamb—leg, best end of neck, breast, shoulder, loin
Pork—whole fillet, spare rib, hand and spring, belly, loin, blade
Veal—loin, leg, shoulder, breast, best end of neck
Poultry—chicken, poussins, turkey, duck, guinea fowl
Game (young)—wild duck, pheasant, pigeon, grouse, venison.

Roasting times and methods
There are three basic methods of roasting (see chart for methods and timing).

Method A
The meat is first roasted at 230°C (450°F) mark 8, for 15 minutes, and the heat is then reduced to 180°C (350°F) mark 4, for the remainder of the cooking time.

Method B
The meat is roasted at 190°C (375°F) mark 5 for the whole cooking time.

Method C
The meat is roasted at 160°C (325°F) mark 3 for the whole cooking time. This long slow method of roasting is most suitable for large turkeys, and for joints which are not considered prime roasting joints like, for example, silverside of beef, hand and spring of pork and breast of lamb.
Remember to allow extra roasting time if foil and/or stuffing are used, and to weigh joints and birds *after* stuffing in order to calculate accurate cooking time.

	Methods A & B	Method C
Beef (whole fillet, rump, sirloin, ribs, topside, silverside)	15–20 minutes for every 450 g (1 lb) plus 20 minutes	30 minutes for every 450 g (1 lb) plus 30 minutes
Lamb (leg shoulder, loin, best end of neck, breast)	20–25 minutes for every 450 g (1 lb) plus 25 minutes	35–40 minutes for every 450 g (1 lb) plus 40 minutes
Pork (whole fillet, loin, leg, sparerib, hand and spring, belly, blade)	30 minutes for every 450 g (1 lb) plus 30 minutes	40–45 minutes for every 450 g (1 lb) plus 45 minutes
Veal (loin, leg, shoulder, breast, best end of neck)	25–30 minutes for every 450 g (1 lb) plus 30 minutes	35–40 minutes for every 450 g (1 lb) plus 40 minutes
Chicken (whole bird)	20 minutes for every 450 g (1 lb) plus 20 minutes	30 minutes for every 450 g (1 lb) plus 30 minutes
Turkey 2.25–3.5 kg (5–8 lb)	20 minutes for every 450 g (1 lb) plus 20 minutes	30 minutes for every 450 g (1 lb) plus 30 minutes
3.5–6.5 kg (8–14 lb)	—	20 minutes for every 450 g (1 lb) plus 20 minutes
Over 6.5 kg (14 lb)	—	15 minutes for every 450 g (1 lb) plus 15 minutes
Duck	15 minutes for every 450 g (1 lb) plus 15 minutes	20 minutes for every 450 g (1 lb) plus 20 minutes

BARBECUING
Barbecuing is a wonderfully easy way of cooking food out of doors. It lends itself perfectly to entertaining, since you can get delicious results with the minimum of effort.
A barbecue is like an outdoor grill, depending on charcoal for its fuel. The grill needs to be heated first and then the meat or fish which is to be cooked is placed either directly on the grill or first in foil and then on the grill.

Preparing food for barbecuing
● Always use good-quality meat; poor quality meat does not cook very well on a barbecue
● Marinate the food for at least 1 hour before barbecuing it. This enhances its flavour and ensures moistness
● Allow chilled foods to come to room temperature before putting them on the barbecue; chilled foods give off moisture which can cause spitting
● Brush foods with oil to prevent them from sticking to the barbecue grill
● Season meat and poultry with salt after cooking as salt draws off the meat juices
● Watch food carefully once it is on the barbecue, and test from time to time
● As well as barbecuing directly on the barbecue grill, food can also be wrapped in foil and cooked either on the grill or in the coals

Good foods for barbecues
Beef—lean steaks, good stewing (kebabs)
Lamb—chops, leg steaks, fillet (kebabs)
Pork—chops, spare-ribs, fillet (kebabs)
Bacon and sausages
Veal—chops, leg fillet (kebabs)
Chicken—drumsticks, legs, split poussins
Offal—kidneys
Fish—firm-textured fish such as halibut, monkfish and cod; whole fish such as bass, bream, trout,

mackerel and sardines
Shellfish—split lobster, large prawns and scallops
Vegetables—corn on the cob is particularly good
Fruit—particularly bananas, cubes or slices threaded on skewers, in their skins or skinned and wrapped in foil

POT ROASTING
This is a one-pot method of cooking larger pieces of meat, whole birds and fish. It involves the minimum of preparation and long, slow cooking. Simply brown the meat all over in hot fat in a heavy pan, remove from the pan while browning vegetables in the fat. Place the meat on top of the vegetables; add a little liquid, cover and cook in a moderate oven.

For an even quicker pot roast use the cold start method and simply put all the ingredients in the pot at once and place in the oven. The cooking time will be longer.

Good foods to pot roast
Brisket or topside of beef; boned, stuffed and rolled breast of lamb or veal; stuffed hearts; rolled shoulder of venison and chicken.

CASSEROLING
With very little preparation and long, slow cooking you have a dish that can be prepared in advance and then reheated as required. Casseroles freeze very well and can be brought to the table in their casserole dish. In short, they save you a great deal of time.

There are two types of casseroles—brown (fry start) and white (cold start). To make a brown casserole, fry small chunks of meat in fat until browned all over. Remove and drain on absorbent kitchen paper. Add vegetables to the pan and fry until well coated. Add seasoning, stir in some flour, put back the meat and add some liquid. Cover tightly and simmer either on top of the cooker or in a slow to medium oven until tender. A white casserole is

quicker to prepare. Simply layer the same ingredients as for a brown casserole into your dish and place in a slow to moderate oven, cooking until tender.

Good foods for casseroling
Beef—leg, shin, chuck, flank, blade, skirt, joints of topside, top rump, brisket, silverside
Lamb—breast, scrag, middle or best end of neck, loin. Shoulder and leg may be cooked as joints or boned and cubed
Pork—hand, spare rib, belly (trimmed of fat). Also, loin chops, spare rib chops and fillet. Gammon steaks and joints and cooked, cubed ham
Veal—breast, neck, shoulder, shin, leg, knuckle
Offal—ox and sheep's kidneys; calves' and sheep hearts; lambs' and sheep's tongues; oxtail
Poultry—joints
Game—grouse, rabbit
Pulses

BOILING
Boiling is an easy technique that involves covering the food in a liquid, heating it until it comes to boiling point and then, more often than not, lowering the heat and simmering it. The cooking time will depend on what type of food is being cooked as well as its size. You can boil meat, fish, grains, pulses and vegetables.

Boiling meat and poultry
Tie or truss joints and poultry carefully with string, so that they retain their shape during cooking. Smoked and salty gammon and ham should be soaked in cold water before hand and the soaking water should be discarded. This gets rid of some of the saltiness. Place the meat or poultry in a large pan with enough cold water to cover. Bring to the boil. Lower the heat and remove any surface scum with a slotted spoon. Add chopped onion, some chopped peeled root vegetables, a bay leaf, a small bunch of parsley, a few peppercorns and a blade of mace.

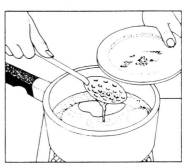

Removing surface scum

(Add salt at the end of the cooking time or the meat will toughen. Don't add it to pickled or cured meat.) Cover the pan tightly and simmer very gently. The exact time depends on the type of meat; with boiling fowl it depends on age. As an approximate guide, allow 30 minutes for every 450 g (1 lb), plus an extra 30 minutes.

Suitable meats for boiling
Beef—brisket or silverside
Lamb—leg of mutton
Pork—belly
Gammon and bacon—corner gammon, middle gammon, gammon slipper, boned and rolled hock
Poultry—boiling fowl
Grains
Pulses
Vegetables

Equipment for Meat, Poultry and Carving

Good-quality equipment is essential if you are to deal with fresh meat and poultry successfully. And, with a little knowledge and the right tools for the job, carving is a less daunting job than you may imagine. Follow the step-by-step guidelines in this chapter and you will soon find yourself volunteering for the job!

EQUIPMENT

Chopper Has a heavy rectangular blade with a strong edge. A heavy meat chopper will go through most bones and joints, but you will need a little practice to ensure you hit the correct place each time.

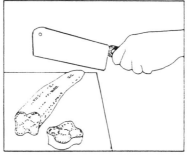

A heavy chopper has many uses

The technique is to use your forearm and not your wrist and to look at the target, not the chopper. A chopper is also useful for flattening steaks and escalopes.

Butcher's knife Usually fairly heavy with a long, firm blade. Useful for slicing raw meat and for trimming and finishing joints before cooking.

Saw Used for cutting a carcass; the only tool which will cut through bones. A hacksaw will cut through most smaller bones, but with a butcher's bow saw you would be able to cut up a carcass yourself, although this is rarely necessary. When sawing through a bone, remove the dust immediately.

Boning knife Used for removing bones from raw meat. A smallish knife with a small, sharp-pointed blade. The knife should be kept very sharp for maximum efficiency.

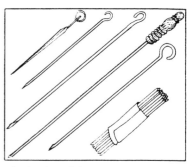

A selection of skewers

Skewers Hold meat firmly in shape during cooking. Both wooden and metal skewers are available in various sizes. Kebab skewers are made of flat strips of steel to prevent the food from swinging around while being grilled.

Larding needle Has a sharp point and a long hollow body for threading small strips of fat through very lean meat.

Trussing needle Like a very large darning needle. The eye must be large enough to take fine string and the point must be very sharp. Useful for sewing up stuffed joints. Check you thread enough string on to the needle to complete the job.

Pounders and tenderisers These tools deal with food that needs to be beaten flat or tenderised. They are usually made of wood and are fairly heavy and strong. A smooth-sided pounder is useful for flattening steaks and escalopes, but for tenderising meat, a meat mallet with pyramid-

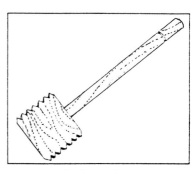

A meat mallet for tenderising

shaped studs is useful. This should be reserved for very tough or thick pieces of steak.

Mincer Made of cast iron or plastic and is attached to the work surface by a suction pad or clamp. Food is dropped into the hopper and falls on to a revolving screw which is turned by a handle. The food is forced towards a cutting blade or cutting discs to give mince of the required texture, from coarse to fine. Electric mincers are available, as attachments to tabletop mixers. Nowadays, food processors have taken the place of mincers in the kitchen, but care should be taken that the meat is not ground to too fine a paste.

Electric carving knife This is very useful for carving large joints quickly and for cutting cold meats very thinly. When using, follow the tips for successful carving, right.

Slow cooker A slow cooker enables you to prepare stews or casseroles and then leave them for up to 12 hours to cook. In this way, you can prepare a dish in the morning and come home to a fully cooked meal—the slow cooker is ideal for making all-in-one meals. There is no risk of burning or boiling dry. Some models have a removable pot which can be used for serving and makes cleaning much easier.

CARVING

THE RIGHT TOOLS

The essential tools for correct carving are a two-pronged carving fork with a finger guard, a large sharp carving knife and an efficient sharpener such as a steel.

- Place the joint on a meat dish, wooden board, or spiked metal carving dish with recesses to catch the meat juices.

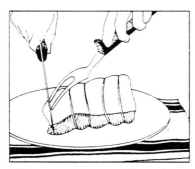

Always carve on a non-slip surface

- Always carve on a non-slip surface. A damp kitchen cloth or tea towel placed under the meat dish helps to stop it slipping.
- As far as possible, loosen the cooked meat from exposed bones, such as rib bones, before starting to carve.
- Aim to cut across the grain of the lean, to shorten the muscle fibres. This makes the meat easier to chew and therefore more tender. Usually, this means cutting at right angles to the bone. The thickness of the slices depends on personal preference.
- Boned and rolled joints are simply sliced through. Boneless joints are likely to take a little longer to cook because the bone, which is a good conductor of heat, has been removed.

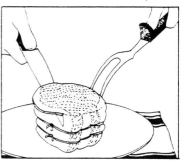

Carve small flat joints horizontally

- Small rolled flat joints are easier to carve horizontally. Since cutting will usually be done in the direction of the hand holding the meat, it is essential to use a fork with a finger guard.

SHARPENING A KNIFE USING A STEEL

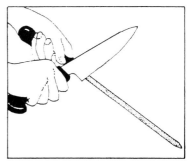

1 Keep the blade of the knife at a 30° angle to the steel and bring the whole length of the edge in contact with it. Use your wrist and forearm, keeping your elbow still. Start with the heel of the knife by the guard, and end with the point at the tip of the steel.

2 Sharpen the other side of the blade under the steel. About 10–12 strokes should be sufficient to sharpen the knife.

HOW TO CARVE A LEG OF LAMB

1 Use a cloth or absorbent kitchen paper to hold the shank end of the joint and place the meatiest side uppermost.

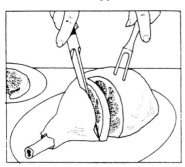

2 Take out 2 slices from the centre of the leg down to the bone. Continue slicing from either side of the first cut, gradually angling the knife to obtain larger slices.

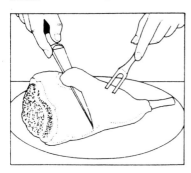

3 Turn the joint over and trim off excess fat. Carve horizontal slices along the leg.

HOW TO CARVE A SHOULDER OF LAMB

1 Use a cloth or absorbent kitchen paper to hold the shank end of the joint and place the meatiest side uppermost.

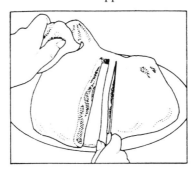

2 Cut a long slice from the centre of the joint down to the bone. Carve thick slices from either side of the initial cut.

3 Carve horizontal slices from the shank bone. Turn the joint over and trim off any excess fat. Carve thin horizontal slices from the remaining meat.

HOW TO CARVE A LOIN OF PORK

1 Remove the crackling from the loin of pork in sections, using a sharp knife.

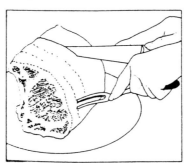

2 Slice the loin, working at a slight angle, cutting down to the bone.

HOW TO CARVE A HAND OF PORK

1 Remove the crackling and detach the rib bones.

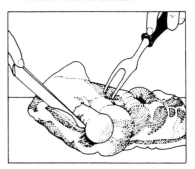

2 Carve downward slices, working from either side of the bone.

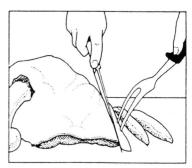

3 Turn the joint over and trim off excess fat. Carve the remaining meat across the grain.

HOW TO CARVE A LEG OF PORK (KNUCKLE END)

1 First, remove the crackling from the knuckle end of pork in sections.

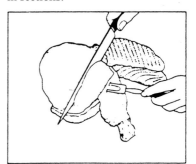

2 Start carving on the thick side at the knuckle end, slice at a slight angle down the bone.

HOW TO CARVE A LEG OF PORK (FILLET END)

1 First, remove the crackling from the fillet end of pork in pieces.

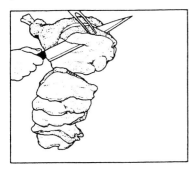

2 Place the joint flat, with the thick side on the right. Carve a few slices from the thick edge towards the centre bone, then turn the joint so that the thin side is on the right and carve in towards the bone until the surface is level.

3 Continue carving the meat, keeping the surfaces as level as possible.

HOW TO CARVE BELLY OF PORK

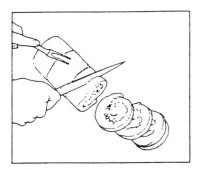

1 Place flat, fat side uppermost and carve downwards in fairly thick slices across the grain of the meat. If boned, rolled and stuffed, carve in the same way.

HOW TO CARVE CHICKEN AND TURKEY

Place the bird on the dish so that one wing is towards your left hand with the breast diagonally towards you. Steadying the bird with the flat of the knife, prise the leg outwards with the fork, exposing the thigh joint. Cut through the joint to sever the leg. On a turkey or large chicken hold the end of the drumstick in one hand and cut slices from the leg in a downward slant away from you, turning the leg to get slices from all round the joint. When the bone is bare set it to one end of the dish. For a medium-sized chicken the leg will not have enough meat for carving but can be divided into two at the joint, giving a thigh and a drumstick portion. If the chicken is small the leg may be served as a single portion.

Next remove the wing that is facing you. Hold the wing with the fork and cut through the outer layer of the breast into the joint. Ease the wing from the body and cut through the gristle. A turkey wing may be divided again; a chicken wing is too small and is served in one piece.

Carve the breast in thin slices parallel with the breast bone. If the bird is stuffed, the outer slices of meat and stuffing will carve together; the rest of the stuffing will have to be scooped out with a spoon. Carve one side of the carcass clean before turning the dish round and starting the process again on the other side of the bird.

CARVING DUCK

Duck have particularly tough leg and wing ligaments and a shorter, heavier knife is needed to cut through these. Place bird on carving dish with legs diagonally

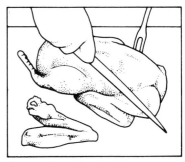

Cutting through wing joint

towards you. Hold the body firmly with the fork and cut down through the wing joint. Move fork closer to leg end and cut firmly through the joint. Leave a duck leg whole; separate a goose leg into two. With a long carving knife carve thin breast slices.

Jointing small cooked chickens
Halve or quarter small chickens such as poussins. Use a strong, heavy knife and cut the bird in two straight through the breast and backbone. Halve each piece crossways for quarters.

Jointing a duckling
Place the bird on a board with the legs facing you. With poultry shears, cut along the top, keeping the blades just to one side of the breast bone. When you reach the wishbone, cut firmly through it and open up the bird. Next cut through the back, just to one side of the backbone. Cut down the other side and discard it.

Lay the two duckling halves skin side up on the board and with a sharp knife cut through the skin and flesh between the wing and leg sections. Leave plenty of breast meat with the leg portion. Use the shears to cut through the bone to divide the portions.

Guide to Buying and Storing Fresh Food

Knowing what to look for and how to select wisely are important factors when buying foods. The following notes will help you in your choice and also provide information on the best ways of storage for perishable foods.

BUYING

BEEF

Beef is available all year round, and offers a variety of cuts to suit all cooking methods and occasions, from large roasting joints to economical braising and stewing cuts. When buying fresh beef look for a fresh, slightly moist appearance. The redness of the meat will vary after cutting and exposure to air, but this need not affect your choice. The lean of roasting joints should be smooth and velvety in texture. Coarse-textured lean beef is usually an indication that the meat is suitable only for braising and stewing. Beef that is very coarse will almost certainly need slow cooking to tenderise it.

The lean should be surrounded by a layer of creamy-white fat. The colour of the fat may vary for a number of reasons, none of which will affect the taste. The fat should, however, always be firm and dry. Marbling, or flecks of fat in the meat, will help to keep the meat moist during the cooking and often gives it a better flavour. Very lean roasting joints are sometimes sold larded with fat to help keep them moist.

VEAL

The colour and quality of veal depends greatly on the age at the time of slaughter, and the method of rearing. Milk-fed calves have very pale flesh that is highly valued. The best veal comes from calves that are fed on a rich milk diet and, as this method of rearing is expensive, the price of veal is high. As the calf is weaned from milk and starts to eat grass, the flesh tends to become darker. When buying veal the flesh should be pinkish beige, with no dark or discoloured particles. It should be very lean and moist with no juice running from it.

POULTRY AND GAME

If buying *fresh poultry*, choose a bird that looks plump and well rounded. The skin should be free from blemishes and bruising. In a young chicken the tip of the breast bone will be soft and flexible; if it is hard and rigid the bird is probably too old to roast satisfactorily although it will be suitable for steaming or boiling.

Modern poultry production methods ensure a moist, tender-fleshed bird. Prompt freezing also guarantees freshness, so you can expect high quality from any of the well-known brands of frozen poultry. Traditionally reared farmyard birds are inclined to have more flavour.

Larger birds generally give the best value as the proportion of meat to bone is higher and the extra meat, particularly chicken and turkey, left over from the first meal is excellent cold or made up in another dish. Remember that packaged poultry, frozen or fresh, is sold by oven-ready weight, but a fresh bird bought from a traditional poulterer or butcher will probably be sold at 'plucked weight'—plucked but not drawn. The butcher will draw it for you, but after weighing and pricing. You will need to allow for this in estimating the size of bird you require.

LAMB

Look for fine-grained, lean meat with a bright red colour tinged with brown. The fat should be creamy white, and not brittle. The bones should be moist and white at the joints. Legs and shoulders should have a thin covering of fat. The fat of some cuts is covered with a thin papery skin. This should be pliable, not hard and wrinkled. Remove from chops before cooking, but leave on roasting joints as it helps the meat to retain moisture. English new season's lamb is available between March and November, although supplies are at their peak between August and November. All joints, except those from the neck, can be roasted, and the individual cuts from them grilled or fried.

PORK

Good-quality pork is available all year round. Look for firm, dry and lean meat with a good pinkish colour. The fat should be firm and creamy white. The rind should be smooth and supple. When deeply scored, the rind forms crackling on roast pork. Ask the butcher to score the meat if you want crackling.

BACON

Bacon should have a pleasant smell, with no stickiness. The rind should be thin and smooth, and the fat smooth and white. Bacon can be bought ready boned and rolled into convenient-sized joints, or it can be cling film wrapped or vacuum packed. Some joints are also sold in convenient boilable bags.

FISH AND SEAFOOD

Really fresh *whole fish* has clear, bulging eyes and bright red gills. Avoid any with sunken, cloudy eyes and faded pink or grey gills. The body of the fish should be firm and springy to the touch, with shining skin and bright, close fitting scales. *Fish fillets* and *steaks* should look freshly cut, the flesh moist and firm-textured, showing no signs of dryness or discolouration. The bones should be firmly embedded in the flesh; if they are loose and coming away from the flesh this indicates that the fish has been cut for some time and is past its best.

When buying *frozen fish*, make sure that it is solidly frozen, clear in colour and free of ice crystals. Any smell should be mild and clean, exactly as for fresh fish. Breadcrumbs or batter coatings on frozen fish portions should be crisp and dry looking. Avoid frozen fish that has a brownish tinge or that is in any way damaged.

Shellfish should be very fresh as they are more perishable than other fish. They should have a clean sea smell and clear fresh colour; avoid any that are dull looking. Prawns and shrimps should have tails curled well under them. Look for tightly closed shells where applicable.

While it is unwise to freeze your own shellfish—since the temperature required for satisfactory preservation of shellfish is lower than that normally obtainable in any domestic freezer—commercially *frozen shellfish* are useful when the type you require is out of season. You can also freeze very fresh shellfish in made-up dishes such as soups, fish pies and quiches.

DAIRY PRODUCE

When buying fresh *milk, cream* and *yogurt*, look at their date stamps, then keep them cool, clean and covered to ensure they stay fresh.

Cheese can be bought from specialist cheese shops and supermarkets. Freshly cut cheese should look fresh, with no dried or greasy areas on the surface. It is important that the cut surface of cheese is always covered and that a mild-flavoured cheese is not kept alongside a strong cheese. If buying pre-packed cheese, check that it does not look sweaty or excessively runny and that it is within the life of its date stamp. If buying a ripened soft cheese, such as Camembert, well before the expiry of the date stamp, you may prefer to keep it to allow it to ripen to your liking.

Prepacked *eggs* in shops now have the date they were laid stamped on each individual egg. From this you can immediately tell how old they are.

FRESH FRUIT AND VEGETABLES

When buying fruit and vegetables always choose them carefully and make sure that they are fresh. Fruits should be bought with unblemished skins. Root vegetables, such as potatoes, carrots and swedes, should be bought firm and unwrinkled. Buy little and often to ensure freshness.

STORING

FRESH BEEF AND VEAL

Freshly cut meat should be stored in a cool place, preferably a refrigerator. Unwrap the meat and wipe the surface with absorbent kitchen paper, then wrap in foil or cling film to prevent the surface drying out. Place the meat in the coldest part of the refrigerator, at the top if you have a larder refrigerator, otherwise on the shelf immediately below the frozen food storage compartment, away from cooked meats and other foods. Fresh meat can be kept for 3–5 days in the refrigerator, although it is advisable to cook smaller cuts within 1–2 days.

COOKED BEEF AND VEAL

Cooked meats should be wrapped or covered to prevent them drying out before they are put in the refrigerator. Leftover stews and casseroles should first be allowed to cool and then put in the refrigerator or a cool place in a covered dish. They should be used within 2 days and reheated thoroughly before they are eaten. Bring the dish to boiling point and simmer for at least 10 minutes.

FRESH POULTRY

To store fresh poultry remove the giblets from inside the bird (except quail) as soon as you get it home. Remove any tight packaging, cover the bird loosely with a bag, and store in the re-frigerator for a maximum of 3 days. The giblets should preferably be cooked straight away as they deteriorate more quickly than the rest of the bird. If storing, keep separate from the rest of the bird.

COOKED POULTRY

Leftover roast poultry should be cooled as quickly as possible. Remove stuffing and wrap meat in polythene or foil before storing in the refrigerator. Eat within 3 days. Use cooked dishes within 1 day.

LAMB

Freshly cut meat should be stored in a cool place, preferably in the refrigerator. Minced lamb should be used within 24 hours. If no refrigerator is available, place the meat on a plate in a cool place and cover with an upturned large bowl. In a refrigerator, wrap the meat in foil or cling film. Never leave fresh meat in the sealed polythene bag in which it was bought. It should be placed on the shelf below the frozen food compartment. Lamb can be stored for up to 4 days in the refrigerator.

PORK

Pork is highly perishable, and should be eaten as soon after buying as possible. If no refrigerator is available, cook on the day of purchase. To store in a refrigerator, wrap in foil or cling film, to prevent the meat drying out. Never leave fresh meat in the sealed polythene bag in which it was bought. Cook within 2 days of purchase.

BACON

Wrap bacon joints in foil and store in the refrigerator for up to 3 days. Green, or unsmoked, bacon rashers can be stored for up to 7 days, smoked for up to 10 days. Wrap in foil or place in a covered plastic food container. Cooked bacon joints can be stored in the refrigerator for up to 4 days.

FISH

Fresh *fish*, from the fishmonger, should be loosely wrapped and stored in the refrigerator. Cook it within 24 hours of purchase. Store frozen fish in the freezer or frozen food compartment in its original wrapping.

DAIRY PRODUCE

Store *cheese* in the bottom of the refrigerator, so it does not get too cold, but it's best to remove it from the refrigerator half an hour before serving to allow it to come up to room temperature and regain its flavour. *Milk, cream* and *yogurt* will keep for several days, but check date stamps when buying them. The same applies to cartons of fresh juice. UHT milk will keep well even without a refrigerator but it is best stored in a cool place.

EGGS

Eggs are best kept in a rack in a cool place. If you have to store them in a refrigerator, keep them well away from the ice compartment (there is often a special egg storage rack) and away from foods like cheese, fish or onions whose smells may transfer to the eggs.

Store eggs pointed end down and use them at room temperature; eggs that are too cold will crack when boiled and are also difficult to whisk. Fresh eggs can be stored for 2–3 weeks in the refrigerator or 1–2 weeks in a cool place.

VEGETABLES

Brassicas and leafy vegetables, which include broccoli, sprouts, cauliflower, cabbages and spinach, don't keep well; 1–2 days in a cool, airy place, 3 days if wrapped in paper and refrigerated.

The **onion** family, which comprises leeks, garlic, shallots and spring onions, need to be chosen carefully. Make sure onions are firm, dry and not sprouting; check that the base of leeks is firm. Onions and garlic can sometimes be bought in strings. They are best stored in a cool, airy place, whereas leeks and spring onions should be wrapped in paper and refrigerated.

Pods and seeds—these are all the beans, peas, okra and sweetcorn. For the best flavour buy peas and beans as young as possible. Okra should be bought with an unmarked skin. Sweetcorn should be clean and green with silky, yellow tassels and plump, tightly packed kernels. Store peas and beans in a cool place or wrap in paper and refrigerate for 1–2 days. (If you shell peas keep them covered in the refrigerator.)

Roots and tubers, like potatoes, swedes, carrots and celeriac, should be bought firm and unwrinkled. If you buy potatoes ready washed in polythene bags it is best to transfer them to a paper bag so that they do not become soft and spongy. Store all these vegetables in a cool, airy place, such as a vegetable rack, so that air can circulate round them.

Stalks and shoots, like celery, artichokes, asparagus and fennel, should be crisp and fresh and any leaf tops should be fresh and green. Keep them wrapped in paper in the refrigerator or upright in a jug of water.

Nowadays many different types of **mushrooms** are available— button, flat cap and oyster are a few of them. Dried ones like porcini can be bought at delicatessens. Fresh ones should have unblemished skins and should be stored in paper in the refrigerator. As they deteriorate they darken in colour, so make sure they are fresh looking.

Salad leaves, like lettuce, chicory and watercress, should be bought as fresh as possible and unwrinkled. Inspect inner as well as outer leaves as the inner ones can sometimes be slimy. Apart from Iceberg lettuces, which are crisp and firm, most salad leaves do not keep well. Always refrigerate lettuce. You can wash it and dry it well and store it for 1–2 days in the refrigerator in a polythene bag.

Some vegetables are known as vegetable fruits; these include: tomatoes, courgettes, aubergines, avocados, cucumber, peppers and olives. All should be bought with unblemished skins. Tomatoes and avocados can be bought under-ripe and left to ripen.

Fruits such as apples and pears are best kept in a fruit bowl.

Freezing and other Handy Tricks

Owning a freezer is rather like having a second pair of hands in the kitchen. You need a pastry case: don't bake one, take it out of the freezer! You want some real stock for a special dish; don't make some, thaw some! If you have a culinary disaster—never mind—here's how to turn it into a success. Plus some tricks of the trade to make the simplest dishes look and taste superb.

FREEZING

Careful and thoughtful use of your freezer not only speeds up your cooking, but it makes it a lot easier. Never be tempted to freeze food for the sake of filling the freezer; you should only freeze food that you and your family like and that you will enjoy serving to guests.

Your freezer should be a great help when it comes to planning menus, especially for parties and other large functions. Food from your freezer should always be complemented by seasonal fresh foods, both to give you satisfaction as the cook, and to offer variety. No one is going to be particularly impressed by eating frozen raspberries when fresh ones are in season. Watch this overlap carefully when planning menus.

Apart from freezing made-up dishes, freezers are immensely useful for storing odd bits and pieces which will speed up food preparation. Things like, for example, breadcrumbs, grated cheese, chopped fresh herbs and leftover wine. All these can be added to the freezer in a spare moment and are indispensable when cooking in a hurry.

Do not be tempted to put food in your freezer and forget about it. Always label foods clearly. Although food that is kept past its recommended storage time is perfectly edible and safe to eat, it will deteriorate somewhat in flavour, texture and appearance.

Always use very fresh ingredients; the food that you take out of the freezer is only as good as the food that you put in. Freeze foods in amounts that you know you will use in one go; it is usually impossible to separate out small quantities from a larger pack. People tend to disagree on which foods can be frozen and which cannot. In fact *all* foods *can* be frozen, but the thawed result is often far from acceptable. It is the water content in food which freezes first; if the water content of a food is very high, the food will collapse on thawing. Two very good examples are raw lettuce and cucumber; it would be an absolute disaster to try and freeze either. However, they can be frozen in the form of soup.

WHAT TO FREEZE

SOUPS

It is a very practical proposition to freeze soups. Always make them in large quantities as they freeze particularly well. Soups based on vegetable purées freeze best of all. Homemade stocks give a better flavour to soup that is to be frozen; any excess stock can always be frozen separately. Cool soup very quickly after making it, pack it in suitable sized containers, and freeze it as soon as possible. If a soup needs cream, it is advisable to add it on reheating, otherwise it may separate.

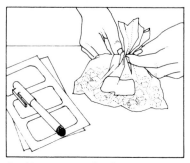

Packing croûtons for freezing

Croûtons are handy soup garnishes and can be frozen, already fried, in freezer bags. They can be 'freshened up' from frozen in a moderately hot oven.

GOOD SOUPS FOR FREEZING

Carrot and orange soup; cauliflower soup; French onion soup and potato and watercress soup.

Recommended storage life: 3 months.

FISH

Fish is a highly perishable food, and even more care has to be taken when you are buying it for the freezer, than when buying it to be eaten fresh. Make a good friend of your fishmonger, so that you can rely on him choosing really good quality fish for you. Always freeze fish the day it is bought. If you are freezing uncooked fresh fish pack it in such a way that you will be able to take out just the quantity that you need; interleave fillets

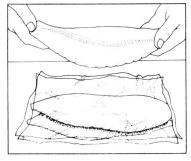

Interleaving fillets with freezer wrap

and steaks with freezer wrap. White fish stands up to freezing far better than shellfish and smoked fish.

GOOD FISH DISHES FOR FREEZING

Cod provençale; fish loaf; home-made fish cakes; smoked fish mousses; smoked haddock croquettes and salmon quiche.

Recommended storage life: 2 months for dishes containing white fish; 1 month for dishes using smoked or shellfish.

CHEESE

Cheese does not freeze very well in its raw state as it tends to lose texture and become crumbly. Bags of grated cheese are useful to have in the freezer — frozen grated cheese is free-flowing and useful when in a hurry. Made up dishes containing cheese freeze most successfully. Some cheese dishes are best frozen uncooked or only partly cooked.

GOOD CHEESE DISHES FOR FREEZING

Croquettes; cheese and ham flan and pizza.

Recommended storage life: 2 months.

MEAT AND POULTRY

Most varieties of meat and poultry freeze extremely well, both raw and made up into complete dishes. Dishes that take time and effort to prepare are the ones to freeze. They are invariably the sort of dishes that are perfect for un-expected dinner guests or for family meals. Pasta-based dishes; cooked meat or poultry in a gravy or sauce; homemade beefburgers or meatballs are all excellent from the freezer. When making cas-seroles for the freezer, reduce the initial cooking time by about 30 minutes. Casseroles are best thawed before reheating; it is safer, and the texture of the ingredients is much better.

GOOD MEAT AND POULTRY DISHES FOR FREEZING

Meat and chicken casseroles; chicken Kiev; meat loaves; pâtés and terrines; meat fillings (to use for pies); pasta dishes such as lasagne; mince based dishes such as moussaka; beefburgers and meatballs; beef olives.

Recommended storage life: 3 months.

TO FREEZE A CASSEROLE

Line a casserole dish with freezer foil and fill with the cooled,

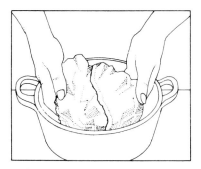

Lifting out parcel of frozen casserole

cooked casserole. Pinch the foil over to seal, and freeze until solid. Lift out the foil parcel with the frozen casserole in it, and over-wrap. Return to the freezer. (In this way you are not minus a cas-serole dish.) When you want to use the frozen casserole: take it out of the freezer, remove the wrap-ping and place the solid casserole back into the casserole dish in which it was originally cooked Allow it to thaw and then reheat. No messy freezer containers, and the casserole looks as if it has been cooked in the dish in which you serve it.

SAUCES AND STOCKS

Sweet and savoury sauces are both very worthwhile items to have in the freezer; they save a lot of time and last-minute effort. Choose sauces that are versatile. Basic white or brown sauces are both good; they are useful in their own right but can also be used as the base for many other simple sauces. Thickened sauces stand up to freezing far better if they are thickened with cornflour rather than with wheat flour. For sweet sauces, freeze those based on a fruit purée or pulp, and smooth sauces like those made from chocolate. Sauces are best frozen in quite small quantities (even in ice cube trays); amounts that you can use in one go. The most con-venient way of packing sauces which are to be served hot, is to use 'boil-in-the-bag' bags; they can quickly be thawed and heated be lowering them into a pan of boiling water.

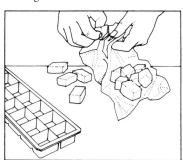

Packing frozen stock cubes

GOOD SAUCES FOR FREEZING

Basic brown sauce; basic white sauce; Bolognese sauce; curry sauce; fresh tomato sauce and onion sauce.

Apple; butterscotch; chocolate and cranberry.

Recommended storage life: 6 months for most, but 2 months for those containing strong flavours such as curry, or perishable ingredients such as meat.

DESSERTS AND PUDDINGS

The perfect puddings to have in your freezer are those which can be taken out and are ready to serve as soon as they have thawed. Dessert 'bases' are also very useful to have on hand in the freezer, such as, pastry cases, sponge cases and choux buns.

Homemade ice creams are easy to prepare when you have a freezer, and are far superior to the bought varieties. Cooked fruit purées are very useful; once thawed they can be topped with pastry lids or crumble mixtures. Pies can be baked before freezing, or left uncooked, in which case they can be cooked from frozen; if you use foil pie plates, make sure that the fruit does not come in contact with the foil as the fruit acid reacts on foil.

GOOD DESSERTS AND PUDDINGS FOR FREEZING

Flans; flan cases; fruit pies and purées; ice creams, homemade and profiteroles (freeze choux buns and chocolate sauce separately); mousses and soufflés.

Recommended storage life: up to 6 months for most puddings and desserts.

DESSERT AND PUDDING GARNISHES

CRUNCHY BISCUIT CRUMBS

Crumble stale biscuits into crumbs; fry in butter with a little demerara sugar. Cool and freeze in a freezer bag. Use frozen to crumble over ice creams or as a cheat crumble topping.

LEMON SLICES

Open freeze thin slices, or half slices, of lemon. Pack into freezer bags. Once thawed they can be used for decorating puddings and desserts, or for adding to drinks.

WHIPPED CREAM ROSETTES

Pipe rosettes of whipped cream

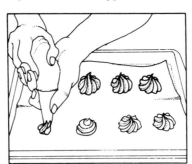

Piping rosettes of whipped cream

onto waxed paper and open freeze. Pack into rigid containers, separating layers and return to the freezer. Thaw on absorbent kitchen paper, before placing on top of the pudding or dessert.

BAKING

Nearly all baked foods, such as cakes, breads and biscuits, freeze extremely well. Many of them are also quite time-consuming to make, so it is a great advantage to be able to freeze them. Baked foods also tend to go stale quite quickly; the freezer keeps them beautifully fresh until required. All baked goods should be really cold before they are packed for the freezer. Thin icings can go very runny on thawing so it is better to stick to the thicker types such as buttercreams and frostings. Cakes or gâteaux which have a piped or elaborate decoration on top should always be 'open-frozen' before being packed.

GOOD BAKED ITEMS FOR FREEZING

Brandy snaps; bread, all types; cheesecakes; chocolate cake; éclairs (unfilled); scones (sweet or savoury); sponge cake layers (ready for assembly).

Recommended storage time: about 2 months.

Breadcrumbs: When you have some slightly stale bread, make it into breadcrumbs, and freeze in freezer bags. (They are very useful in savoury cooking as well as in sweet recipes.

VEGETABLES AND FRUIT

If there is a glut of any particular fruit, or you happen to have it growing in the garden, then it is always worth freezing some down for using later in the year. Raspberries and blackberries are both good choices.

The same really applies to vegetables, as far as freezing them in their natural state is concerned. Some made up vegetable dishes also freeze very well; two good examples are stuffed peppers and stuffed aubergines.

GOOD VEGETABLES AND FRUITS FOR FREEZING

Asparagus, broad beans, broccoli, Brussels sprouts, calabrese, carrots, cauliflower, courgettes, fennel, leeks, mangetout, peas, peppers, runner beans and sweetcorn.

Apples, blackberries, blackcurrants, damsons, gooseberries, greengages, lemons (in slices), peaches, pears, raspberries and rhubarb.

Recommended storage time: 12 months for most vegetables, if blanched, and 12 months for most firm fruits; 4 months for soft fruits.

TRICKS OF THE TRADE

Food should look as good as it tastes, and vice versa. Presentation is very much part of the art of cooking, and it is eye appeal which first sets the taste buds working. Some garnishes and decorations are very time-consuming to prepare, but many are both quick and easy. Ideally the garnish or decoration on any dish should be edible, and echo the ingredients in that particular dish. Garnishes and decorations can also help to balance texture and colour; you would use crisp garnishes with smooth, otherwise soft foods, and rich greens or reds to offset cream-coloured sauces. Keep these 'finishing touches' as simple and uncluttered as possible; the food should never look fussy or contrived.

FINISHING TOUCHES
- If a colourful ingredient is used in a dish, keep a little back before cooking to use as a garnish—a ring or two of green or red pepper, a few peas, feathery tops from fresh carrots, celery leaves or fennel
- Leave the small fresh green leaves on cauliflower when cooking it; it looks much more attractive
- Browned flaked almonds add a crunch to cooked white fish, and a pleasing contrast to grilled whole fish, such as trout

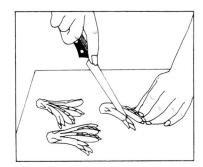

Fanning out asparagus tips

- Use asparagus tips fanned out on top of a cooked chicken breast or lamb cutlet
- Finely snipped crisp bacon adds a pleasing savoury crunch on top of creamed potato
- Sprinkle a mixture of oven-dried breadcrumbs and finely grated lemon rind over cooked green vegetables, such as broccoli
- Give a mimosa garnish to pale vegetables such as cauliflower or Jerusalem artichokes. Chop the whites of hard-boiled eggs finely and sieve the yolks. Sprinkle the white over first of all, and then the sieved yolk
- Black lumpfish roe looks stunning on yellow or cream-coloured dishes, such as egg mayonnaise, or noodles in a cream sauce
- Chop set aspic jelly with a wet knife; use to garnish joints of cold meat or cold fish such as salmon
- If a dish is to be served with a side-serving of mayonnaise or hollandaise sauce; fill a large hollowed out tomato or half a lemon with the chosen sauce

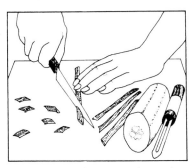

Cutting leaves from cucumber peel

- Cut leaves from cucumber peel to garnish fish mousses and pâtés
- Peel carrots. Using a potato peeler, cut thin spirals of carrot; plunge into a bowl of iced water. Use to garnish portions of pâté and terrines
- Put orange and lemon rind into the liquidiser with granulated sugar; blend until smooth. Use

for sprinkling over the top of fruit pies and crumbles

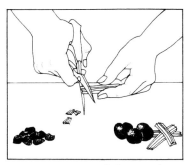

Cutting angelica with dampened scissors

- When using angelica and glacé cherries for decoration, you will obtain a neater finish if you chop both of them with dampened kitchen scissors
- Use mint sprigs for garnishing portions of melon or grapefruit. For a truly sparkling finish, dip the mint sprigs in beaten egg white and then in caster sugar
- A brandy snap filled with a whirl of cream makes a pretty garnish for a fruit mousse or fool
- Try a curl of plain chocolate for a special ice cream or mousse;

Cutting curls of plain chocolate

use chocolate that is firm but not chilled, and form the curls using a potato peeler
- Sandwich ratafia biscuits together with plain chocolate and leave until set. Use to decorate trifles and large mousses

● Clever doiley-dusting looks most effective on plain sponge cakes. Use icing sugar to dust

Dusting icing sugar over a doiley

over a doiley; and then dust cocoa or chocolate powder over another doiley.

ADD A DASH OF FLAVOUR

● For a strong orange flavour, use frozen concentrated orange rather than freshly squeezed orange juice
● Add an extra piquant flavour to canned soups: a dash of white wine to fish or chicken soups, and a dash of sherry to oxtail and other rich brown soups
● If you are making up a salad which contains quite a sizeable quantity of fruit, use orange juice in the dressing rather than white wine vinegar — it is less harsh
● Use chopped fresh coriander as a garnish for soups which respond to a spicy addition; it is good with carrot, mushroom and Jerusalem artichoke
● For potato salad, pour the pre-pared dressing over the potatoes while they are still warm — for an unusual flavour add a dash of Pernod
● Cook vegetables in real chicken stock for a really rich flavour

PRESENTATION

Here are some garnishes and decorations which have that extra panache; they are simple to make but ultra effective.

Slicing oranges into cartwheels

Orange or lemon cartwheels

Using a canapé cutter, cut down the length of the lemon or orange, taking strips out of the rind. Cut the fruit into slices. Use to decorate desserts or drinks.

Stuffed cucumber rings

Cut thickish slices of cucumber, and hollow out the centres. Fill with cream cheese, finely chopped red pepper and chopped spring onion. Chill and then cut into thinner slices. An attractive garnish for Parma ham and salami.

CRAFTY TRICKS

● Not enough cream to go round? Fold whisked egg whites into whipped cream.
● If a soup is too salty, add a peeled potato or a good slice of French bread; simmer for a few minutes to allow some of the salt to be absorbed.
● To mend a cracked pastry flan case, brush all over the cracks with beaten egg white. Return to the oven for a few minutes until the egg white has sealed the cracks.
● If you want to make mayon-naise or white sauce to further, thin it with top of the milk, single cream, natural yogurt or soured cream.

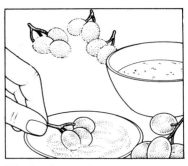

Dipping fruit in frosting mixture

Frosted fruits

They can be used as a most attractive garnish for both sweet and savoury dishes. You simply dip the fruits in a mixture of egg white and icing sugar. Grapes and strawberries look particularly attractive frosted. Use them on platters of cold meat or as a border garnish for elaborate gâteaux.

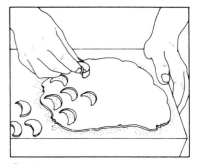

Cutting out pastry crescents

Pastry crescents

Roll out puff pastry trimmings and cut out small crescent shapes. Glaze with beaten egg and bake until golden. Use to garnish fish dishes.

Gherkin fans

Hold the gherkin firmly on a chopping board at one end. Using a small sharp knife cut a series of tongue-shaped slices along the length of the gherkin; do not cut right through the stem end. Fan out each cucumber fan. Use to garnish platters of cold meat and savoury mousses.

QUICK MEALS

With a well-stocked store cupboard, last-minute dishes can be fun to put together, and very satisfying for the cook.

The following ideas are based on store cupboard ingredients, with a few fresh foods as well.

SOUPS

PRAWN AND ASPARAGUS BISQUE

Mix canned asparagus soup with a little white wine; add peeled prawns (frozen or canned). Heat through and swirl in cream.

QUICK VICHYSSOISE

Blend drained canned celery with drained canned new potatoes; add chicken stock and cream to give a smooth soup-like consistency.

STARTERS

MARINATED ARTICHOKES WITH MUSHROOMS

Make a dressing with orange juice, olive oil, chopped mint (fresh or dried) and seasoning. Add drained canned artichoke hearts and button mushrooms and chill. Serve with bread.

MAIN DISHES

MEAT

CHINESE CHICKEN

Cook chicken drumsticks until tender. Add canned sweet and sour sauce and sliced canned water chestnuts. Heat through.

SAUSAGE CASSEROLE

Mix cooked sausages with canned red cabbage, canned red wine sauce, sliced green peppers, dill seeds and seasoning. Heat through in the oven.

FISH

FISHERMAN'S PIE

Mix a can of flaked salmon with a can of mushroom soup and some fried sliced onion; top with made up instant mashed potato mixed with egg yolk and grated cheese. Bake until golden.

SMOKED SALMON FONDUE

Heat canned smoked salmon soup with a little white wine, cream and chopped fresh herbs.

EGG

EGG RISOTTO

Heat ready cooked canned rice in butter with chopped spring onion; add chopped hard-boiled egg, chopped parsley and a little cream and heat through.

PASTA

NOODLE BAKE

Mix cooked green noodles with soured cream, thawed frozen peas, chopped ham, grated Parmesan cheese and seasoning. Place in a gratin dish, sprinkle with extra cheese and bake until golden.

SUPPERS AND SNACKS

CHICKEN AND POTATO GRATIN

Mix canned chicken soup with chopped canned chicken breast and finely chopped red pepper. Put into a gratin dish and top with frozen potato balls. Sprinkle with grated cheese and a few dried breadcrumbs. Bake until golden.

PIZZA-STYLE FRENCH BREAD

Cut lengths of bread and split in half; brush with or dip in oil. Top with drained canned tomatoes, slivers of cheese and/or salami, anchovy fillets and black olives. Brush with oil and bake.

VEGETABLES

Wrap *frozen potato croquettes* in rashers of streaky bacon, and bake until crisp.

Mix thawed and drained *frozen spinach* purée with bottled tartare sauce; heat through in the oven in a covered dish.

Toss blanched almonds in melted butter until lightly golden; add frozen *brussels sprouts*, and heat through.

Lightly cook *button mushrooms* and stir in sufficient canned curry sauce to bind lightly. Delicious with steak and other grilled meats.

PUDDINGS AND DESSERTS

BUTTERED PINEAPPLE PASTRY

Roll out thawed frozen puff pastry to a rectangle; brush with beaten egg white. Top with canned pineapple slices, well drained (or slices of fresh pineapple) and knobs of butter. Scatter with demerara sugar and bake until well puffed and golden. Serve hot with cream.

PEACHES WITH MELBA SAUCE

Use canned whole peaches or skinned fresh ones. Blend raspberry jam with orange juice and a little brandy until smooth. Put peaches into glass dishes and spoon over the sauce.

RASPBERRY ROMANOFF

Crush packet meringues coarsely or, alternatively, use sponge finger biscuits. Mix with lightly whipped cream and well drained canned raspberries. Spoon into stemmed glasses and garnish with a twist of orange.

Basic Recipes

This chapter is packed with all the basic recipes you need to make up the dishes in this book. From simple things with basic methods like stocks, gravy, sauces and dressings, to pastry recipes and how to prepare and cook vegetable accompaniments (there's even a whole page devoted to cooking potatoes).

SHORTCRUST PASTRY

175 g (6 oz) plain white or wholemeal flour
pinch of salt
75 g (3 oz) butter or block margarine and lard
about 30 ml (2 tbsp) cold water

1 Mix the flour and salt together in a bowl. Cut the fat into small pieces and add it to the flour.

2 Using both hands, rub the fat into the flour between finger and thumb tips until the mixture resembles fine breadcrumbs.

3 Add the water, sprinkling it evenly over the surface. Stir it in with a round-bladed knife until the mixture begins to stick together in large lumps.

4 With one hand, collect the mixture together and knead lightly for a few seconds to give a firm, smooth dough. The pastry can be used straight away, but is better allowed to 'rest' for about 30 minutes. It can also be wrapped in cling film and kept in the refrigerator for a day or two.

5 *To roll out:* sprinkle a very little flour on a working surface and the rolling pin, not on the pastry, and roll out the dough evenly in one direction only, turning it occasionally. The ideal thickness is usually about 0.3 cm ($\frac{1}{8}$ inch). Do not pull or stretch the pastry. When cooking shortcrust pastry, the usual oven temperature is 200–220°C (400–425°F) mark 6–7.

BAKING BLIND

Baking blind is the process of baking a pastry case without the filling—essential if the filling is to be uncooked or if it only requires a short cooking time. First shape the pastry into the baking tin. Prick the pastry base with a fork. For large cases, cut a round of greaseproof paper rather larger

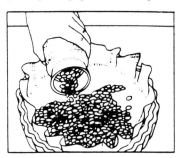

than the tin. Use this to line the pastry and weight it down with some dried beans, pasta or rice. Alternatively, screw up a piece of foil and use that to line the base of the pastry case. Bake the pastry at the temperature given in the recipe for 10–15 minutes, then remove the baking beans and paper or foil lining and return the tin to the oven for a further 5 minutes to crisp the pastry. Leave the baked case to cool and shrink slightly before removing it from the tin. (The baking beans can be kept for use again.)

For small cases, it is usually sufficient to prick the pastry well with a fork before baking.

Baked unfilled pastry cases can be kept for a few days in an airtight container.

PUFF PASTRY

450 g (1 lb) strong plain flour

pinch of salt

450 g (1 lb) butter

about 300 ml ($\frac{1}{2}$ pint) cold water

15 ml (1 tbsp) lemon juice

beaten egg, to glaze

1 Mix the strong plain flour and pinch of salt together in a large bowl.

2 Cut 50 g (2 oz) off the butter and pat the remainder with a rolling pin into a slab 2 cm ($\frac{3}{4}$ inch) thick

3 Rub the 50 g (2 oz) butter into the flour with the finger and thumb tips. Stir in enough water and lemon juice to make a soft, elastic dough.

4 Turn the dough on to a lightly floured surface, then knead until smooth. Shape into a round and cut through half the depth in a cross shape.

5 Open out the flaps to form a star. Roll out, keeping the centre four times as thick as the flaps.

6 Place the slab of butter in the centre of the dough and fold over the flaps, envelope-style. Press gently with the rolling pin.

7 Roll out into a rectangle measuring about 40 × 20 cm (16 × 8 inches). Fold the bottom third up and the top third down, keeping the edges straight. Seal the edges by pressing them with the rolling pin.

8 Wrap the pastry loosely in greaseproof paper and leave it to rest in the refrigerator or a cool place for about 30 minutes.

9 Put the pastry on a lightly floured surface with the folded edges to the sides and repeat the rolling, folding and resting sequence five times.

10 After the final resting, roll out the pastry on a lightly floured surface and shape as required. Brush with beaten egg before baking. The usual oven temperature for puff pastry is 230°C (450°F) mark 8.

PANCAKES (CRÊPES)

Makes 8 pancakes

125 g (4 oz) plain flour

pinch of salt

1 egg

300 ml ($\frac{1}{2}$ pint) milk

lard or vegetable oil

1 Mix the flour and salt together in a bowl. Make a well in the centre and break in the egg. Add half the liquid, then gradually work in the flour from the sides of the bowl. Beat until smooth.

2 Add the remaining liquid gradually. Beat until the ingredients are well mixed.

3 Heat a little lard or oil in a small frying pan, running it around the pan to coat the sides. Pour in a little batter, tilting the pan to form an even coating.

4 Place over moderate heat and cook until golden underneath, then turn with a palette knife and cook the other side. Slide the pancake on to a plate lined with greaseproof paper. Repeat.

BASIC PIZZA DOUGH

This mixture will be very sticky initially, but is soon worked into a soft, smooth dough. Don't be tempted to add more flour—it won't be needed.

350 g (12 oz) strong plain white flour

1.25 ml ($\frac{1}{4}$ level tsp) salt

5 ml (1 level tsp) fast-action dried yeast (no need to reconstitute in water)

30 ml (2 tbsp) olive oil

1 In a warm, medium bowl, stir together the flour, salt and yeast. Make a well in the centre of the dry ingredients and add 225 ml (8 fl oz) warm water and the olive oil.

2 Stir the mixture by hand until it forms a wet dough. Beat for a further 2–3 minutes.

3 Turn out the dough on to a well floured surface and knead for about 5 minutes, or until the dough becomes very smooth and elastic.

4 Place in a bowl and cover with a clean tea towel. Leave in a warm place until doubled in size, about 45 minutes.

5 Turn out the dough on to a floured surface and knead again for 2–3 minutes.

STOCKS, GRAVIES, SAUCES AND DRESSINGS

BEEF STOCK

Makes about 1.4 litres (2½ pints)

450 g (1 lb) shin of beef, cut into pieces

450 g (1 lb) marrowbone or knuckle of veal, chopped

1.7 litres (3 pints) water

bouquet garni

1 onion, skinned and sliced

1 carrot, peeled and sliced

1 stick celery, washed and sliced

2.5 ml (½ tsp) salt

1 To give a good flavour and colour, brown the bones and meat in the oven before using.

2 Put in a pan with the water, bouquet garni, vegetables and salt. Bring to the boil, skim and simmer, covered, for 5–6 hours. Or pressure cook on High (15-lb) pressure for 1–1¼ hours using 1.4 litres (2½ pints) water. If using marrowbones, increase the water to 1.7 litres (3 pints) and cook the liquid for about 2 hours.

3 Strain the stock thoroughly, discarding the vegetables, and leave to cool. Remove fat.

CHICKEN OR TURKEY STOCK

Makes 1.1–1.4 litres (2–2½ pints)

1 roast chicken or turkey carcass plus scraps

1.4–1.7 litres (2½–3 pints) water

roughly chopped celery, onions and carrots

bouquet garni (optional)

Put the carcass, bones and scraps in a pan with the water, flavouring vegetables and herbs, if used. Bring to the boil, skim and simmer, covered, for 3 hours. Strain the stock and, when cold, remove all traces of fat.

FISH STOCK

Makes about 900 ml (1½ pints)

450 g (1 lb) fish heads, bones and trimmings

6 white peppercorns

bouquet garni (page 351)

1 onion, skinned and sliced

1 Put the fish bones in a large pan with the peppercorns, bouquet garni and onion. Cover with 900 ml (1½ pints) cold water. Bring to the boil.

2 With a slotted spoon, skim off any scum that forms.

3 Lower the heat, cover and simmer for no longer than 20 minutes.

4 Strain the stock into a bowl. Use on the same day, or store in a covered container in the refrigerator for no longer than 2 days, thereafter it must be brought to the boil and boiled for 10 minutes every 2 days if it is to be kept longer. It will keep in this manner for 2–3 weeks as long as it is boiled every 2 days. It can be frozen for up to 6 months. Use for fish soups.

VEGETABLE STOCK

Makes about 1.2 litres (2 pints)

30 ml (2 tbsp) vegetable oil

1 medium onion, skinned and finely chopped

1 medium carrot, washed and diced

50 g (2 oz) turnip, washed and diced

50 g (2 oz) parsnip, washed and diced

4 celery sticks, roughly chopped

vegetable trimmings such as: celery tops, cabbage leaves, Brussels sprout leaves, mushroom peelings, tomato skins and potato peelings

onion skins (optional)

bouquet garni

6 whole black peppercorns

1 Heat the oil in a large saucepan, add the onion and fry gently for about 5 minutes until soft and lightly coloured.

2 Add the vegetables to the pan with any vegetable trimmings, outer leaves or peelings available. If a dark brown coloured stock is required, add onion skins.

3 Cover the vegetables with 1.7 litres (3 pints) cold water and add the bouquet garni and peppercorns. Bring to the boil.

4 Half cover and simmer for 1½ hours, skimming occasionally with a slotted spoon.

5 Strain the stock into a bowl and leave to cool. Cover and chill in the refrigerator. This stock will only keep for 1–2 days, after which time it will begin to go sour.

THIN GRAVY

A rich brown gravy is served with all roast joints. If the gravy is properly made in the roasting tin, there should be no need to use gravy mixes, or extra colouring.

Remove the joint from the tin and allow it to stand while making the gravy.

1 Pour the fat very slowly from the roasting tin, draining it off carefully from one corner and leaving the sediment behind.

2 Pour in 300 ml (½ pint) hot vegetable water or stock (which can be made from a stock cube). Stir thoroughly with a wooden spoon until all the sediment is scraped from the tin and the gravy is a rich brown.

3 Place the tin on top of the cooker, bring to the boil, stirring, then simmer for 2–3 minutes. Season to taste with salt and pepper. Serve very hot.

This is the 'correct' way of making thin gravy, but some people prefer a thicker version.

THICKENED GRAVY

1 Pour the fat very slowly from the roasting tin as for thin gravy (left), but leaving behind 30 ml (2 tbsp) of the fat.

2 Using a flour dredger to give a smooth result, shake in about 7.5 ml ($\frac{1}{2}$ tbsp) plain flour.

3 Blend well with a wooden spoon and cook over the heat until brown, stirring constantly. Slowly stir in 300 ml ($\frac{1}{2}$ pint) hot vegetable water or stock, bring to the boil, then simmer for 2–3 minutes. Add plenty of salt and pepper to taste, strain and serve very hot.

Notes

1 If the gravy is greasy (due to not draining off enough fat) or thin (due to adding too much liquid), it can be corrected by adding more flour, although this weakens the flavour.

2 When gravy is very pale, a little gravy browning may be added for colour.

3 For extra flavour, meat extracts are sometimes added to gravy, but they do tend to overpower the characteristic meat flavour. A sliced carrot and onion cooked with meat in the gravy will give extra 'body' to the taste without impairing it, and 15 ml (1 tbsp) cider or wine added at the last moment is excellent.

GRAVIES AND SAUCES FOR POULTRY

The best gravies are made with stock based on the giblets, with any bones that are available. After cooking your poultry, never throw away the bones but use them to make a stock for next time; either freeze it or store in the refrigerator, boiling every 2–3 days.

The lighter meats, such as chicken and guinea fowl, are usually served with a thin gravy, turkey and goose are served with a richer version (see Giblet gravy).

Sauces for poultry may be made with stock or milk, or with a mixture of the two.

GIBLET GRAVY

Makes 600 ml (1 pint)

| poultry giblets |
| 1 small onion |
| 1 small carrot, peeled |
| 1 stick of celery, trimmed and cut into chunks |
| bacon rinds |
| salt and freshly ground pepper |
| 1.1 litres (2 pints) water |
| 15 ml (1 tbsp) flour |
| butter |

1 Put the gizzard, heart and neck (not the liver) in a saucepan with the vegetables, a few bacon rinds, seasoning and the water. Bring to the boil, cover and simmer for about 2 hours.

2 Strain the giblet stock into a basin. Discard the vegetables and bacon rinds and, if you wish, set aside the cooked giblets for use in another dish.

3 When cooked, remove the bird to a warm plate and pour off most of the fat from the tin, leaving behind sediment and about 30 ml (2 tbsp) fat.

4 Blend the flour into the fat in the roasting tin. Cook until it turns brown, stirring continuously and scraping any sediment from the bottom of the tin. Slowly stir in 600 ml (1 pint) giblet stock. Bring to the boil, stirring.

5 Meanwhile, sauté the liver in a knob of butter until just cooked. Remove from the pan, drain and chop into small pieces.

6 Add the chopped liver to the gravy and simmer for 2–3 minutes to heat. Check the seasoning. Pour into a gravy boat and keep hot until needed.

WHITE SAUCE

Makes 300 ml ($\frac{1}{2}$ pint) pouring sauce

| 15 g ($\frac{1}{2}$ oz) butter |
| 15 g ($\frac{1}{2}$ oz) plain flour |
| 300 ml ($\frac{1}{2}$ pint) milk |
| salt and freshly ground pepper |

1 Melt the butter in a saucepan. Add the flour and cook over low heat, stirring with a wooden spoon, for 2 minutes. Do not allow the mixture to brown.

2 Remove the pan from the heat and gradually blend in the milk, stirring after each addition to prevent lumps forming.

3 Bring to the boil slowly and continue to cook, stirring all the time, until the sauce comes to the boil and thickens.

4 Simmer very gently for a further 2–3 minutes. Season the sauce with salt and freshly ground pepper.

—— VARIATIONS ——

COATING SAUCE

Follow the white sauce recipe above, but increase **butter and flour to 25 g (1 oz) each.**

CHEESE SAUCE

Follow the recipe for white sauce or coating sauce above. Before seasoning with salt and pepper, stir in **50 g (2 oz) finely grated Cheddar cheese, 2.5–5 ml ($\frac{1}{2}$–1 tsp) prepared mustard and a pinch of cayenne pepper.**

TRADITIONAL BOUQUET GARNI

| 1 bay leaf |
| 1 sprig of parsley |
| 1 sprig of thyme |
| few peppercorns |

1 Tie in a small piece of muslin. You can, of course, choose some other fresh herbs.

BÉCHAMEL SAUCE

Makes 300 ml (½ pint)

300 ml (½ pint) milk
1 slice of onion
1 bay leaf
6 black peppercorns
1 blade mace
20 g (¾ oz) butter
20 ml (4 tsp) flour
salt and freshly ground pepper

1 Put the milk into a saucepan with the onion slice, bay leaf, peppercorns and mace. Heat gently for 5 minutes, then strain.

2 Melt the butter in the rinsed-out pan. Add the flour and cook gently for 1–2 minutes, stirring. Remove pan from the heat and gradually blend in the milk. Bring to the boil, stirring and simmer for 2 minutes until thick. Season with salt and pepper.

SIMPLE TOMATO SAUCE

Makes enough to dress 4 servings of pasta

450 g (1 lb) tomatoes, skinned and roughly chopped, or 397 g (14 oz) can tomatoes, with their juice
1 small onion, skinned and roughly chopped
1 garlic clove, skinned and chopped
1 celery stick, sliced
1 bay leaf
sprig of parsley
2.5 ml (½ tsp) sugar
salt and freshly ground pepper

1 Place all the ingredients in a saucepan, bring to the boil and then simmer, uncovered, for 30 minutes until thickened. Stir occasionally to prevent sticking to the bottom of the pan.

2 Remove the bay leaf and purée the mixture in an electric blender or food processor until smooth or push through a sieve using a wooden spoon. Reheat and then taste and adjust seasoning. Serve the sauce hot with freshly cooked pasta.

CUSTARD SAUCE

Curdling can be a problem with egg custards. It occurs if the custard is boiled, so as soon as the mixture coats the back of a wooden spoon it must be removed from the heat. To help prevent curdling, add 2.5 ml (½ tsp) cornflour to every 300 ml (½ pint) milk.

Makes 300 ml (½ pint)

2 eggs
10 ml (2 tsp) caster sugar
300 ml (½ pint) milk
5 ml (1 tsp) vanilla flavouring (optional)

1 In a bowl, beat the eggs with the sugar and 45 ml (3 tbsp) of the milk. Heat the remaining milk to lukewarm and beat into the eggs.

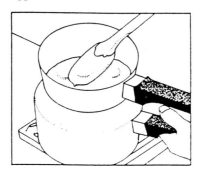

2 Pour into a double saucepan or bowl standing over a pan of simmering water. Cook, stirring continuously, until the custard is thick enough to thinly coat the back of a spoon. Do not boil.

3 Pour into a cold jug and stir in vanilla flavouring, if liked. Serve hot or cold. The sauce thickens slightly on cooling.

VINAIGRETTE

Makes about 300 ml (½ pint)

75 ml (5 tbsp) red or white wine vinegar*
10 ml (2 tsp) Dijon or made English Mustard
10 ml (2 tsp) salt
5 ml (1 tsp) freshly ground pepper
10 ml (2 tsp) sugar (optional)
2 garlic cloves, crushed (optional)
200 ml (⅓ pint) oil†

For a creamy dressing blend the ingredients in an electric blender or food processor. For a thinner dressing, shake in a screw-topped jar.

—————— VARIATIONS ——————

* Try also **tarragon vinegar** in dressings for tomatoes or potatoes; **thyme vinegar** with eggs or mushrooms; **cider vinegar** with fruits. **Lemon juice** can be substituted for vinegar as well. **Garlic vinaigrette:** add **2 garlic cloves**, skinned and crushed. † **Sunflower oil** alone or half and half with **olive oil** is pleasant. **Walnut oil** adds interest to strongly flavoured ingredients.

HORSERADISH SAUCE

Makes about 225 ml (8 fl oz)

75 g (3 oz) grated horseradish
5 ml (1 tsp) mustard powder
5 ml (1 tsp) sugar
10 ml (2 tsp) white wine vinegar
150 ml (¼ pint) double cream, lightly whipped

1 Mix all the ingredients together and leave the sauce to stand for 20 minutes before serving.

MAYONNAISE

Makes about 400 ml (12 fl oz)

3 egg yolks

7.5 ml (1½ tsp) dry mustard

7.5 ml (1½ tsp) salt

2.5 ml (½ tsp) freshly ground pepper

7.5 ml (1½ tsp) sugar (optional)

450 ml (¾ pint) sunflower oil or ½ olive oil and ½ vegetable oil

45 ml (3 tbsp) white wine vinegar or lemon juice

1 Put the egg yolks in a bowl with the seasonings and sugar and beat with a whisk. Continue beating and add 150 ml (¼ pint) of the oil about a drop at a time.

2 Once the mixture starts to thicken, continue in a thin stream. Add the vinegar or lemon juice, beating constantly.

3 Add the remaining oil 15 ml (1 tbsp) at a time or in a thin stream, beating continually until it is completely absorbed.

―――――― VARIATIONS ――――――

Tomato mayonnaise: Prepare as above, but add 2 tomatoes, skinned, seeded and diced; 3 small spring onions, trimmed and chopped; 3.75 ml (¾ tsp) salt and 15 ml (1 tbsp) vinegar or lemon juice.
Garlic mayonnaise: Skin 2 medium-sized garlic cloves and crush with some of the measured salt, add to the finished mayonnaise.
Cucumber mayonnaise: Prepare as above but add 90 ml (6 tbsp) finely chopped cucumber and 7.5 ml (1½ tsp) salt.
Lemon mayonnaise: add the **finely grated rind of 1 lemon** and use **lemon juice** instead of vinegar.

BLUE CHEESE DRESSING

Makes about 350 ml (12 fl oz)

150 ml (¼ pint) mayonnaise

142 ml (5 fl oz) soured cream

75 g (3 oz) blue cheese, crumbled

5 ml (1 tsp) wine or cider vinegar

1 garlic clove, skinned and crushed

Mix all the ingredients well together. Allow to stand for several hours.

SOURED CREAM DRESSING

Makes 150 ml (¼ pint)

142 ml (5 fl oz) soured cream

30 ml (2 tbsp) white wine vinegar

¼ small onion, skinned and finely chopped

2.5 ml (½ tsp) sugar

5 ml (1 tsp) salt

freshly ground pepper

1 Mix together the soured cream, vinegar, onion and sugar. Season with salt and freshly ground pepper and mix again thoroughly.

PUDEENE KI CHUTNEY
(MINT CHUTNEY)

Fills a 350 g (12 oz) jar

50 g (2 oz) fresh mint leaves

60 ml (4 tbsp) fresh coriander leaves

1 medium onion, skinned

juice of ½–1 lemon

2.5 ml (½ tsp) sugar

2.5 ml (½ tsp) salt

1 Wash the mint and coriander leaves and dry thoroughly with absorbent kitchen paper.

2 Work the onion in a blender or food processor with a little lemon juice until minced.

3 Add the mint and coriander, sugar, salt and remaining lemon juice and blend to form a smooth paste.

4 Turn into a bowl, cover tightly and chill for about 1 hour before serving. Store for up to 2–3 days in the refrigerator.

RAITA
(CUCUMBER WITH YOGURT)

Serves 4

½ small cucumber

300 ml (½ pint) natural yogurt

15 ml (1 tbsp) chopped fresh mint

salt and freshly ground pepper

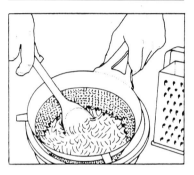

1 Coarsely grate the cucumber. Put in a sieve and squeeze out as much of the water as possible.

2 Put the yogurt in a bowl and stir in the cucumber, mint and pepper to taste.

3 Cover and chill for about 1 hour. Sprinkle the raita with salt before serving.

―――――― VARIATIONS ――――――

Substitute fruit for the cucumber such as 1 sliced banana or 1 finely cubed dessert apple. If liked, add 1 seeded and very finely chopped green chilli. Substitute 15 ml (1 tbsp) chopped fresh coriander for the mint.

PREPARING AND COOKING VEGETABLES

The choice of vegetables available in shops today is enormous. By importing from different parts of the world at different times of the year there is always a wide selection from which to choose. Buy vegetables carefully as quality is important. Bruised, damaged or old, tough vegetables can be picked over and cooked gently in soups, but for boiling and salads you need the best you can buy.

STORING AND PREPARING

Store vegetables in a cool, airy place such as a vegetable rack in a pantry or in the salad drawer of a refrigerator.

Green vegetables should be used as soon as possible after buying, when their vitamin C value is at its highest. Prepare all vegetables as near to their cooking or serving time as possible to retain both flavour and nutrients. Because vitamin C is water-soluble, vegetables should not be put into water until ready to be cooked.

Serve vegetables as soon as they are cooked – they deteriorate through being kept hot. When serving more than one vegetable at a meal try to balance the colours and textures. Slightly under rather than overcook, to preserve nutrients and keep a good texture and colour. Steaming and stir-frying are good methods of preserving texture and flavour.

IDEAS FOR SEASONING

Add seasoning to cooked vegetables, especially if they have been steamed or fried without salt. Fresh herbs combine well if sprinkled in just before serving. Try caraway on carrots, tarragon on peas, oregano on courgettes. A little grated nutmeg improves cabbage, spinach and mashed potatoes.

GETTING THE BEST FROM GREENS

Cooked properly, stretched with all manner of ingredients – meat, fish, cheese, rice, vegetables – greens can take pride of place in a varied diet. Prepared greens will keep for a day in a damp plastic bag in the refrigerator. Home-grown greens usually need shorter cooking time than bought ones.

All greens taste better cooked with sea salt. Use about 5 ml (1 tsp) to 300 ml ($\frac{1}{2}$ pint) water and 450 g (1 lb) greens. Don't keep greens hot after cooking; if necessary let them cool and reheat when needed. Reheat with a dab of butter and some freshly ground black pepper or grated nutmeg.

Broccoli Never buy broccoli that is yellowing. The stem snaps easily if the vegetable is fresh. To prepare, trim the stems, cut large heads and stems through lengthways and wash. The stem of calabrese (or purple broccoli) can be cut off to 2.5 cm (1 inch) so that the heads don't overcook. Steam or boil bundles of trimmed broccoli in a little boiling salted water for 10–15 minutes so that the stalks boil and heads steam. When cooked the broccoli should be crisp to the bite. Drain and serve with melted butter and a squeeze of lemon juice or garnish of toasted flaked almonds. It can also be served with a rich hollandaise sauce.

Brussels sprouts need to be perfectly fresh when bought and don't keep for long. Look for firm, compact sprouts and avoid any that have a trace of yellow or that are open. Good sprouts don't need much trimming. Cut a cross on the stems of larger ones and wash them all in cold water. Use a wide, shallow pan that takes them in one layer, otherwise those underneath will overcook. Cook for 5–8 minutes in about 2.5 cm (1 inch) of gently boiling salted water and · leave the pan lid slightly open to keep a good green colour. They should still have a little crunch at the core when done. Drain

thoroughly and toss in melted butter with nutmeg and ground pepper. They are also delicious almost cooked then fried in bacon fat with a few crumbled chestnuts. For a richer dish, turn fully cooked sprouts in gently warmed cream, then garnish with tiny fried croûtons, flaked almonds or buttered crumbs. To accompany roast chicken, purée sprouts with a spoon or two of cream, 25 g (1 oz) butter and generous seasoning.

Cabbage Discard rough leaves, quarter and cut away hard core. Shred finely and wash in cold water. Use just enough salted water to cover. Add cabbage to boiling water and cook for about 5 minutes. Drain thoroughly, turn well in butter and season with pepper and nutmeg. Sour cream or natural yogurt make a good finish for cabbage.

Spinach should be young with small leaves. Allow 225 g (8 oz) per person. Tear away coarse ribs and wash well with plenty of water. Cook over moderate heat in just the water that clings to the leaves after washing and a sprinkling of salt, stirring occasionally for about 5 minutes until tender and reduced. Alternatively, boil small amounts gently in plenty of salted water for about 5 minutes, drain then press with a potato masher. Serve whole or chopped, with melted butter and grated nutmeg. Can be puréed and reheated with cream, pepper, nutmeg and a dusting of grated Parmesan cheese.

Spring greens, kale and curly kale should be bought very fresh. Discard coarse dark leaves, remove any thick ribs, shred roughly, wash. Cook spring greens in a little boiling salted water for 5 minutes; drain well. Serve with butter and nutmeg. Kale needs 10–15 minutes cooking time. To serve, drain well, press out surplus water, chop finely.

POTATOES

All potatoes taste better and keep their shape well if cooked in their skins, which also helps preserve the vitamin C content. The skins can easily be removed after cooking. If you do peel potatoes ahead of time, don't store them in water for long as some vitamins and starch will be lost.

Allow 175 g (6 oz) per portion.

DUCHESSE POTATOES

900 g (2 lb) potatoes
salt and freshly ground pepper
50 g (2 oz) butter or margarine
pinch of grated nutmeg
2 eggs, beaten

1 Boil the potatoes. Drain well, then sieve or mash. Beat in the butter with plenty of seasoning and a pinch of nutmeg. Gradually beat in most of the eggs, reserving a little for glazing.

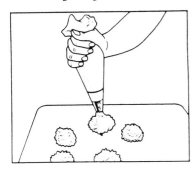

2 Cool the potato mixture then spoon into a piping bag fitted with a large star nozzle. Pipe the mixture in pyramids on a greased baking sheet.

3 Brush carefully with the remaining egg to which a pinch of salt has been added. Bake in the oven at 200°C (400°F) mark 6 for about 25 minutes or until golden brown and set. When cooked, place in a serving dish.

CHÂTEAU POTATOES

Serves 4

900 g (2 lb) small new potatoes
50 g (2 oz) butter or margarine
salt and freshly ground pepper

1 Scrape the potatoes, wash and drain well. Pat dry with absorbent kitchen paper.

2 Melt the butter in a shallow flameproof casserole. When it is foaming, add the potatoes and fry gently until golden brown.

3 Add the salt and pepper, then cover the casserole. Cook in the oven at 180°C (350°F) mark 4 for 20–25 minutes, or until the potatoes are quite tender.

GRATIN DAUPHINOIS

1.4 kg (3 lb) old potatoes, peeled
1 garlic clove, crushed
300 ml (½ pint) single cream
salt and freshly ground pepper
pinch of grated nutmeg
100 g (4 oz) grated Gruyère cheese
watercress, to garnish

1 Cut the potatoes into small pieces and parboil for 5 minutes; drain well and place in a lightly greased pie dish or shallow casserole.

2 Stir the garlic into the cream, with the salt, pepper and nutmeg. Pour this seasoned cream over the potatoes and sprinkle with the cheese.

3 Cover with foil and bake in the oven at 180°C (350°F) mark 4 for about 1½ hours. Remove the foil and place the gratin under the grill to brown the cheese. Serve garnished with watercress.

HASSELBACK POTATOES

Serves 8

16 small potatoes
vegetable oil
salt and freshly ground pepper

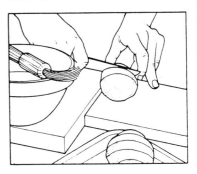

1 Peel and cut the potatoes across their width at ¼-inch intervals three-quarters of the way through.

2 Place in a single layer in an oiled baking pan. Brush with oil and season well.

3 Roast, uncovered, in the oven at 180°C (350°F) mark 4 for about 1 hour or until cooked through. Serve immediately.

ROAST POTATOES

Serves 4

700–900 g (1½–2 lb) potatoes, peeled
lard or bacon drippings
chopped fresh parsley, to garnish

1 Cut the potatoes into evenly sized pieces, place them in cold salted water and bring to the boil. Cook for 2-3 minutes and drain.

2 Heat lard in a roasting pan in the oven. Add the potatoes, baste with the fat and cook at 220°C (425°F) mark 7 for 45 minutes or until golden brown. Sprinkle with chopped parsley.